INEXACT
SCIENCE

INEXACT SCIENCE

THE SIX MOST COMPELLING
DRAFT YEARS IN NHL HISTORY

EVAN DOWBIGGIN &
BRUCE DOWBIGGIN

Published by ECW Press
665 Gerrard Street East
Toronto, Ontario, Canada M4M 1Y2
416-694-3348 / info@ecwpress.com

Editor for the Press: Michael Holmes
Cover design: Michel Vrana
Cover photo © Frank Prazak/Hockey Hall of Fame
Evan Dowbiggin author photo: Precious Aguila of Precious Images
Bruce Dowbiggin author photo: Canwest News Services

LIBRARY AND ARCHIVES CANADA CATALOGUING IN PUBLICATION

Title: Inexact science : the six most compelling draft years in NHL history / Evan Dowbiggin & Bruce Dowbiggin.

Names: Dowbiggin, Evan, author. | Dowbiggin, Bruce, author.

Identifiers: Canadiana (print) 20210219351 | Canadiana (ebook) 2021021936X

ISBN 978-1-77041-530-0 (softcover)
ISBN 978-1-77305-666-1 (ePub)
ISBN 978-1-77305-667-8 (PDF)
ISBN 978-1-77305-668-5 (Kindle)

Subjects: LCSH: National Hockey League. | LCSH: Hockey players—Selection and appointment. | LCSH: Hockey players—Recruiting.

Classification: LCC GV847.8.N3 D69 2021 | DDC 796.962/64—dc23

This book is funded in part by the Government of Canada. *Ce livre est financé en partie par le gouvernement du Canada.* We also acknowledge the support of the Government of Ontario through the Ontario Book Publishing Tax Credit, and through Ontario Creates.

PRINTED AND BOUND IN CANADA

PRINTING: MARQUIS   5   4   3   2   1

FSC
www.fsc.org
MIXTE
Papier issu de
sources responsables
FSC® C103567

To Mom,
Always the enforcer I needed,
even when most weren't willing
to drop the gloves over me.

TABLE OF CONTENTS

INTRODUCTION

Scratch any hockey lifer and they'll tell you a great NHL draft story. One who got away. One who couldn't miss. One a team stole from under the eyes of the rest of the league. Hall of Fame reporter Eric Duhatschek remembers the 1984 draft, when he was covering the Calgary Flames for the *Calgary Herald*, and a random encounter that he had in that long, long day of drafting:

> Back then the draft was just one day. They would start at nine in the morning. They always took a break after—I'm going to say round five. I remember seeing (Flames head scout) Ian McKenzie in the break and asking him how things were going. He tells me, "I can't believe Brett Hull hasn't been taken yet. This guy had an unbelievable year, and I've been pushing, pushing, pushing for him and he's still on the board!" Sure enough, I think it was 10 or 12 names that came off the board before the Flames came up at number 117. And of course, that's where they did draft Hull. I always trusted scouts who were enthusiastic about somebody beforehand rather than a year later. Saying, "Wow, this guy's a really great pick, and I'm a genius"? Ian was never like that. He was pretty honest and forthright about it. He wasn't right all the time, but he was right more often than you'd think.

So Ian was asked afterwards by a bunch of people, including a reporter from *Sports Illustrated*, about why they drafted Brett Hull. The main question was "Did you draft him because he's Bobby Hull's son?" And Ian's answer was "No, it's because he scored 105 fucking goals in the B.C. Junior League!" Remember how *SI* used to have that section called "They Said It"? Well, that quote became the one they chose, without the "fucking" part, of course. And Ian was very proud of that. It was the only time in his life he ever got quoted in *Sports Illustrated* magazine.

Now fast-forward to August. In those days, the Flames were producing a newsletter that they sent out to their fans. It was just a four-page publication that you got if you were a season ticket holder. Ian calls me up and says, "Can you ghostwrite it for me? I'll pay you 100 bucks for it." And I agreed to. I was doing it more as a favour than as an actual freelance assignment. Anyway, I interviewed him to get what I needed for the write-up. We went through all the players the Flames had taken, such as Gary Roberts, Paul Ranheim, Hull. Then, near the end, he says, "I want to talk about this kid we took in the ninth round, Gary Suter."

This was still 1984, and it was more than a year before he'd played an NHL game, so it wasn't just after-the-fact BS. It was just two months after the June draft. No one had paid even one word of attention to Suter. Ian pointed out that he had been an older player, being drafted at age 20 after being passed over a couple times. But mostly it was because of size. In those days, very few NHL teams drafted defencemen who were under six feet tall. Ian told me he had been scouting the University of Wisconsin and was in the corridor talking to a coach or staffer when a player walked by. Ian asked, "Who is that?" And the guy he was talking to said, "Oh, that's Gary Suter." Ian replied, "*That's* Suter!?"

Then Ian went back to look at Central Scouting, and they were still listing him at five-foot-nine or whatever. Well clearly, he'd had a growth spurt! Ian watched him play as well, and it looked like he was very close to six feet tall, if not over. So basically, the Flames were sitting on him because they had this information, all based on a chance encounter while talking to somebody outside the dressing room and having Suter walk by. That's how they ended up drafting him when they did. I put this story in the newsletter article, then typed it up and sent the draft of it over to Ian. He told me a funny story afterwards. He called me up one time and started laughing, saying, "Yeah, I get all kinds of positive responses to that newsletter that you wrote in my name. Most of the time people are saying, 'Wow, you should do this for a living! You're so much better than those fucking sportswriters who don't know what they're talking about.' I can't tell them you are the one who actually wrote it. Thanks for making me look good!"

Suter went on to make McKenzie look more than merely good, nabbing the Calder Memorial Trophy as the NHL's top rookie in 1985–86, playing in four All-Star Games and serving as a key member on the blue line for Calgary's Stanley Cup championship team in 1989. Even after his days with the Flames were over, Suter would be a relied-upon contributor to the Blackhawks and Sharks and go on to play over 1,000 games in the NHL despite a bit of a late start in being drafted. At the time of his retirement, he was considered one of the greatest U.S.-born defencemen ever (before the current era, where there have been far more U.S. blueline stars than there were in Suter's early days as a pro).

Yes, the draft puzzle can be defined many ways. It is the way to victory. And the road to ruin as well. From Guy Lafleur to Sidney Crosby to Connor McDavid, the annual draft of hockey's most talented young prospects has been considered the way to riches for top talents and the path to great heartache and disappointment as well. Each June, the hockey world convenes to see the game's young stars chosen by their future employers (or the first of their NHL employers). Callow juniors and their parents wait for the call that will shape their destiny. Though owners and general managers have attempted to use trades and/or free agency to build their clubs into winners over the years, it's the NHL draft that has proven the special sauce in creating a championship-calibre operation. Since the introduction of a hard salary cap in 2005, an even greater onus has been placed on drafting.

Inexact Science will tell the curious and captivating events of the NHL draft's five-plus decades through the six most compelling years in its history. In addition to analyzing these top draft years, *Inexact Science* will show the lessons learned from the process of guessing hockey horoscopes, how it changed the business of the game and finally where the draft is headed. By looking at what history has shown, the epilogue will demonstrate how the best organizations in pro hockey today have expertly played the crapshoot of the draft. The inexact science of sure shots or diamonds in the rough, but also of the supposed can't-miss prospects who indeed did somehow miss—and the general managers who paid the price for getting it so wrong.

There have certainly been controversies, blockbuster trades, innovative ideas and/or plain old bad judgement in these six most intriguing years. As *Vancouver Province* columnist Tony Gallagher put it, riffing on infamous words from Todd Bertuzzi, "The draft is what it is. Read, watch and listen to whatever you like, but make sure the bullbleep filter is cranked to the max when consuming this piffle." For example, just how did the Detroit Red Wings get the jump on the European talent bonanza (namely the Russian revolution) to propel them to a quarter century of runaway success? Why were Sam Pollock's Montreal Canadiens able to exploit the inexperience and mismanagement of the NHL's bumbling expansion teams to their benefit at the draft, en route to Stanley Cup after Stanley Cup? And why is 1979 considered perhaps the greatest draft of all time, and how did it come to be seen that way?

The NHL draft itself took over in the 1960s from a long-practiced system of junior sponsorship and the signing of amateur talent to exclusive agreements. Though the first draft began in 1963, the earliest iterations were decidedly minor affairs and not taken any more seriously than a waiver or intra-league draft. The first six years are often a footnote to what emerged in the '70s and beyond. Simply put, the amateur draft, as it was labelled at the time, didn't resemble much of what we've come to know.

Just ask Garry Monahan, selected first overall in the inaugural NHL Amateur Draft of 1963. "I didn't know there was a draft. Certainly, my parents and my older brother, Pat, didn't know. The phone rang after the fact, and I don't even remember if it was the next day or the next week (that Sammy Pollock called). We were all sort of flabbergasted . . . My recollection is that my dad told Sammy, 'You mean Pat, Garry's (18-year-old) brother?' Pat was the better player."

Back then, the draft was designed for teams to claim only players who weren't already on sponsored lists or signed to C-forms. And that was slim pickings at the time. Selections in those days were not the prime properties that they became a handful of years later. Most years saw a snake format used, meaning those that ended a round would pick first in the next. Teams could defer their pick to another round or to another team. Also prior to 1969, players could still be signed to C-forms that locked in their rights with an NHL team at ages as young as 12 (as in the case of Bobby Orr, who was inked by the Bruins).

Kinks were eventually ironed out in the set-up, such as the Canadiens being allowed to snap up two of the best Quebec prospects before any other team had a chance to pick them. Contrary to popular belief—often perpetuated by those rationalizing the Habs' 15 Stanley Cups in a 24-season span from 1956 to 1979—this privilege was only really utilized in 1969 to gain the rights of Réjean Houle and Marc Tardif. Once created to help Montreal survive in their time of need during the Great Depression and early 1940s, by 1969 the Quebec priority clause was an unnecessary chestnut that was scrapped in time for the highly touted Gilbert Perreault to go first overall in 1970.

Today's version of the universal draft strives to provide an equal chance for all teams to find the best young talents the hockey world has to offer. Thanks to a combination of factors, though, equality hasn't always been the case, as even the greatest of talent evaluators and teachers often get it wrong and, only occasionally, strike it rich. And that lottery hasn't always ensured turnarounds for sad-sack clubs; the upper-class teams often dig up gems in lower rounds, where the success rate has traditionally been minimal. Once in a while, future stars have slipped through the cracks and come to the NHL as free agents following a different road (Adam Oates,

Curtis Joseph, Martin St. Louis). This is just a slice of why the draft is far from foolproof (especially when fools are running the ship).

With one major exception (see chapter 2), hockey's biggest and brightest stars in the post-expansion era (1967–68 to the present) began their pro careers via the draft. The rules skew heavily toward helping the weakest-performing clubs each season. But when that wasn't enough, NHL commissioner Gary Bettman adopted one of the practices of his former employer the NBA, instituting a draft lottery starting in 1994.

In the draft's early days, many teams were slow to grasp its importance. In the 1970s and throughout much of the '80s, few teams properly recognized the value of stockpiling picks through trades. Not until the Canadiens, Islanders and Oilers had created dynasties from their drafting wizardry did most teams finally catch on. Even then, these copycats could not capture that secret sauce of scouting and development. Teams fell flat on their face, and still do, trying to replicate what the select successful organizations do through the draft. Much of the time, it's a mighty task to undertake and master the art of drafting well. And what worked today doesn't necessarily work five years from now.

Certainly, there are very few surprises anymore, says Calgary Flames radio analyst Peter Loubardias:

> Twenty-five years ago, we didn't live in an era where you can consume what you can consume now from afar. Every game and every league, everywhere, happens to be on TV or online now. So in some ways there's less of an excuse for missing out on talent. If you really want to dig into some of the amateur stuff in a lot of different areas, it's there for you if you bother to watch. For instance, I'm fairly certain that 1991 was the first year where we saw every Canadian game at the World Juniors. And I think that was also one of the first years that we got to see not just the Memorial Cup Final, but *every* game in the tournament. It's about technology and the ability to just see more players and be exposed. And it's like anything else, if you see a guy maybe once or twice a year, you might be able to go, "Well, I don't know, is this guy

really better than the guy that we've watched in Sault Ste. Marie 50 times?" But now you're exposed to those people more than once a year.

But drafting is just the first hurdle. What teams do subsequently in training and development with their hits is what counts. And not to downplay understanding and exploiting the parameters of the draft, but luck often turns out to be the prevailing factor. That luck can come in bunches, then vanish just as fast. For example, legendary teams like the Oilers and Islanders of the '80s were able mine for gold for a few years at the draft table but then lapsed into prolonged funks where hardly anything went right (even though both have seen many top 10 picks handed their way thanks to awful season after awful season).

Truly, the draft beast can giveth—but just as easily it can taketh away. While the rules, parameters and trends of the draft have evolved, this cruel reality remains the same. Our aim is to encapsulate the many compelling, wild and captivating stories to be borne out of five-plus decades of NHL draft history.

CHAPTER 1

CARRYING A TORCH (1971)

1. Guy Lafleur, Montreal
2. Marcel Dionne, Detroit
3. Jocelyn Guevremont, Vancouver
4. Gene Carr, NY Rangers
5. Richard Martin, Buffalo
6. Ron Jones, Boston
7. Chuck Arnason, Montreal
8. Larry Wright, Philadelphia
9. Pierre Plante, Philadelphia
10. Steve Vickers, NY Rangers

ALONG THE NORTH SHORE OF THE Ottawa River, not far from its confluence near Montreal with the even mightier St. Lawrence, there sits a small Quebec town called Thurso. Historically known for its major employers, the Fortress paper mill and the Lauzon sawmill, Thurso lies in Quebec's mountainous Outaouais region. Situated in a flatter valley portion along the river at the base of the Laurentians' rolling hills, Thurso is in fact closer to the Canadian capital of Ottawa than it is to Montreal. But no one would think it's anything but Quebecois to its roots. Like the boys of small towns throughout Quebec in the mid-20th century, Thurso's young skaters possessed a burning desire to suit up with the beloved Montreal Canadiens. Making the NHL with any other club was unthinkable. The legendary exploits of Maurice Richard in the 1940s only intensified that feeling among the province's youth, influencing even more stars to come up through the ranks of hockey. Which means that late in the career of the "The Rocket," Richard enjoyed unparalleled success, with five straight Stanley Cups from

1

1956 to 1960—featuring Richard playing alongside many of the same young men he'd inspired with those earlier exploits on the "Flying Frenchmen."

This Cup domination only exacerbated the devotion many held toward this revered équipe de hockey. By the middle of the 1950s, when the Canadiens exerted their vice-like grip, hockey was considered Quebec's top religion after Catholicism. (Once the Quiet Revolution eroded the influence of the Catholic Church in favour of more secular values, hockey arguably became the province's primary mode of worship.) Within a generation, expatriate Quebeckers from coast to coast would still consider themselves devotees of *Le Tricolore* and witness Stanley Cups as a rite of passage every spring.

The 1950s NHL royalty of Rocket and the Canadiens were a far cry from their lowly estate fewer than 20 years earlier. Having barely survived a losing product coupled with the crippling economic effects of the Depression, the Habs ultimately emerged alone in the pro hockey scene of Montreal when the Anglophone-supported Montreal Maroons closed up shop in 1938. The 1940s started off no better for the Habs, with star player and newly named head coach Babe Siebert drowning in Lake Huron before he ever got to step behind the bench. But then the turnaround began, as Richard transformed from a notably injury-plagued prospect to NHL superstar alongside "Punch Line" mates Toe Blake and Elmer Lach. Coach Dick Irvin and his successor, Blake, stabilized the coaching position between 1940 and 1968. At the management level, the Canadiens in 1946 acquired a godsend in general manager Frank Selke, who'd been fired from the Maple Leafs front office in a fit of pique by team GM and owner Conn Smythe. By 1968, this Selke-Irvin-Blake collaboration had captured nine Stanley Cups (on top of the two won in the Punch Line's heyday, before Selke's arrival when Tom Gorman manned the GM post). The fanatical interest in the Canadiens produced the new generation of talented, hockey-mad kids in Quebec during the 1960s and '70s, a groundswell that made prior generations of Quebecois pro stars look meagre by comparison. Youths growing up around Thurso could now dream of avoiding working in the factories whose noxious odours attacked their olfactory senses. But one of those youths went on to achieve heights seldom seen in pro hockey before or since.

It seemed accepted from a tender age that Guy Lafleur, Thurso's prodigal son, would excel at the highest level of the sport. At five, the boy was given his first pair of skates as a Christmas gift. By seven, he was so passionate for the sport that he actually slept in his hockey equipment just so he could be ready to hit the ice right after waking up in the morning. To go along with this love of the game, he developed an inordinate amount of skill for a child so young. The son of Réjean and Pierrette Lafleur began to torch competition at every level. He also worked even harder than most kids his age at becoming such a supreme hockey machine.

At the same time, about 200 kilometres away along the Saint-François River southeast of Montreal, another prodigy was growing up in Drummondville. Tykes' fantasies weren't much different in this mill town, even if the population was 20 times larger than that of Thurso. Just as the name Thurso was derived from a Scottish burgh's, Drummondville too was a reminder of the British heritage in 18th-century Lower Canada, as it was named after Sir Gordon Drummond—Upper Canada's lieutenant-governor from 1813 to 1816. One can travel through southern Quebec today and still spot towns with English names, particularly in the Eastern Townships. Settled by Loyalists who left the U.S. after the American Revolution, towns in Quebec earned names such as Brownsburg, Hudson, Sutton, Knowlton, Cowansville, Sherbrooke and yes, Thurso and Drummondville.

Born a month earlier than Lafleur, in August of 1951, Marcel Dionne would parallel Lafleur's rise to stardom. A child from a typically large French-Canadian family of eight, Dionne was not tall as elite prospects go (Patrick Kane notwithstanding). Yet from the start, he never let height deter his ambition, frequently dominating against larger players. Even though he topped out at just five-foot-eight, Dionne's tremendous accomplishments would eventually earn him the moniker "The Little Beaver," since his diminutive build reminded fans of the legendary "midget" wrestler of the same name. Dionne wasn't easily pushed around, even though he largely played in an era when goons began to overrun the sport.

Like soccer legend Diego Maradona, Dionne utilized superb lower-body strength—what they call core strength today—that made him extremely difficult to catch, knock down or force into surrendering the puck. All are attributes essential for a centre to succeed. Future Canadiens star Steve Shutt suited up in the OHA with the Toronto Marlboros over the last two seasons of Dionne tearing up the league with the St. Catharines Black Hawks. In an interview with Ted Mahovlich for his 2004 book *Triple Crown: The Marcel Dionne Story*, Shutt recalled, "All you'd hear about (in those days) was Marcel Dionne, Marcel Dionne, Marcel Dionne . . . I go and get a look at (him). Well, here's this little wee, short guy and I said 'That's Marcel Dionne?' Once I saw him play, I said 'Oh, *that's* Marcel Dionne. But he certainly doesn't look like a hockey player.'"

Summing up Dionne's enormous ability combined with exemplary perseverance, Mahovlich writes, "As a result of his proportions, Dionne was questioned, doubted, overlooked and misread. And so, while the nonbelievers dismissed him, he quietly set out to do what his deceptively blessed physique would allow." Indeed, Dionne's style was notable in how it contrasted to Lafleur's. Where Dionne was a centre and an expert set-up man with a sneakily great release, Lafleur was a winger and a top-notch finisher first and foremost. He overwhelmed opponents with his blistering slappers—shots so hard and accurate that even the best goalies could look like fools, on sharp-angle blasts along the ice going off the post and in (laughably exploiting the stand-up style of the era's netminders). Though renowned for his shooting, Lafleur—similar to Wayne Gretzky, a noted playmaking wizard who just happened to be the most prolific goal scorer ever (almost as a footnote to his passing abilities)— is actually one of the few right wingers in the NHL's history to post multiple seasons of 70-plus assists.

While graceful, quick and elusive himself, the Flower resembled more of a middleweight boxer, with his sinewy, chiselled physique; he took advantage of skating, reflexes and intuition over muscle and brawn. Gliding on the wing like a gazelle, Lafleur belied his frame with a repertoire of powerful blasts. Meanwhile, Dionne is one of the greatest goal getters ever at the centre position, only dwarfed by Gretzky and, arguably, in terms of peak/prime, by Phil Esposito and Steve Yzerman. Yet, like the "Great One" (who took over the MVP mantle from him and ran with it), Dionne could fool you by being a shorter player who didn't seem to blow you away with speed and yet still found all the open areas, still exploited the defenders' weaknesses and still managed to beat everyone on the ice to the puck. A modern comparable would be the aforementioned Kane, albeit with a more devastating release and an even more pronounced scoring touch.

Superior to their peers at every step, the twin phenoms of Lafleur and Dionne would stand, without interruption, above the field from a very young age. Their paths crossed at various tournaments throughout Quebec's youth hockey landscape, and they often won championships for their respective hometown teams. Naturally, one of them was destined to become the projected top selection in 1971 once draft-eligible at 20 years of age (the youngest an amateur player could be taken at that time). It wasn't long before scouts, fans and media were captivated by the idea of which NHL teams would scoop up this pair born just a month apart.

In the pre-draft era of the 1950s and '60s, a talented Quebecois kid could logically expect to be scooped up by the Canadiens. In the CHs' halcyon "Flying Frenchmen" days of the 1920s, Howie Morenz's home town of Mitchell, Ontario, was about as far away as one could expect a Canadiens great to come from. Once Frank Selke took over running the organization, he paved the franchise's way to NHL hegemony by instituting the modern-day farm system concept in pro hockey. Not dissimilar to what baseball executive pioneer Branch Rickey did for the Cardinals and Dodgers organizations, Selke's machinations allowed the Canadiens to capitalize on all the tremendous talent that was developing not just in their backyard, but abroad as well. Former NHL GM Cliff Fletcher—who cut his teeth in Selke's system as a young man—recalled driving into the Quebec hinterland with Canadiens head scout Claude Ruel to a town called Port-Alfred to scout a blueline prospect by the name of Jean-Claude Tremblay. A future All-Star (and, considering who has been let in, one of the most curious Hockey Hall of Fame snubs to date), J.C. was one of 13 children in his family, and Fletcher remembered walking into the family home and thinking he was in a school as the Tremblay siblings all crowded into the kitchen to see the mighty Canadiens sign their brother. There was no doubt that day that they wouldn't be allowed to leave without getting J.C.'s signature on a C-Form contract.

As mentioned previously, when the NHL carved out territorial rights for teams, it allotted the right for the Habs to sign the top two Quebec prospects. This was done to keep the Canadiens thriving in the Great Depression, knowing that snapping up famous *gars de chez nous* would drive fan interest and therefore increase revenue for a business that had fallen on hard times both on (and especially) off the ice throughout the '30s. However, the arrival of the universal draft format in 1969, when that right was revoked, could have reasonably spelled the end of the dominance. With the NHL finally nixing that provision (one not entirely more beneficial than the Leafs owning most of Ontario as their region of priority), promising prospects from Quebec could now just as easily wind up in the uniform of another NHL club when the time came for their names to be called at the draft. Alas, the notion that this would cause the Habs empire to crumble turned out to be wishful thinking. While the NHL was pleased to see its newer franchises propped up by Quebec talent, Montreal's mastery would not fade for quite a while. Contrary to the popular narrative, it was the weak Canadian dollar, changing pro sports economics, free agency, language issues and provincial taxation—not the loss of a so-called divine right to French Canadians—that was most detrimental to the Canadiens' eventual downturn.

Under the stewardship of general manager Sam Pollock, Les Habitants continued to reign supreme over the league in the 1970s, despite now dealing with competition for talent closer to home. Culling prospects from all over North America, the Canadiens proved more than adept at not relying solely on the best prospects from their home province. They even outdid some teams in their own respective territories. For example, it can be argued that the Canadiens dug up more eventual stars out of Ontario in the '70s than did the Leafs, Sabres (who played across the border from Fort Erie) and Red Wings (who played across the border from Windsor). They also featured more American-born players during Pollock's time than nearly any U.S. team.

But that was in the future. For Lafleur and Dionne, there would be a wide array of potential suitors: in October 1967, when they were just 16 years old, the NHL had officially doubled in size from six to twelve teams. Even before the '60s were over, it boiled down to a simple question: Who would go number one and who would go number two? Montreal Junior Canadiens superstar Gilbert Perreault had been the consensus top pick leading up to his 1970 selection, when the expansion Buffalo Sabres picked him over their expansion brethren Vancouver Canucks. In 1971, there was certainly no easy decision like Buffalo had in taking Perreault over Dale Tallon.

The journey toward draft day, meanwhile, took the grassroots hockey rivals in very different developmental directions. Lafleur at age 15 would relocate from Thurso to the provincial capital of Quebec City to enhance his progress, commencing a journey parallel to that of one of his biggest hockey idols, Jean Béliveau. Following a Junior A career that saw the Trois-Rivières native excel for the Victoriaville Tigres and Quebec Citadelles, Béliveau had made a name for himself in the provincial capital city by dazzling for the senior-level Aces in the early 1950s. (He was reported to be making more with the Aces than most NHLers were making at that time. The joke was that the Canadians wanted Béliveau, but he couldn't afford to take the pay cut.)

While the Canadiens would compete on territorial rights contracts that allowed call-ups to the big club between 1950 and 1953, "Le Gros Bill" was still not a permanent member of the organization. He continually rebuffed offers from all around, including from Montreal. With Elmer Lach in his twilight years and his second-in-command centre Ken Mosdell unable to rival the great middlemen of that period, Frank Selke was aware he needed that superstar to match names like Boston's Milt Schmidt, Detroit's Sid Abel and Toronto's Ted Kennedy, not to mention future centre stars on those teams such as Alex Delvecchio, Don McKenney and Bronco Horvath. So, as the story goes, Canadiens ownership bought a majority stake in the Quebec Senior League to secure exclusive signing rights to Béliveau, most likely paying a lot more for that opportunity than they did when negotiating his actual annual salary. (Toronto would follow suit by later purchasing a league to secure exclusive control of Frank Mahovlich in Schumacher, Ontario.)

Fittingly, the team Lafleur would join was dubbed the Quebec Junior Aces. Two years after Lafleur's arrival in Quebec City, the Quebec Major Junior Hockey League was established, absorbing the strongest teams from the Junior A Quebec Junior Hockey League and the Metropolitan Montreal Junior Hockey League. With this transformation in time for 1969–70, Lafleur's Junior Aces were reborn under new ownership interests as the Quebec Remparts. This new league would then set the stage for many historic head-to-head showdowns between Lafleur and Dionne, right? Well, no, actually. Though they'd competed against each other in their adolescent years, a rivalry between Lafleur and Dionne wouldn't materialize in the Q.

This was because Dionne bolted from Drummondville to try the supposedly more challenging Ontario Hockey League as part of his quest to reach NHL stardom. Dionne may have been a Quebec product, but his path to prized-prospect glory took a very different journey. He had initially starred at the Junior A level in his own backyard with the Drummondville Rangers of the QJHL. Instead of remaining closer to home, the 17-year-old Dionne travelled to join the Ontario Hockey Association's St. Catharines Black Hawks in 1968. Knowing few words of English, he would nonetheless go on to establish some of the most impressive records anyone has ever had on the Ontario circuit, before or since. Authoring a career scoring mark not surpassed at the OHA level until Dale McCourt a decade later, Dionne became the early favourite for the number one pick according to several hockey writers and scouts, primarily those who followed the OHA more closely. Others, however, championed Lafleur.

By comparison, Dionne finished second in the OHA for points as a 17-year-old rookie in 1968–69 by posting exactly 100. A year later, he'd top the league with 135 points and then do so again in 1970–71 with 143, despite playing in only 46 of the possible 62 games. If Dionne had been a year older and born in 1952 (from which Billy Harris emerged as the top choice in 1972) or even a year younger and born in 1950 up against the flashier Perreault, Marcel likely would have been looking at definite number-one-overall-pick status. By sheer luck, he happened to be in the draft cohort of Lafleur, another once-in-a-blue-moon phenom.

By then recording his own special achievements in Quebec, Lafleur would register gaudy goal-scoring numbers that rewrote the record book and would not to be touched until Mario Lemieux arrived a decade and a half later. Donning the No. 4 of his hero Béliveau, Lafleur would light it up in ways previously thought unimaginable at the highest junior level. He would advance from 30 goals and 49 points in 43 games during 1967–68 (when still just 16 years of age) to 50 goals and

110 points in 49 games the year after. His pure dominance culminated with an effort of 103 goals and 170 points in only 56 games in 1969–70. Because he had to wait until he was 20 to be drafted, Guy followed that with an unthinkable 130 goals and 207 points in 62 games during his final amateur campaign of 1970–71.

When it comes to the draft, timing is everything. Guy's teammates would learn that, reaping the benefits of a generational junior superstar on their line. Jacques Richard would play as Lafleur's centre at times during four of his five years with Quebec, parlaying it into becoming the first draft selection in Atlanta Flames history (number two overall in 1972). Likewise, André Savard would get to play down the middle with Lafleur and put up similar giant numbers that led to going sixth overall to the Bruins in 1973. While neither enjoyed the lofty heights in the NHL that "The Flower" did, their journeys could be tied to their hundreds and hundreds of productive shifts playing alongside him.

During his time in St. Catharines, Dionne benefitted from playing with, and helping to enhance the allure of, future pros such as defenceman Dick (brother of Mickey) Redmond, centre Bobby Sheehan (a 1969 Canadiens selection and, briefly, Dionne's NHL teammate with the Kings in 1981–82) and wingers like Bob MacMillan. But there was no doubt who was really inflating the numbers of others on the junior Black Hawks. Given the less outrageous scoring of the OHA, several writers and scouts believed Dionne's numbers were actually more impressive than the ones Lafleur was putting up in the freewheeling Q. Also, given that Lafleur's teammates turned out to be much higher-ranked prospects in their draft years, it seems Dionne was doing it with slightly less aid as well.

With both teams' success throughout 1970–71, a collision was widely predicted between Lafleur and Dionne in the Memorial Cup. At the time, that championship's format still pitted the OHA and QMJHL champions against each other in a series to determine the Eastern representative, who would then face the Western champion (the tournament became a three-team affair starting just a year later). As many expected, the Hawks and Remparts won their respective leagues, with both phenoms meeting the high expectations and easily slicing through the competition of their respective playoff brackets.

The much-hyped Eastern Championship Final was set as a result. The series would turn out more volatile than anyone expected—and not because of hatred between the opposing sides, either. Fittingly, the Remparts head coach at the time was Maurice Filion—the same bench boss Dionne had toiled under with Drummondville as recently as 1968 (Filion would ascend to become the off-and-on GM of the Quebec Nordiques between 1972 and 1990 during both their WHA and NHL existences). He had moved behind the Remparts bench a year and half earlier, just in time for their first season in the newly formed Q. He frequently told the media in the lead-up to the Memorial Cup semifinal series that he wanted payback on Dionne and his Black Hawks, as he was still stinging from the defection of his best player to the rival Ontario circuit almost three years earlier. According to sports columnist Claude Larochelle, as quoted by Craig MacInnis in the 2004 anthology *Remembering Guy Lafleur*, that departure was "consummated in the midst of a barrage of insults"— one of which saw Filion bark, "Go to Ontario, Dionne. One day I'll beat you with a team from Quebec."

Many hockey fans in the province of Quebec felt the same way as Filion about Dionne's defection to Ontario. This would produce a series featuring violence and animosity stoked by the fans' provincial and linguistic grudges. With the Hawks' alleged intimidation tactics on the ice, fans of the Remparts became increasingly incensed about anything Hawks and/or Dionne-related. All in all, Canadian junior hockey would witness one of the more controversial and fearsome playoff series in its history.

After the first two games in St. Catharines were split, Game 3 back in Quebec City saw over 100 penalty minutes combined. The majority of those (77 to be exact) were given to St. Catharines, which sought to rough up the more finesse-oriented Quebec champs. Remparts fans were none too pleased by the intimidation tactics, which persisted even as their side skated to a 3–1 series lead thanks to a 6–1 win in Game 4. That contest saw Lafleur rack up a hat trick before the Hawks turned to mixing it up physically in the later going, much to the consternation of referee Jack Bowman (brother of famed head coach Scotty), who would whistle six misconduct penalties to St. Catharines over the final five minutes.

As MacInnis reports, Filion was incensed afterward, declaring St. Catharines "a disgrace to hockey. Why try to injure players when they're on the doorstep of a pro career? Have you noticed that none of my players have gone out of their way to hurt Dionne? Why should we?" The vitriol toward the Black Hawks would notably see Dionne's parents caught up in the fury, with Quebec fans reportedly accosting them in the crowd—while directing their venom at Dionne and the Hawks' other francophone "traitor," Pierre Guité.

It wasn't just hockey hatred that ran deep in this series. During these years, Quebec's Quiet Revolution was in full swing. Dionne was portrayed as an appeaser to the English over his decision to "take his talents" (excuse the turn of phrase, LeBron James) to Ontario instead of keeping them where the *"maîtres chez-nous"* (masters in our own house) advocates held sway.

The tension even spilled into the political realm when the Front de Libération du Québec (FLQ) terrorist group reportedly pledged that the Hawks would not be safe if they bothered to show their faces in the provincial capital again—a threat to be taken seriously after the previous year's October Crisis, when FLQ members murdered Quebec trade minister Pierre Laporte, and prime minister Pierre Trudeau decided to invoke the War Measures Act for the first and only time in Canada's history. After Game 4, a police escort was required for the Black Hawks to exit Le Colisée and return to their hotel. There they were confronted by an angry mob surrounding the team bus. The nastiness worried St. Catharines team personnel and parents so much that they refused to play Games 6 and 7 anywhere in the province of Quebec. Rather than attempt to finish off a valiant comeback, St. Catharines opted to forfeit the rest of the series once negotiations failed in convincing the Remparts to play the final two games at a neutral site. While the unexpected conclusion to the Richardson Cup series didn't detract from what Dionne had accomplished as a junior, Lafleur certainly added to his resumé when his Remparts went on to sweep a best-of-three Memorial Cup over the West representatives, the Edmonton Oil Kings.

Lafleur may have been the biggest reason for the Remparts' triumph, but unlike so many projected top selections in the years to follow, he was not destined to be picked by a struggling, uncompetitive franchise just looking for respectability in a weak hockey market. If anything, his predicament would be far more pressure-packed than stepping in to save a fledgling expansion team. Dionne, meanwhile, would end up on a team that was anything but a world-beater at the time.

The mystery of who would be taken first overall was already tantalizing heading into that fateful 1971 draft day at Montreal's Queen Elizabeth Hotel. Enhancing the mighty grandeur, the hometown Habs a mere few weeks earlier had become surprise Stanley Cup champions by riding a rookie goalie named Ken Dryden to an upset defeat of Bobby Hull and the Chicago Black Hawks for the franchise's 17th Cup. And now, amazingly enough, fans of *Le Tricolore* were presented with adding the number one NHL prospect to their already abundant riches.

You might ask: How in the world can a championship organization from the season before ever get into possession of the draft's first overall selection? Imagine a scenario where just weeks after hoisting the Cup, the 2018–19 Blues got to draft Jack Hughes first overall, or if the 2019–20 Lightning were set to grab Alexis Lafrenière. In 1971, the equivalent situation faced Montreal after they pulled a Brinks job on the weak and vulnerable Oakland Seals. Since there was no draft lottery at the time and the worst record from the season before automatically earned a club the first crack at the top-ranked amateur players, the result was left much less up to chance. The number one pick could involve any team owning the rights to that pick via trade, back before there were provisions to a transaction such as "lottery-protected" or "deferred to the next year."

The Seals were one of the six 1967 expansion entries into the NHL—one that didn't fully comprehend the value of holding on to their draft picks. Of all the additions from that massive league growth, the Seals seemed to be the most caught up in chaos. Lost in a cycle of poor ownership and shaky management that would persist until the franchise's 1976 move to Cleveland, the Seals demonstrated their incompetence in spades during the 1970–71 NHL season. At the time the infamous trade happened, however, it was anything but a certain outcome. After a dreadful 15–42–7 last-place campaign in their inaugural season of 1967–68, the Seals had actually made the playoffs in the West Division in 1968–69. But then, with expectations of further improvement, the Seals crashed hard by going 22–40–14 in 1969–70. Amazingly, this got them back to the post-season—thanks to a quirk of the silly expansion playoff set-up that saw the Habs in the East Division miss out with 92 points despite having six more than the first-place Blues in the West (an outcome that prompted the NHL to move the Chicago Black Hawks to the West, while the expansion Sabres and Canucks were added to the East Division to level off the imbalance in teams and competitiveness). Once they barely qualified for the 1970 playoffs, though, the Seals suffered a swift exit at the hands of the Pittsburgh Penguins—a series that would end up being the final playoff action the franchise would ever see.

As alluded to, 1969–70 had been an up-and-down year for the Canadiens too, as they shocked many in the hockey world by missing the playoffs for the first time since 1948. Fans and media were calling for the team to do something significant to restore excellence. What ended up happening was more dramatic and earth-shaking than most could have predicted at the time. Wily Canadiens general manager Sam Pollock knew one of the ways he could set about turning things around was to pry a first-round pick from one of the weak-sister franchises. On May 22, 1970, he managed to achieve that by swapping a promising 22-year-old prospect from Regina named Ernie Hicke along with his team's first-round pick in the 1971 Draft for stay-at-home defenceman François Lacombe and the first-rounder of the Seals (soon to be rebranded as the California Golden Seals). With a year to go before the 1971 draft, the Seals' disaster-to-be was still an abstract concept. No one knew just how much worse they would become over the next 12 months.

Ironically, the Oakland GM that Pollock would fleece was Frank Selke Jr., the son of the man who had mentored Pollock all those years prior and groomed him to become his successor in time for 1964–65. The close ties make it perhaps more understandable how Pollock could have pulled off such a swindle. This trade also may partly explain the junior Selke's resignation from his GM post in November 1970—one of several tumultuous events for the struggling Bay Area hockey operation. At the time of the 1971 draft, the team was under the guidance of the eccentric Charlie O. Finley, then running MLB's Oakland Athletics—a team about to unleash a run of three straight World Series championships, yet all the while resenting the meddling of the man who sat at the very top of the organization. Finley's purchase of the Seals in 1970 represented the third ownership change during the Seals' tattered history. Calamity was often the order of the day under any owner for the misbegotten franchise, but Finley's zany ways added a new dimension to this facet.

On the Montreal side of the 1970 trade, Lacombe proved a generic throw-in, as he would never take part in a single regular season game for Montreal. What the Seals got in return would hardly help the already lagging organization either. Hicke joined his older brother Bill in Oakland for two years before bouncing around with three other teams until his pro career ended in 1978. Meanwhile, the Habs' first-rounder was used by California to take Chris Oddleifson—a depth scorer who mostly played out his NHL career in Vancouver and Boston without ever taking part in a single game in Seals colours (which were changed in 1970 to green, gold and yellow in order to resemble Finley's much more successful A's; for a time, the team also donned white-painted skates so as to create the appearance that the players were "floating" along the ice. Both colour schemes proved unpopular with most players and fans).

In this—at the time, seemingly minor—transaction, it was the Seals' first-rounder sent to Montreal that wound up as the true mother of all draft picks and a treasure chest of a return arguably unparalleled in NHL draft history before or since. The bumbling California squad saw to that by winding up dead last in 1970–71 with a mark of 20–53–5 and therefore handing the number one pick to the Habs on a silver platter.

Pollock was first given an in-depth preview on Lafleur's mighty potential by his primo talent evaluator, Claude Ruel. If there were a Hall of Fame for hockey scouts, Ruel might be the first inductee. As a consequence of his heightened stature within the organization, he also was sent behind the Canadiens bench—a role he always felt uncomfortable with—on two separate occasions. As Montreal's head coach, the Sherbrooke native had guided the team to a Stanley Cup in his first season after taking over from Toe Blake in 1968–69. But despite making the very most of an unenviable position (imagine, for example, whoever has to follow Bill Belichick with the New England Patriots or Gregg Popovich with the San Antonio Spurs) for his debut season, Ruel garnered a very opposite reaction as the Habs cratered in 1969–70 (albeit with a team that finished 16 games over the .500 mark, which represented a "crash" only because they'd been 27 above it .500 the previous year). The next year began with similar inconsistency, leading Ruel to quit his post partway through the season. Montreal had started at "only" 11–8–3 and were on track to perhaps miss the playoffs once again in the ultra-competitive East. Such were the seemingly impossible expectations of the Montreal scene by this point that Ruel was being routinely criticized for his inability to inspire the team—which, to be fair, was in an awkward transition between an aging core and the future of the franchise while suffering a litany of unlucky injuries along the way (mostly to the beleaguered Serge Savard, who due to the trauma of several serious leg injuries went from the French-Canadian answer to Bobby Orr in 1969 to more of a sublime stay-at-home defenceman by 1972).

Ruel's harshest critics deemed him to be nowhere near the immortal Toe Blake's equal, as if that was a designation to be ashamed of. They weren't entirely wrong, given Ruel's uneasiness with coaching in general even if his record is a glittering one compared to the majority of bench bosses in NHL history. The fact that his predecessor had never needed to put his team among the top four or five of the 12 NHL teams (since the West Division winner always had fewer points than the last playoff-seeded Eastern team did in those early expansion days) was lost on most Ruel doubters. Also commonly forgotten was the fact that the 1967–68 Blake-led team had—coming off a Stanley Cup Final loss to an over-the-hill-gang Leafs (spoiling a second Montreal "five-peat")—started a "disastrous" 8–12–7 in his final campaign as coach. (Perhaps this led Toe to realize it was best to go out on top. His team shook off the slow start and rallied to go a combined 46–11–3 the rest of the way, authoring a ludicrous 22–1–2 run from December 27 to February 22 then going 12-1 in the playoffs to claim the Cup with ease and let Blake retire a champion).

No matter; Hector "Toe" Blake was a legend now best remembered for his conquests, while Ruel was castigated for his shortcomings such as his lack of deftness with the media and approval among his players. With the tension mounting, Ruel had decided enough was enough, and on the morning of December 2, he handed over the reins to assistant and former Hab Al MacNeil (one of the last Habs bench bosses to date who wasn't fluent in French) who debuted that night in a tie vs the Penguins. Out of a position in which he had always been a bit shackled feeling, Ruel would immediately go back to his bread and butter as a scout and help the Habs in a talent-evaluating role.

Not long after his resignation in 1970, Ruel became convinced that he'd seen the ultimate hockey prospect in the world, and that the Canadiens needed to somehow secure him. While this wizard on the ice was certainly no deeply kept secret in the late fall of 1969, Ruel had never seen Lafleur first-hand until then. Months after the fact, he would relate to Ted Blackman of the *Montreal Gazette* that "by December 6, I was on the phone from Quebec City to Sam Pollock. I saw Guy Lafleur that night and I knew right away. I told Sam that night . . . well, I told him something . . . You could guess." Whatever was said by Ruel, Pollock was likely salivating over the possibilities when it became obvious that the Seals were basement-bound. California's disastrous move that cost them Lafleur was another example of the foolish short-sightedness many 1967 expansion teams displayed in those early years of expansion. (A lesson not repeated by future expansion teams such as the Islanders, Oilers and Vegas Golden Knights.)

Such was the reputation of Pollock that a myth has developed over the years, asserting that he made a second trade only so he could help the moribund Los Angeles Kings rise out of the NHL cellar and leap past the Seals in the standings. That deal came on January 25, 1971, when he shipped veteran Ralph Backstrom—a long-time, once-vital centre in the Habs attack who was now disgruntled over his playing time—to the Kings for spare parts Gord Labossiere (dealt a day later for Rey Comeau and cash), Ray Fortin and future considerations. An unremarkable trade at the time, it was supposedly pulled off to ensure that the Kings wouldn't finish in last place, and so the first-round pick Montreal had acquired from the Seals would remain of the number-one or number-two variety. The thing is, this transaction wasn't as sly a maneuver as the myth has built it up to be. In actuality, the Kings were not a bottom-three team at the time of the deal and, while the 33-year-old Backstrom was quite solid, his 14 goals and 27 points in 33 games didn't single-handedly vault the Kings to competency overnight. In fact, L.A. was 14–23–8 at the time of the deal and were barely better over the balance of their schedule. That this has developed into one of the more persistent Canadiens myths truly speaks to the managerial genius of Pollock.

Decades later, as quoted by Frank Orr in *Remembering Guy Lafleur,* "Sad Sam" would modestly brush off the "genius" label assessing that "in 1969–70, the Seals finished fourth in their division after a strong second-place finish the previous season. They definitely were a team on their way to good things, and many thought they could win the West Division . . . There's no way I could have predicted that the Seals would be last in the NHL, and we would have their draft pick, No. 1 overall. Sometimes in hockey, it's better to be lucky than good." Pollock may have been a bit charitable to the aimless Seals organization, somehow forgetting that the Black Hawks were moved into the West in 1970–71 and that a California first-place outcome was next to impossible because of that, but he was correct that he couldn't have predicted they would finish dead last in the entire league.

Considering the presence of two expansion teams in the Sabres and Canucks, not to mention that the 1967–70 West outside of the Blues was full of mediocrity (with a 14–52–10 Kings team registering the worst single-season winning percentage the NHL had seen since the miserable Hawks of 1953–54), the Seals certainly weren't pegged to be the abject worst when 1970–71 rolled around. Most predicted that L.A., Vancouver and Buffalo would occupy the league's bottom three in 1970–71—a scenario which could have put Lafleur in Hollywood, Western Canada or playing on the wing alongside Gilbert Perreault on a truly ferocious French Connection fantasy line.

Pollock also responded to the theory that he traded Backstrom to help the Kings as "fiction, pure fiction, and stronger words if you want them. Ralph will verify this. For personal reasons, Ralph wanted to move to a team on the West Coast, and we talked about it . . . The Kings were the only team to make an offer for him." But when it comes to Montreal hockey lore, the famous phrase from *The Man Who Shot Liberty Valance* applies: "When the legend becomes fact, print the legend." Expounding on the subject around the 1971 All-Star game—and speaking in a tone that would make Gary Bettman's heart swell with pride—NHL president Clarence Campbell opined that "if we are ever going to get parity in the NHL, some embargo must be placed on the trading of amateur draft choices . . . Sammy Pollock needs the first draft choices for five years like I need another hole in my head." The importance of the top draft pick that the Canadiens now held, meanwhile, was that they were not just being presented with a chance to land a franchise player, but they also would have a chance to hand the proverbial torch of French-Canadian icon from one adored legend in Jean Béliveau (who took it over from Maurice Richard upon the Rocket's retirement in 1960) to potentially another in Lafleur or Dionne.

With its junior-level greatness, 1971 produced perhaps the hottest debate ever over the top two draft picks. Many other years have seen the first and second picks end up almost equal, while a select few have seen the top two picks both become superstars such as Pierre Turgeon and Brendan Shanahan in 1988, Joe Thornton and Patrick Marleau in 1997, Alex Ovechkin and Evgeni Malkin in 2004, Steven Stamkos and Drew Doughty in 2008 or even Taylor Hall and Tyler Seguin in 2010. But no year saw two future legends come so close to each other in scouting praise as they did in 1971. Leave it to "Trader Sam" Pollock to pull off a coup to acquire that top pick in the first place. Easily the shrewdest of any executive during the early post-expansion era of NHL upheaval and instability, Pollock had risen from success in Frank Selke's junior coaching and executive ranks to become the Canadiens' director of player personnel in 1959.

Receiving the ultimate grooming process from the originator of the modern-day NHL farm system, Pollock would hone his craft until his chance came to run the entire operation. Having set a very high bar for expectations, Selke retired suddenly before 1964–65. Coming off an "unacceptable" fourth straight Cup-less season running the Habs, Selke was made to see that it was time to step down at age 71 and hand over the controls to a ready and experienced (by the standards of a 38-year-old hockey management figure, that is) Pollock. Selke only did it because he believed he had bequeathed the position to a very capable individual, who would not squander what he had spent years to build. His premonition proved spot-on, and this choice—his last as Canadiens GM—proved to be one of his greatest decisions ever. It stands in contrast to when Pollock himself retired from the post in 1978, as his choice of successor (Irving Grundman) turned out to be a classic dud.

From the very first universal amateur draft in 1969 until his own retirement as the Habs' GM, Pollock would routinely exploit desperate and poorly run franchises for their first-round picks. Comprehending the innate advantages that the draft would present going forward in that it provided cheap young talent that would make veterans expendable and also raise the level of internal competition among players, Pollock was intent on proving that drafting, not trading, was the way to build a winning franchise in the draft era.

With the support of Canadiens ownership, he set about stockpiling picks via his trades from 1969 onward (in the days when draft selections cost each team a set amount of money). While Pollock was given the luxury of taking over a team with the deepest farm system in the NHL, he didn't let it lapse either, and he arguably left the Canadiens with as strong an arsenal as he had inherited 14 years earlier. This happened in spite of challenges such as competition from the free-spending WHA (who pillaged stars such as J.C. Tremblay, Réjean Houle, Marc Tardif and Frank Mahovlich) and the NHL expanding from 6 to 18 clubs during his tenure. After Pollock talked them up, anyone who wore the *tricolore* was soon judged to be at least twice as valuable in the trade market. Thus, he often jettisoned veteran players he regarded as expendable once their best days had come and gone. It was a masterful racket, and he exercised it to perfection.

Even with Montreal chalking up eight Stanley Cups during his tenure as GM (and with a ninth coming the year after he retired from the role and was just on the board of directors before leaving hockey altogether in 1979), Pollock somehow continually ended up with multiple first-round picks once draft day rolled around. He remained keenly aware of how a good chunk of top draft selections were unlikely to become stars, or in some cases not pan out as viable NHLers at all. So, he made a concerted effort to assemble as many selections as he could to account for all the chum. He sometimes manufactured trades as many as three years in advance to secure a potentially high draft pick that he thought was on the rise. Arguably his most glaring example of banking on future draft yields was his September 13, 1976, trade of AHL scoring star Ron Andruff and career minor league Sean Shanahan to the Colorado Rockies for the right to swap first-rounders in 1979 or 1980.

It's been speculated that this particular trade was perhaps done because Pollock thought that Wayne Gretzky could be the draft prize in one of those years. Thanks to a variety of circumstances (see chapter 2), that wasn't meant to be. But the transaction did earn Montreal the first overall pick following the 1979–80 season (why the Habs went with Doug Wickenheiser to be their franchise lynchpin is a different question). As the decades have passed, Pollock's strategies and approaches look either more visionary or more larcenous, depending on your point of view. While Pollock was never forced to draft and develop under the unforgiving grind of the salary cap, few doubted he could have been in the forefront of that era also.

Thanks to this artful opportunism, Montreal ran the NHL almost like a house league—not unlike what CSKA Moscow, a.k.a. the Red Army team, was doing at the time in the USSR, with the core of the great Soviet international teams playing for it (Pollock didn't have the ability to send anyone to Siberia, just the press box). No wonder Sam's disciples like Cliff Fletcher and Bill Torrey were in hot demand and soon headed off to run a few of the NHL expansion outposts. Even players Pollock managed—and in some cases, drafted—during his tenure—Bob Gainey, Glen Sather, Serge Savard, Ken Dryden, Rogie Vachon, Doug Risebrough and yes, Réjean Houle—would go on to serve as NHL GMs, while others would come close to that level of management in their thriving post-playing stints (Jacques Lemaire, Larry Robinson, Jacques Laperriere, Keith Acton).

The other operations in this era eventually figured out how to avoid perpetual second-class status by rarely trading their prized picks—especially not to Pollock, who was always eager to utilize the art of the deal. As a result, the Flames, Islanders, Flyers and Oilers went on to compete for and win Stanley Cups in subsequent years. Perhaps the best example of this self-discipline was Torrey's Islanders, who went from a dreadful 12-win expansion team in 1972–73 to a semifinalist in a mere three years, then a perennial top-five team for the next four seasons before finally becoming a Cup champion (the first of four in a row) in just their eighth season as a franchise. Stepping into the New York market as the "second-class" team to the established Rangers, the Isles became a model organization while their city rivals continued to come close but blunder at the worst possible times amidst a 54-year Cup drought. Learning from the Seals' mistake with Lafleur, Torrey rebuffed trade package offers from other teams (including the Habs themselves) for his 1974 first overall pick, which became one of the great defencemen ever in Denis Potvin. The majority of GMs, though, were not so fortunate when they decided to chance making moves with the Canadiens' mastermind wheeler and dealer. Broadcaster Mitch Melnick, a veteran of the Montreal sports scene with a distinguished 40-plus-year career in radio, asserts that:

> I'm sure Sam would've been able to make that trade if Torrey was willing, because he had so many prospects and stars to offer other teams. It was like the Yankees in that every prospect was so overhyped that he was able to snooker gullible GMs into giving away high draft picks and promising players. Shows you how good Torrey was and why the Isles became so dominant themselves, huh? The story goes that Sam took him for a walk around the block, and each time they circled the Forum, he'd add a new player to sweeten the pot. Some big names were mentioned, even Cournoyer, I think. All to get Denis Potvin. But Torrey came up with Montreal when he got into scouting, like Cliff Fletcher had. It was like a remarkable scouting factory with the '50s and '60s Habs. Obviously, both learned well from the master.

But in June of 1971, that still lay in the future. Meanwhile Pollock was presented with a serious dilemma. Just weeks before the epochal 1971 draft, Pollock's underdog Canadiens garnered yet another Stanley Cup title in a 3–2 Game 7 comeback win on Chicago Stadium ice. Alongside the fact that the Habs also ousted the powerhouse Bruins along the way to the final, this championship was likely the most surprising of any that the storied franchise had won. The magical journey of 1971 occurred primarily due to the heroic efforts of rookie goalie Ken Dryden. However, the leadership of 39-year-old captain Béliveau proved essential to this famed "Cinderella" run as well.

With his most unexpected of conquests yet, Le Gros Bill had earned a then-unprecedented 10th Cup ring as a player (for Henri Richard, it was his 10th of a record 11 Cups). In the midst of the dressing room euphoria, Béliveau was besieged. Was he truly hanging up his skates for good? No better symbolism could have been found than to have Les Habitants replace Béliveau with yet another Quebecois wunderkind. No French-Canadian star from the 1970–71 Habs—Jacques Lemaire, Yvan Cournoyer or Serge Savard—could "carry that torch," despite their experience and abilities. Instead, the pressure would be deferred from actual proven hockey super-stars and be placed on an unproven rookie, either Lafleur or Dionne. It sounds wacky today, but it totally made sense to the demanding Habs fan base in the summer of 1971.

Just 22 days after the sweet victory of May 18, Béliveau confirmed publicly that his pro career was over. Lafleur's top draft selection would fittingly come just a day after Béliveau's official June 9 announcement. Though fans saw it as a slam dunk, the choosing of Lafleur was not quite a sure thing once the 1971 playoffs ended. Hockey scribes puzzled over which French-Canadian prospect would go to the Canadiens, and Pollock agonized over the important decision as well. Scouting wisdom deemed both to be "can't miss" superstars of the future, if not right away. Lafleur was the more explosive, electrifying and raw talent while Dionne was perhaps the more pro-ready. Many asserted that Lafleur owned the higher ceiling of the two but would have to be worked on by coaching in order to improve his two-way game and iron out the bad habits that one can get away with at the amateur/junior level.

Upon Pollock's passing in 2007, Eric Duhatschek wrote a *Globe and Mail* obituary and spoke to Scotty Bowman, who recalled that:

> The night before the draft, we met for three hours, and Sam grilled everybody in the room—Al MacNeil, Ronnie Caron, Claude Ruel and a couple of scouts—What should they do with Lafleur and Dionne? Then he excused himself and made a call to coach/GM Ned Harkness, in Detroit, to propose a trade . . . Sam offered the Wings goalie Phil Myre, plus either Terry Harper or J.C. Tremblay and something else, to get the

second pick. Hapless Detroit was willing to do it, because they were going to get three players who could help them immediately. I remember Sam came back in the room and said, "If I make this deal, could it be another Béliveau and Geoffrion for ten years?" But nobody would stand up and say yes. So, he didn't make the deal—because that's how Sam worked. If there were five people in the room, he would never do anything until he talked all five people into doing what he wanted to do.

Despite a tongue-in-cheek "time out" called by Pollock when the Canadiens' turn to pick came around, it was Lafleur whose name was uttered first on June 10, 1971. The ultimate determination to select Lafleur came after a whirlwind 24-hour period in which not only had Béliveau retired, but Bowman had been hired to take over as Habs head coach after Al MacNeil resigned following clashes with veterans such as Henri Richard, who called him the "worst coach I ever played for" upon a benching during their Cup Final series with Chicago. The Red Wings would still get to select the "consolation prize" of Dionne at second overall, after all was said and done.

Dionne certainly felt no disappointment about being passed over, half-facetiously observing to Ted Mahovlich in *Triple Crown* that he "didn't even want to go to Montreal . . . Looking back, Detroit was the right place for me to go. If I had gone to Montreal, I probably would have committed suicide—jumped off the Jacques Cartier Bridge. I had too much emotion, they would have destroyed me in Montreal." The pressures in Detroit were still there, obviously, given Dionne was joining the Wings right after their GOAT (Greatest of All Time) Gordie Howe had "retired" at age 43. Nonetheless, it paled next to the expectations in a pure hockey town like Montreal, where winning had become second nature and Cup memories were very fresh—unlike in Motown, where such glory had become a fleeting memory and the franchise was entering a hellish period from which it wouldn't fully escape until the early 1990s.

Some felt that taking Dionne would have been a publicity disaster at the time for the Canadiens too. Asked about it in *Triple Crown*, Dick Irvin pointed out that "Lafleur was *the* guy in Quebec. If Sam Pollock had drafted Dionne (instead), they would have run him out of town . . . I think it was just so much Lafleur, and that was the whole story. And I don't think there was a blinking of an eye or wringing of hands that Marcel Dionne went to the Red Wings." With the benefit of modern perspective, Craig Button—a former scout, director of player personnel and GM in the NHL (and now a TSN scouting insider)—points out, "If you go back and ask the principals involved, I don't think that there was a debate of who they were taking. It was Lafleur all the way."

Mitch Melnick was just 12 when the Canadiens drafted Lafleur but recalls that, while it may have been analyzed a bit behind closed doors, out in the public sphere the choice was clear: "There was never any debate in Montreal that it was going to be Lafleur and not Dionne. If you were a fan of the Canadiens back in 1970–71, you weren't only following them, you were following the Remparts as well because there were game reports every day on what he was doing. And there was a lot to report, since he scored 130 goals!"

The apparent decision to make Lafleur the number one selection lends credence to the theory that Pollock also wanted to acquire the number two pick so he could get Dionne to be Lafleur's centre. While Jacques Lemaire was already in place and Pete Mahovlich would play that role to a tee later on, neither could quite hold a candle to Dionne's offensive exploits during his prime years from the mid-1970s to mid-'80s.

While Dionne figured he'd be waiting past the selection of Lafleur, the prized Flower himself was late to the actual draft ceremony itself, as he arrived a few minutes after the announcement of his name. And the Canadiens after taking Lafleur weren't entirely finished digging up key pieces on that late spring day in downtown Montreal. In an example of the draft's crapshoot nature, they held the number eight pick, and used it on Chuck Arnason, who failed to catch on in Montreal and barely carved out a respectable pro career after being traded away. But as luck would have it, a rangy defenceman with decent wheels for his size and a cannon shot would be available in round two.

Lafleur had noticed this particular red-headed "beanpole" while playing peewee teams from across the Ottawa River in Ontario. He was Larry Robinson, born in a town just south of Ottawa called Winchester, and raised in the small village of Marvelville (part of the township of Metcalfe). Growing up on a dairy farm, Robinson was pure Eastern Ontario country stock. In his 1990 book *Overtime: The Legend of Guy Lafleur*, Georges-Hébert Germain reports that upon arriving at the draft ceremony to see all the teams and media assembled, Robinson remarked to his father, "It's like a livestock auction, don't you think?" much to the amusement of those who heard the comment.

Looking back on the draft experience in his 2014 book *The Great Defender: My Hockey Odyssey*, Robinson admitted that it was only the third time he had ever travelled to Montreal; because of his family's unfamiliarity with big-city traffic, they only showed up halfway through the first round. His famous cattle comment, according to his 1988 book *Robinson for the Defence*, was inspired by the resemblance of the 14 NHL teams at their tables to buyers at an auction, while the cattle were the "strapping young men in new, ill-fitting suits or blazers and slacks. You had never seen so many flowered shirts and paisley ties outside San Francisco . . . Mr. (Clarence) Campbell was on a raised platform, addressing each team's spokesman as his turn came up, much like the auctioneer who would have cattle paraded for inspection before a group of farmers."

Robinson for the Defence also chronicles what it was like to wait around for the calling of his name: "I looked around the room, occasionally nodding or waving to teammates and opponents I'd known. We were studies in feigned nonchalance—occasionally we would lock eyes and roll them upwards, as if to silently say across the room: 'What a crock of shit, this is,' while deep inside a little voice was saying 'Pick me! Pick me! Pick me! I don't care.'"

Robinson wouldn't have to wait long, though—he would be chosen as 20th overall—to become the Canadiens' fourth selection of that year's draft. In what would represent one of Pollock's classic "project picks," Robinson was called to the draft floor earlier than most experts had expected him to be. After all, here was a player who hadn't quite gone through years of dominating the OHA like glitzy picks such as Dionne, Jocelyn Guevremont, Rick Martin and Steve Vickers had. But he did exhibit some interesting potential, enough to make it hard for the Habs brain trust to pass him up once they'd selected the phenom Lafleur plus some scoring winger skill in Arnason and Murray Wilson. By 1971, "Big Bird" had come off just a single year of Junior A experience with the Brockville Braves and another of major junior experience with the Kitchener Rangers. He was a bit raw for a 20-year-old, but certainly had proven adept each time he advanced a level on the junior hockey ladder.

Once announced as the Canadiens' newest selection, Robinson claims he quipped to his father, "Hold me up Dad, I think I'm going to faint!" He would later joke in *Robinson for the Defence* that:

> When you are 6' foot 3", your jaw has a long way to go to hit the floor. How wide open was my mouth? Picture a three-car garage . . . It was all a blur . . . I kept mumbling "thanks" and floated along through a sea of outstretched hands at a speed that approached a single-frame advance. Inside, however, my mind was on fast forward . . .
>
> "The Montreal Canadiens? Not on your life. J.C. Tremblay. Terry Harper. Jacques Laperriere. Guy Lapointe. Serge Savard. Pierre Bouchard. I'm going to spend my life in the American Hockey League" if I was lucky; the Canadiens also had a busload of talented young defencemen playing in Halifax (with the Nova Scotia Voyageurs).

At the same time, Robinson did acknowledge that he had received a good lot in his hockey life by not being taken where anyone would expect miracles at the outset—unlike Lafleur, who went 19 spots ahead of him. Robinson even asserted, "I wouldn't have traded places with him for the world."

While being drafted by the most talent-rich franchise in pro hockey posed a daunting challenge for Robinson, he knew he was entering an organization that owned the most productive farm system in the NHL at the time too. While he could have enjoyed a quicker succession to the NHL if claimed by a weaker team such as the Seals, Canucks or Kings, it's almost a guarantee he wouldn't have enjoyed the same sort of illustrious career. The Habs owned the uncanny ability to develop elite talents at the minor-league level, and did it thanks to tremendous competition for jobs and ice time. It had worked like a charm in the Frank Selke days of the 1950s and '60s and didn't miss a beat in the '70s either. Craig Button recalls that "one of the great things about Montreal was that they had this philosophy: 'We're not going to trade our players until we *test* our players.' They didn't just trade them after one game or 10 games, they really tested them first. Then they knew *exactly* what they had."

Robinson would be one of the decade's great success stories for Montreal, advancing to the big club late in his second season with the Voyageurs and sticking there for the rest of his Hall of Fame career—one that saw him become the next great Canadiens leader during the club's post-dynasty years, a stalwart for 20 seasons in the NHL (when players in their late 30s were often phased out due to the young legs in the game, not to mention their often lucrative contracts that proved dispensable) and one of the great defencemen his generation ever produced. To say nothing of a draft legend that rival clubs—some of whom passed twice on Big Bird— lived to regret not selecting.

As for Robinson's long-time teammate Lafleur, he was a 19-year-old in the summer of 1971 himself, though one dealing with far bigger expectations placed upon him. It wouldn't help matters that, throughout his junior career, he had worn the same No. 4 jersey that Jean Béliveau had worn. (Jean allegedly even offered No. 4 to the new phenom.) As it turns out, the decision would be out of Lafleur's hands as he had to switch to No. 10 because Béliveau's number would be raised to the rafters of the old Montreal Forum during the 1971–72 season (another honour on top of his induction into the Hockey Hall of Fame, when it waived its customary minimum three-year waiting period for entry).

Even though Montreal was loaded with established stars up front, such as the Mahovlich brothers, Cournoyer, Lemaire and Richard, conventional thinking from fans and media was that "Le Démon Blond" would quickly soar past them on the depth chart, and instant success would be his. Whatever number he would wear, many expected *la crème* to quickly rise to the top and establish himself as a 50-goal and/or 100-point superstar in his first season. After all, he was supposed to be Quebec's answer to Bobby Hull. Akin to the "Golden Jet," Lafleur was a hard-shooting, fast-skating streak of excitement who could entertain and captivate crowds wherever he went. (It didn't hurt that, like Hull, he was considered somewhat of a sex symbol, too.)

By this point, Montreal had been consistently spoiled not only by team glories but by youngsters making the jump seamlessly from junior to pro. In the prior two decades, Bernie Geoffrion, Ralph Backstrom and Bobby Rousseau had all won the Calder Trophy as rookie of the year. And though he didn't win that honour—thanks to an injury-shortened 1942–43 season—Maurice Richard would become a superstar winger in his first full NHL campaign of 1943–44. Béliveau, too, had become a top-10 scorer in the league during his second full season, in 1954–55. And now Lafleur in 1971 was being hailed as potentially more dominant than all those Calder winners ever had been, not to mention a successor to the gargantuan legacies of the Rocket and Le Gros Bill themselves. It was quite the burden for anyone, even a player with the supreme confidence and skill of a young hotshot like Lafleur. Mitch Melnick recalls the scenario:

> There was big pressure, for sure. I mean, the last game that Béliveau played was only a few weeks before that draft in Chicago. When he won the Stanley Cup and became—at least, I believe so—the first player to take it for a victory lap on the ice. So he went out on top, and that was the lasting final memory of Jean's playing career that Guy had to step into. There's been nobody like Béliveau in the history of hockey in Montreal, and I don't think anywhere else in terms of the dominance and elegance, almost like a statesman for the game. Even among kids at the time, we knew there was something magical about him. Now you're passing the torch to Lafleur. There was even talk of switching him to the middle in his first year, to basically move into Béliveau's spot as the number one centre of the Canadiens. And before the goalie became the dominant position in Habs lore, that was *the* marquee role to have. Lafleur was basically walking into a large shadow. I mean, that's tough. You're the next French superstar and you're replacing a legend who maybe would never be topped in the history of the franchise in terms of a

persona. (Lafleur) had a very good rookie year too! Scored 29 goals and had 64 points. Anywhere else in the NHL, that's a very good rookie season, but I think people were expecting 30 to 40 goals and a point a game.

As we know now, it was no surprise that Scotty Bowman would saddle a young player with challenges that put his two-way abilities to the test. And he certainly put his star pupil to the test in those early, often underwhelming years. The newest impact rookie to enter the NHL, Lafleur found himself shuffled around the lines, and sometimes he was indeed tried out at centre—a designation that required much more responsibility than his natural right-wing slot and also didn't exactly guarantee prime ice time given that Jacques Lemaire, Pete Mahovlich and Henri Richard were natural centres too.

All these challenges produced a modestly successful debut season for Lafleur. At the time, it was actually one of the higher-scoring rookie campaigns in NHL history (partly attributable to the 78-game schedule, whereas an NHL season before 1967 never extended beyond 70 games). However, for a player who had averaged over two goals per game in his draft year as a junior, 1971–72 was considered underwhelming and led to some questions about just exactly what the big fuss was all about. Sure, the Flower offered up flashes of his game-breaking talent by recording three hat tricks in that rookie campaign. However, he only managed to pot 18 goals in the 70 other games he suited up for. This inconsistency confused onlookers, who could see that the amazing talent was there but the production often wasn't. The eager hockey world was expecting a lot more than the frustrating boom-or-bust rookie year they saw.

Worse for Pollock, his selection may have had one more tally and just seven fewer points than Dionne, but it was the perception that mattered also. And the perception was that Lafleur didn't match up to his draft "adversary." Making matters worse was that Buffalo's number five overall pick, Rick Martin, achieved the heights Lafleur supposedly should have reached in 1971–72 by amassing an NHL rookie record 44 goals—still tied today as the seventh-highest such total in league history. Lost in the nagging criticism was the fact that Martin got to play alongside a better centreman

(Perreault) than anyone Lafleur had at his disposal in Montreal. Martin and Dionne would be runners-up to another Hab in Calder voting though, as Dryden followed his 1971 playoff MVP star turn with more hardware the next season. Even though he was the odds-on favourite when training camp had rolled around, Lafleur wasn't even a finalist for the award. The dashing of these rather lofty expectations naturally begat skepticism of Lafleur's greatness.

It was a questioning that would only get more intense over the next two seasons, as Lafleur's production actually declined in each of the two seasons afterward. The reduction would happen despite the fact that the Habs were forming their '70s dynasty core and would win a very convincing Cup in the middle of Lafleur's first three seasons by going a gaudy 52–10–16 then topping it off with a 12–4 playoff record in 1972–73. That 1973 title was a perfect confluence of many of their stars developed back in the 1960s (Lemaire, Lapointe, Cournoyer, Savard, Laperriere) still chugging along atop the depth chart beside the future stars knocking on the door (Lafleur, Steve Shutt, Robinson). It was a year that proved the Habs were capable of being as dominant as they had ever been and, according to Craig Button, helped Lafleur in a way, in that it "(took) the pressure off. Guy still wasn't anywhere near his peak yet, but that incredible season and that convincing Cup win afforded him an opportunity to grow, because he had the right support group around him. Just look at that roster. What a group to learn from, study under and develop chemistry with too. I think Sam Pollock also was key in this situation. He understood that if you had more, it *gave* you more possibilities. Why not use the rules, and your economic might, to your advantage if you could?" Indeed, the crowded depth chart, combined with Bowman's detailed and disciplinary style, meant Lafleur would remain a secondary and sometimes tertiary scorer bubbling under the surface of stardom without quite breaking out enough to meet his true potential.

To the exasperation of Habs fans, Lafleur's closest peers continued to outdo him in every way but in championship rings. Dionne avoided any sophomore jinx by posting 90 and 78 points in the next two campaigns, compared to Lafleur's 56 and 55, while Martin reeled off 37 and 52 goal campaigns to show his freshman output had been no beginner's luck. To add insult, even the number 10 pick of 1971, Steve Vickers—debuting for the Rangers in 1972—reeled off back-to-back 30-goal seasons to start off his career. When Lafleur bottomed out with only 21 goals in his third NHL season, 1973–74, there were whispers that maybe he was just a fluke, a flash-in-the-pan who peaked too early, spoiled by the weaker defences of the junior game and perhaps too mentally fragile to handle the immense pressure of being the next supposed legend in Canadiens lore.

Despite his stalled progress, the World Hockey Association's Nordiques were still interested in pouncing to get him, believing his name carried enormous cachet and that those otherworldly skills could be better re-channelled back in the city of his greatest exploits, to be revealed against the inferior pros of the WHA. "As a young fan, I remember being very, very worried that it seemed plausible Lafleur could leave," remembers Melnick. "We all knew Sammy Pollock was intelligent, so he couldn't be so dumb as to allow Lafleur to leave for Quebec even though he was underachieving, right? There was some insecurity out there among people like me, just knowing how good he was and just waiting for him to show up but worried that he might now do it in Quebec instead of Montreal."

Reports indicated at the time that the Nordiques initially had made a three-year, $90,000-per-year offer but that it had been rejected. They came back with an offer that paid $125,000 in the first year, $135,000 the next and $150,000 in the third, with a $60,000 signing bonus. While the move would have provided Guy the chance to really light up the fledgling WHA, it would also have been for better money than Montreal was initially offering up. Instead, the Canadiens hurried to lock up their young star, and soon.

What ultimately won him over was the Canadiens stepping up to offer a mammoth 10-year deal that would give him $100,000 per season on a sliding scale. Also influential was Montreal's place in a higher-level league and superior situation for earnings off the ice. Lafleur at the time opined that he "could get better endorsement deals in Montreal . . . I realize that I'm losing $55,000 per year, maybe more (to go to Quebec over Montreal). But I've secured my future for many years, and that's important to me. My money is guaranteed, so if I break my leg in a year or two, for example, my earnings will continue."

Lafleur would sour on the deal later on however, as he felt he had been pressured into a less lucrative offer from the Canadiens than the one

Quebec had ponied up—a five-year, $1 million pitch that had come too late after Lafleur's pact with the Habs. As Andrew Zadarnowski reports on the *Eyes on the Prize* blog, Lafleur eventually chafed against the theory that off-ice earnings should be irrelevant to the actual structure of a contract for his on-ice work. His deal had to be reconfigured several times once he became displeased with lesser players earning more than him, the best player in the world. The bitter pill of his initial contract led to Lafleur changing agents and taking more hardball stances in his negotiations down the road.

Nonetheless, Lafleur had to live up to the 1974 signing first . . . and live up to it he definitely did. As Melnick says:

> Something certainly came together there after that contract, and it just seemed to free him. But I don't recall people think-ing, "Oh Jesus, this kid's a bust" before that, because it was pretty obvious to anybody who was watching the game that he had *everything*. It's just there was something above and beyond performance level that was affecting his play, and I think I'd like to point to a moment that turned it around, but I can't recall one specific thing. I don't remember who his linemates were originally, and I think it was probably a revolving door of guys really, but I know as soon as it was Mahovlich and Shutt put with him, it clicked . . . and also the departure of Frank Mahovlich to the WHA really seemed to spark Guy to that elite level.
>
> The number one left winger spot going up for grabs because Frank left is what gave Shutt a chance too. He really took the mantle and ran with it and therefore he got the ice time to become the perfect foil for Guy. He became the line-mate who could bury his open looks, put home the so-called garbage goals while Guy unleashed his moves and that dev-astating shot. Meanwhile, Pete was the consummate slick, graceful and creative playmaker they both needed. And to this day, he holds the record for most assists in a season by a Canadien (82, in 1974–75), and that came playing with Lafleur and Shutt for the most part. Meanwhile Guy just was playing

so much better that Scotty couldn't ignore it, so he finally wrestled away that top line right winger slotting from Yvan Cournoyer. It was then that, at long last, we got to see the same superstar we had all witnessed in junior.

Helping pave the way for this major breakout by Lafleur were a number of factors, but what gets overlooked by most are the key defections to the WHA with its tempting high pay. In addition to Mahovlich signing with the Toronto Toros in 1974, the prior off-season had seen 1973 Cup team members Marc Tardif and Réjean Houle go to the Los Angeles Sharks and Nordiques respectively (Houle came back to the Habs in 1976). All this really did was open up more ice time in Bowman's system for younger, hungry names to burst through. Chiefly achieving this with Montreal was Lafleur, who cast off the shackles in 1974–75 and became the superstar many had anticipated from the outset he'd be. Ditching the helmet that had been worn since his NHL debut, he chalked up what would be one of his best ever seasons in per-game production by tallying 53 goals and 119 points in 70 games before following it up with 12 markers in only 11 playoff contests.

That magical 1974–75 campaign would not be a one-off fluke or even a career-best either, as the breakthrough kicked off a historic run of dominance—a player recording at least six consecutive seasons of both 50-plus goals and 100-plus points (bettered by Wayne Gretzky, who did it in eight straight from 1979 to 1987, and matched by Mike Bossy from 1980 to 1986). After all the early fretting over whether he was a bust or not, Guy had transformed himself into the Canadiens' last superstar forward to date.

Lafleur would not just reel in individual awards—three Art Ross scoring titles, three Hart Trophies, three Pearson Awards and one Conn Smythe— but he also shared in team success by winning five Stanley Cups and four Prince of Wales Trophies (back when that was an award for first overall in the NHL standings and not simply the conference championship).

While it's true that he had a tremendous career with an even longer prime and more notable consistency than Lafleur, Dionne's legacy would be diminished by the sorry playoff fortunes of both team and individual, as he never got to compete beyond the second round of the Stanley Cup playoffs. Fair or not, those failures would come to define him. Despite impressive stats, his name isn't often mentioned when people rank the top 20 greatest players ever. While much of the failure was out of his control, there's truth to the adage that your best players must be your best players in crunch time. Dionne's somewhat average (especially for the high-scoring era) 45 points in 49 career playoff games showed that he still owned a stake in the Kings' perennial playoff disappointments. While closer checking in the playoffs obviously led to teams targeting Dionne's line and more effectively neutralizing him (sometimes clearing the track for secondary scorers like Butch Goring, Mike Murphy and Daryl Evans to excel), he still proved largely unable to take his game to the next level. And when he was able to do that, the Kings were usually doomed by their annual (post–Rogie Vachon) goaltending and defence inadequacy.

Dionne's L.A. teams would only win a pair of best-of-three preliminary round series (both 1976 and 1977 against the Flames) and a single best-of-five series (the shocking "Miracle on Manchester" 1982 Smythe Division semifinal upset vs the Oilers) during his tenure of nearly 13 full seasons. Yes, that's right: Marcel Dionne never won a single best-of-seven Stanley Cup playoff series. Even more jarring, he only *played* in two best-of-seven series (the 1982 Smythe Division Final versus the Canucks and, with the Rangers, a 1987 Patrick Division Semifinal against the Flyers). Even when given quality linemates—such as wingers Dave Taylor and Charlie Simmer, on the dominant "Triple Crown" line—or supplied forward depth to take the burden of scoring off of his unit (Goring, Murphy, Bernie Nicholls, Jim Fox) or even respectable goaltending (Vachon; Mario Lessard, for a brief period), something always tripped up Dionne's Kings to give them ho-hum regular seasons and/or short playoff appearances. Sometimes it was thin scoring depth that did them in, but when it wasn't that, the consistently mediocre Kings would be a tire fire on their back end. Residing in the Smythe Division from 1981-82 onward—constantly having to be bombarded by the offensive attacks of the Oilers, Flames and Jets—certainly didn't help matters for the Kings.

Back in 1974–75, when the sky seemed the limit for both, it should be noted that Dionne wasn't exactly left in Lafleur's dust. He too broke out in a large way and notched even more points (121) than Lafleur, despite being saddled with yet another mediocre Red Wings squad. All four seasons he skated for Detroit ended with the team failing to qualify for the playoffs. Showing the same determination that he had when transferring from Drummondville to St. Catharines in 1968, Dionne said sayonara to the winged wheel once he realized his true worth. A trade demand came about when he entered into a contract dispute with Wings management following his rookie deal running out in the spring of '75. In swooped Kings owner Jack Kent Cooke, who tendered a five-year offer worth $1.5 million ($300,000 per year) to the free agent Dionne—a price tag that stingy Detroit was unwilling to match.

In one of the first episodes of testing free agency in NHL history, Dionne would move to the City of Angels in a unique sign-and-trade brokered by agent Alan Eagleson and NHL president Clarence Campbell. The deal sent Terry Harper, Dan Maloney and a second-rounder to Detroit for Dionne and journeyman defender Bart Crashley. History would prove it to be a steal for the Kings—even if it was not the answer to Dionne's dreams of playing constant winning hockey.

Burdened with a slighter shade of mediocrity in L.A., "Le Petit Castor" put up one of the quietest legendary careers maybe in sporting history. Despite his incredible stats, Dionne is still not as famous as contemporaries such as Lafleur, Mike Bossy, Bryan Trottier, Denis Potvin or even less productive players like Gilbert Perreault, Denis Savard, Peter Stastny and Dale Hawerchuk, whom he rivalled in terms of scoring even during his 30s. These players earned a little more love partly due to their markets and partly due to seeing more playoff exposure. During Dionne's prime, the Kings hadn't yet acquired the glamour that would come when owner Bruce McNall brought Wayne Gretzky on the scene in 1988—just over a year after Dionne had been dealt to the Rangers. When ruling as the alpha dog of his club, Dionne often played to less-than-packed crowds at the Great Western Forum.

Looking back, it seems criminal how little attention and success he received for his efforts. Even though NHL hockey may have been a tenant at the "Fabulous Forum," the building was commonly regarded as the home of NBA's "Showtime" Los Angeles Lakers. Often hockey was a consolation prize for a sports fan spending a night out on the town, as going to see the Kings instead of the fabled "Lake Show" or the Dodgers or even the

Rams at the decrepit L.A. Coliseum, was considered second- or third-rate sports entertainment. Even when the Raiders played out of the Coliseum in the 1980s in front of a blue-collar, often vicious and raucous fanbase, they were a more attractive commodity than a Kings team that paraded around in purple and gold like the opening attraction at a circus. While the colours truly looked royal on their basketball brethren, they somehow looked cheap and tawdry on the Kings. Maybe perception is everything though, as perhaps all that losing did the trick of altering perceptions given that L.A loves a winner and virtually ignores anything else. And all the aforementioned teams did their share of title-winning back then, except for the Rams—but even they made several deep playoff runs, while the Kings didn't even pass the second round.

Dionne's greatness with Los Angeles makes one shudder to think how far down the trash heap the reputation of the team would have fallen in the late 1970s to mid-'80s without him. He also had held them afloat in front of minuscule television audiences compared to those of Lafleur, who could be seen weekly in millions of households on *Hockey Night in Canada* and often would be viewed right from October through to his Habs' inevitable late-May championships. On the West Coast, Dionne was mostly impossible to find on national TV or in game highlights outside of Western Canada and California. The best exposure he would get would be when *Hockey Night in Canada* decided to air a Canucks, Oilers, Jets or Flames game against the Kings—especially if that clash was of the playoff variety (which it rarely was).

Because most of his games were played in the Pacific time zone, North American TV networks didn't have the highlight videotape via satellite to play until the next morning, if at all. Though there was plenty of missed potential for team achievement in his career, Dionne may yet go down as the greatest number two overall draft pick of all time (although Evgeni Malkin has made quite a strong case in recent years).

In a dash of serendipity, he and Lafleur eventually became teammates outside of tournaments such as the 1976 and 1981 Canada Cups or All-Star games. This memorable union arrived in 1988, when Lafleur came out of retirement to make the Rangers out of training camp—the same Rangers who had acquired Dionne via trade from L.A. late in 1986–87. By this point both were no longer at their best, yet it was still a curious sight considering how they had always been pitted as major rivals from childhood right up until their NHL drafting. Compared to his prime, Lafleur's final three seasons after his comeback (following a controversial retirement partway through 1984–85) were a happy-go-lucky excursion just to prove he could still hack it and go out on a more positive note than he originally had. No one mistook the returned Lafleur for the superstar he had once been, since his timing, endurance and reflexes were diminished, and he was given less ice time than ever in his playing career.

This time, there was no abruptness about his decision to quit, as Guy announced the decision early enough in the 1990–91 season to allow a farewell tour of sorts. Being rewarded with standing ovations, lavish gifts and pomp and circumstance wherever he went (but especially Montreal, where, showing the same flair for the dramatic that had seen him score twice in his return to the Forum as a Ranger in 1989, he notched a goal in his final visit), Lafleur got to bask in the adulation much more than he had during the sad departure over six years earlier. It was a more appropriate, fitting finale than his original exit from pro hockey.

As for Dionne, his career closed out in 1989 and brought many "what if?" questions from hockey fans who felt he was one of the greatest never to sip from the Cup. If he had been a Hab, that wouldn't have been the case. Dionne reflected on this in *Triple Crown*, opining that "all through my career, it's like people feel sorry for me. They tell me that it was too bad, that Montreal should have drafted me. Well, I played eighteen years in the NHL. What do you want me to do about it? . . . The reality is, we can't *all* play for the Montreal Canadiens."

Mitch Melnick finds that, while Dionne had a fabulous career, it was highly unfair that he never got to experience anything close to the team success a player of his magnitude deserved:

> I remember the deeper into his career he went, the more I
> started cheering for Marcel Dionne to at least get to a Cup
> Final or something. It was nice to be able to do that for the
> '76 Canada Cup because, even if it was a brief showcase, he
> was finally on a really, really good team and playing a pretty

prominent role on it too. I was watching the '76 boxed set on DVD . . . and I had forgotten that Scotty Bowman benched Phil Esposito in that final game because Dionne was quicker and just having a better night. The only times over the last couple games of the tournament where he would use Phil was on the power play, and Phil was pissed about that and hated Scotty for it. (Laughs.) But hey, they won and Dionne *was* a better fit. That was really cool to be able to cheer for both Lafleur and Dionne on the same team and the same line. It's too bad we didn't get to see a ton more of that.

In *Remembering Guy Lafleur*, the Flower suggested to Craig MacInnis that "maybe (Marcel) is luckier than me in some ways, to play his whole career without having the pressure . . . no Stanley Cups, but maybe saner." So, would he have suffered a similar if not worse experience stepping onto those early-1970s Habs? "I doubt it would have been different," says Melnick:

> I have a great respect for Dionne, but if he stepped in to replace the great Béliveau and was not being given first-line minutes right away either? It probably would have been the same as what Lafleur went through if not worse, because here he was a natural centre and not just a goal scoring winger like Lafleur. It's kind of like when Patrick Roy was traded and Jocelyn Thibault had to come take his spot there in 1995. He was a real good prospect, a really smart kid and very likable, but that was just an impossible situation. To go out of your way to not only get a goalie who was going to have to replace Patrick Roy, but to get one out of your own backyard? It's like the Habs were setting him up to inevitably fail. And he was like that sacrificial lamb. Thibault would have been a great goalie for a long time in my opinion, if he hadn't been traded to the Canadiens to follow Roy. I think this similar kind of situation existed in '71 post-Béliveau. There was just no winning for a couple of years there. Whether you were Lafleur or

Dionne, the expectations were just insurmountable at first. But they would have had it a lot better than Thibault at least, because the team was strong either way whereas by the time Roy left the Habs it was more like a sinking ship.

Though he had played to an older age than Dionne—suiting up for his final game around four months before his 40th birthday—Lafleur was often defined by Dionne's career. They will always be inextricably linked to that fateful day where the Canadiens selected one phenom over the other, despite the great Sam Pollock's attempts to somehow land both—a day that sent their careers off in terrific yet wildly differing directions.

RE-DRAFT OF 1971 FIRST ROUND (TOP 7)

#	PLAYER	TEAM	ORIGINAL	ACTUAL
1	GUY LAFLEUR	CANADIENS	#1 (MTL)	SAME
2	MARCEL DIONNE	RED WINGS	#2 (DET)	SAME
3	LARRY ROBINSON	CANUCKS	#20 (MTL)	JOCELYN GUEVREMONT
4	RICK MARTIN	BLUES	#5 (BUF)	GENE CARR
5	TERRY O'REILLY	SABRES	#14 (BOS)	RICK MARTIN
6	RICK KEHOE	BRUINS	#22 (TOR)	RON JONES
7	STEVE VICKERS	CANADIENS	#10 (NYR)	CHUCK ARNASON

CHAPTER 2

PERSONAL SERVICES (1979)

1. Rob Ramage, Colorado
2. Perry Turnbull, St. Louis
3. Mike Foligno, Detroit
4. Mike Gartner, Washington
5. Rick Vaive, Vancouver

6. Craig Hartsburg, Minnesota
7. Keith Brown, Chicago
8. Ray Bourque, Boston (from L.A.)
9. Laurie Boschman, Toronto
10. Tom McCarthy, Minnesota

THE NHL CELEBRATES PLENTY OF ICONIC DATES. Not only for Stanley Cups won or historic playoff performances, but also moments that occurred in the regular season and even off the ice. But if you were to ask the most loyal followers of the sport the significance of November 2, 1978, they'd likely be stumped. That was the day Nelson Skalbania, owner of the Indianapolis franchise in the World Hockey Association, would sell three of the Racers' best players to his pal Peter Pocklington, owner of the WHA's Edmonton Oilers. For the sum of either $700,000 or $850,000 (depending on whom you ask), Wayne Gretzky, goalie Eddie Mio (the best man at Gretzky's fabled 1988 wedding to actress Janet Jones) and Peter Driscoll went westward from the hockey wasteland of Indianapolis to the hockey hotbed of Edmonton. As the story goes, the trio was sent on a flight that would arrive either in Winnipeg or Edmonton, based on the best deal that Skalbania could cut at the 11th hour. He later would inform the 17-year-old future "Great One" the final two options for his destination.

Skalbania reportedly offered Jets part-owner Michael Gobuty the chance to land Gretzky first.

As Wayne would recall years later in an interview with Dan Robson of Sportsnet, "Nelson called me and said, 'I'm going to trade you. I'm going to give you the choice if you want to go to Winnipeg or Edmonton.' I'd never been to Winnipeg or Edmonton, so I had no idea. I called Gus Badali, who at the time was my manager and my agent, and asked what I should do. 'Edmonton has an 18,000-seat arena,' he said. 'They have a better chance of getting into the NHL. Tell them you want to go to Edmonton.'" As it turns out, Badali's prediction was right on. Though both franchises made the NHL, Edmonton survived tougher economic times in the NHL for longer than the Jets could hold out—in no small part due to having a bigger, more modern arena than the Jets, who were done in by an outdated facility in the Winnipeg Arena and could not break ground on a new one before their demise in 1996.

Not only did this particular trade shift the balance of power in the pro hockey to Edmonton for the next decade, it also led to having Gretzky—arguably the greatest prospect ever—avoid the clutches of eager GMs at the NHL draft in 1979. This was just one of the many remarkable features of that year's draft, held in Montreal just after the completion of the NHL/WHA merger.

It would be a watershed moment that changed the structure of the NHL draft forever. To fit Gretzky into their template, the NHL now had to make available many of the WHA's under-20 stars—who hadn't been drafted as yet—while also allowing teams to scour the amateur levels for the best under-20 kids, too. As a result, the 1979 draft would go on to be lauded as perhaps the most fruitful in NHL history—despite Gretzky's name never being called. A combination of multiple draft classes condensed into a "one-time-only" set-up, all contained in a six-round snake format. Draft day itself came rather late in the summer on this particular occasion, arriving early in August instead of on its traditional mid-to-late-June calendar date (the delay coming about mainly because the NHL Board of Governors had been meeting on the issue of what to do with the previously forbidden underage WHA players now suddenly freed up and available).

The 1979 draft witnessed a depth of talent selected that had never been seen in a draft—with one very large omission. That omission, of course, was Gretzky—a young man who was to become the greatest offensive star in the league's history. To Edmontonians of the late 1970s, Gretzky was also their city's ticket into the professional promised land of the NHL. With this skinny, seemingly frail, but also unstoppable scoring machine already on the Oilers payroll, it was widely expected that the Oilers would force their way into the impending merger. Why so much confidence that the Oilers were bound for NHL inclusion? Well, for one, they were situated in the capital city of Alberta at a time when the oil industry was booming (before the controversial National Energy Program instituted in 1982 by prime minister Pierre Trudeau gutted the provincial economy). Based on population, they did play in the fourth-biggest Canadian hockey market at that time. And considering how underwhelming the NHL's Canucks had performed during their 1970s and the less-than-fervent fan support that went along with that, Edmonton might even be the strongest market for pro hockey outside of Montreal and Toronto (both superior-sized urban centres that had been on the pro hockey scene since the early part of the century).

Always a strong supporter of various levels of junior, minor pro and semi-pro, the Greater Edmonton area had churned out hockey legends over the history of the game, such as Neil Colville and Johnny Bucyk. But once the NHL had secured the exclusive rights to the Stanley Cup in 1927, Edmonton's hometown heroes had to head east to make their name. As a result, the Cup went from the Holy Grail of amateur hockey to a Canada-wide professional chalice to a strictly pro-league property in the span of less than 35 years. Edmonton and major Western cities like it were left in the dark by economic realities that kept the NHL as a strictly Northeastern circuit. Those being the days of rail travel only, a transcontinental sports league was impractical and still a few decades away from being reality.

Though the NHL had improved by leaps and bounds after its humble 1917 beginnings, this "monopoly" on the Cup was arguably a regression when it came to crowning hockey's best club (not that the "Original Six" NHL owners saw it that way, of course). Shut out from this exalted trophy, a series of Western-based leagues would rise to fill in the gaps. However, most did not survive. There were several incarnations of the Pacific Coast

Hockey League between 1928 and 1952, but the most prosperous was a cross-border 1944 version that would turn pro in 1948 (picking up a few senior clubs along the way) and rebrand itself as the Western Hockey League in 1952. This particular WHL managed to find stability enough to stick around for over two decades, scaring the NHL enough that it finally explored the idea of expansion in the mid-1960s.

Through it all, the city of Edmonton housed successful clubs such as the Eskimos—a consistently top-performing WCHL/WHL franchise and a name that would find its way to several other Edmonton semi/minor pro franchises in the years to come. Then came the Flyers, who took part in a variety of leagues starting in 1940 (lastly in the WHL) until its folding in 1963. But until strong financial backing and suitable train/plane travel advancement came, leagues based in the wide-open western half of North American were doomed to struggle and be shaken down for a quick buck for most of the investors. The 1950s and '60s success of the WHL would prove to the NHL at long last that expansion west of Chicago was truly a viable idea. (So did pressure from the U.S. Justice Department on the NHL's monopoly status.) But it took some time to get the growth kick-started; western expansion in MLB then the NBA and NFL arrived from the late 1950s to mid-'60s, but the change took a frustratingly longer time to arrive in the hidebound NHL.

For the years leading up to 1967, the NHL not only rebuffed efforts to conduct any so-called "best-on-best" series for the Cup, but it also turned down any expansion bids outside of the Eastern Seaboard. The economic failures of teams during the Great Depression made the league office hesitant to allow any pitches from new cities. (Later, they also were loath to divide TV money from *Hockey Night in Canada*). By the time of 1967's long overdue doubling of the number of teams, that hesitation finally came to an end. Controversially, none of the new six franchises for 1967–68 was awarded to a Canadian city. The so-called hockey homeland was ignored by a league that instead sought to tap into American hockey venues beyond the enclave that they had mined over the course of their history. It would be a familiar scenario over the next decade too. While Vancouver would receive a team in 1970, the growing metropolises of Winnipeg, Edmonton and Calgary weren't considered and still had to accept senior and amateur hockey until 1972. The formation of the World Hockey Association that same year gave a chance for these supposedly "minor-league" cities to witness supposedly elite-level hockey at last.

A charter franchise of the WHA, the Oilers (along with the Quebec Nordiques and New England Whalers) were one of only three teams still playing in their original locale since the "renegade" league's inception. Known as the Alberta Oilers in their debut season (original plans were to split home games between Edmonton and Calgary), they would be crammed into the outdated Edmonton Gardens at the outset. It spoke to the humble origins of the WHA and the Oilers themselves that they began play in a 5,200-seat venue that had been in use since 1913. It was soon apparent that the team couldn't survive there long term, and the city knew a new arena was needed not just for the sake of pro hockey but also for attracting major conventions and music concerts. That all changed when construction on Northlands Coliseum (later the Skyreach Centre and then Rexall Place) was completed in 1974. Moving in during November of the 1974–75 WHA season, the Oilers were suddenly vaulted from one of the league's oldest, smallest-capacity buildings to its newest and biggest at over 16,000 seats.

The on-ice fortunes of the club stayed mediocre, though. The journey from also-ran to contender had its genesis in 1976, when the Oilers acquired a 33-year-old Alberta-born veteran winger named Glen Sather. A member of several NHL/WHA teams by this point in his pro journey, Sather was turned into the team's player/head coach for the 1976–77 season (he would take over the bench boss role exclusively for the following season). An even bigger cause for the turnaround was the famous swindle pulled off by team owner Peter Pocklington.

While the Oilers had been founded by hockey maverick "Wild" Bill Hunter and his business partner Dr. Charles A. Allard, Pocklington would eventually come into the picture after the club was sold in 1976 to Nelson Skalbania. Still shy of his 40th birthday, Skalbania was a tycoon who flipped franchises in the sporting world like he had the real-estate properties that built his fortune. Shortly after his purchase of the team, Skalbania would bring in the even younger (35-year-old) entrepreneur Pocklington as his main business partner. Having made his fortune in car dealerships in

Ontario and Alberta during the 1960s, the Saskatchewan-born Pocklington was a boy wonder who spring-boarded from his early accomplishments into even more financial rewards through a variety of company and real-estate holdings. Most famously, he would turn all that prosperity into becoming majority owner of a pro hockey club. And not just any club, but one that wound up becoming the toast of the NHL for a good decade or so.

Pocklington's rise from humble business beginnings to a position of fortune and fame within 25 years was a true Canadian success story; his eventual fall from grace by transitioning to a hated villain in Edmonton? Just as remarkable. Ever the betting man, Pocklington was known to make deals based on his many assets. Native Edmontonian and NHL play-by-play legend Gord Miller was covering the Oilers in the mid-1980s as a young reporter. He remembers that Pocklington was somewhat of a distraction, quipping, "(Pocklington) did interfere a lot. He was a pain in the ass. He'd do things like walk into the dressing room and throw down $2,000 or say, 'Whoever scores the winning goal gets a side of beef.' He drove (the players) nuts! He really was a meddler." After commencing his nearly two decades of Oilers ownership in 1976, Pocklington became the majority owner after Skalbania sold him his own shares, ostensibly to purchase the fledgling Indianapolis Racers instead.

Like his stint owning the Oilers, Skalbania's experiment in Indiana proved brief, with his debts proving insurmountable. There was some local speculation that Skalbania had intentionally mismanaged the Racers with the intention of moving the struggling franchise to a Canadian city—and to that end, get his foot in the NHL's door once an eventual merger occurred. He was soon disabused of the notion. (Skalbania eventually realized his NHL dream in a way when he bought the struggling Atlanta Flames in 1980 and flipped them to a group of investors out of Calgary.) When the WHA denied his attempt to transfer the Racers north of the border, Skalbania needed to bolster his ever-weakening asset in the Hoosier state.

Looking toward the ranks of Canadian junior hockey, he landed the rights to a gangly teenage prodigy who had just wrapped up his rookie (and as it turns out, only) season in the Ontario Hockey Association. Though younger than the majority of his teammates or foes in the OHA during 1977–78, a 17-year-old Wayne Gretzky had still put up an absurd 182 points (72 goals, 110 assists) for the Sault Ste. Marie Greyhounds. Falling just 10 points shy of the association's scoring title behind 20-year-old Bobby Smith (the 1978 first overall pick by the Minnesota North Stars), Gretzky confirmed his reputation as the most fascinating minor hockey product ever seen to that point. So dominant was he that most scouts believed if Gretzky were draft-eligible, many would take him over the seasoned and accomplished Smith. Still two years shy of legal adult status, the prefab Great One was pegged as the best under-20 player anywhere in the world.

Already a Brantford, Ontario, legend, Gretzky had been chronicled by sports reporters ever since scoring 378 goals in 1970–71 at age 10 (in games that featured 10-minute non-stop periods—a goal every five and a half minutes of real time!). No matter what age bracket he was playing in, wunderkind Wayne was the youngest player when he started out. Doing that at every level (playing peewee at just five years old, bantam at age 11, Junior B at 14 and major junior at 16), he dominated the competition easily. Many marvelled that he looked thoroughly prepared before ever stepping into each new age group of play.

They weren't wrong, considering the hours of dedication from Wayne and the innovative hockey practice techniques employed by his father, Walter. In the fall of 1978 in Indianapolis, Gretzky was again cast in the role of "that frail-looking kid" among a group of older and more experienced players. This time becoming the youngest WHA player at 17 years and eight months old, Gretzky would be surrounded by grizzled teammates who were nearly the age of his father at that point (i.e., 38-year-old Jim Neilson and 37-year-old Dave Dryden; Walter turned 40 the same week his teenaged son debuted in the WHA).

Skepticism would still follow the prodigy to the WHA. Then Jets (and future NHL) coach Tom McVie years later would tell Ed Willes in his book *The Rebel League*, "Everyone else will probably tell you 'Oh yeah, I saw it right away.' They're lying. To me, he looked like somebody's little brother. It looked like he was going to get fucking killed." While there were raves from a majority of fans and scribes, hard-boiled coaches, scouts, managers and other meat-and-potatoes hockey types didn't fully fathom the greatness nor did they buy into the hype. Even if he looked like sitting prey for the more vicious, speedy and aggressive pro world, Gretzky was not at all dominated by it.

Through no fault of his own, the teen's tenure in Indianapolis lasted just eight games.

Even with the Gretzky gambit, Skalbania saw his season ticket base increase by a mere 200 after the announcement. He may as well have signed a star Indiana college or high school basketballer to strap on some skates and suit up as a publicity stunt. It just may have attracted a bigger boost of ticket sales to Market Square Arena. Unfortunately for Skalbania, he was quickly realizing the impending failure facing his investment in the state's biggest metropolis. Pro sports was not the behemoth it would later become in Indiana, as the Pacers of the ABA and then NBA struggled to keep up with the state's massive college and high school hoops obsession. The Racers would also grapple with another college phenomenon in Notre Dame football—situated closer to Chicago than most of the state's other programs and reigning supreme on the state's gridiron scene. Even the tried-and-true sport of baseball failed to take MLB roots in Indianapolis, with the minor leagues remaining as the only presence after major league outfits failed to thrive there between the 1870s and 1910s.

Essentially, the Racers—named in an obvious attempt to appeal to the popularity of the auto racing Indy 500—were doomed from the start. So, early on in Gretzky's short Indianapolis stint, Skalbania decided he would engineer a fast trade to recoup some of his losses before the team went belly up for good (which occurred not long after, naturally). That was the background to how No. 99, the greatest offensive player in NHL history, arrived aboard his legendary flight on November 2 to either Edmonton or Winnipeg.

The Oilers may have provided the more tantalizing chance to be in the NHL someday, but there was still the potential of Gretzky playing with a sporting legend in Winnipeg by the name of Bobby Hull—now looking for elite linemates after Ulf Nilsson and Anders Hedberg had bolted to the NHL's Rangers the prior summer (as it transpired, a different Nilsson—a non-Ulf-relative named Kent—would take the top centre role in Winnipeg with the aging Hull, who, due to injuries, would only play 34 total games over his last two pro seasons, from 1978 to 1980). As attractive as the

Hull/Gretzky pairing might sound, a deal with the Jets never materialized. As Gobuty described it to Dan Robson, he accepted the advice of his hockey men, telling Skalbania that his "partners say no. Rudy Pilous (Jets GM at the time) says no. (It was the) Biggest mistake. Huge mistake. Because, as you know, Wayne was the best. And I didn't do it."

Indeed, it would turn out to be a critical error and major source of regret in Manitoba when Gretzky and his Oilers routinely dismantled the overmatched Jets throughout the 1980s. Even when Winnipeg iced good teams—a rather inconsistent happening in their NHL existence—they would inevitably be defeated by the talent of the Oilers who would always score the right goal at the right time or make the right save at the right time even when off their A-game.

Meanwhile, the three players themselves—travelling on a Learjet that goalie Mio had to pay for on his credit card (under the impression he'd be reimbursed)—made their way from Indy to Minneapolis, where they would stop to refuel and learn their next destination. During this leg of the journey, the party on board discovered that Winnipeg was now out of the equation, and they were Edmonton-bound. Once landed in the Alberta capital, they were met by a big media gathering. Long-time sportswriter Jim Matheson of the *Edmonton Journal* chronicled their arrival, capturing Gretzky commenting on the audaciousness of his situation. "It's funny really. Here I am only 17, with three years' start on most guys (his own age) and already I've been traded."

In his 2009 book, *I'd Trade Him Again*, Pocklington conceded that Wayne certainly was just "a skinny little kid. But you know what? I didn't give a damn. I knew he could play." Dropped into new surroundings with his fourth different hockey club in just under two years' time, Gretzky set to work and shut up any doubters he still had left. Turning 18 partway through the 1978–79 season, Wayne achieved greatness as the greenest kid on the block yet again, posting a combined 46-goal, 110-point rookie year (43 and 104 of those, respectively, over 72 games in an Oiler uniform). Most observers realized the gem with which they now were dealing. Here's how the Oilers game program artfully described him during 1978–79: "Watching (Gretzky) play hockey probably is a little like hearing Mozart play a piano at five or Einstein recite mathematics tables at seven."

By starting for the previously unenticing Oiler franchise, Gretzky bucked the odds that said any soaking wet teenager would need a long NHL adjustment before becoming a pro superstar. Realizing he now had his meal ticket to the NHL with this brilliant youngster, Pocklington quickly acted to protect the new asset and keep Gretzky in Oiler blue and orange for life (or at the very least, through any NHL/WHA merger process). Prior to his Edmonton arrival, Wayne had negotiated a seven-year, $1.75 million deal to join the Racers—orchestrated between Skalbania; Gretzky's first agent, Gus Badali; and his father, Walter (with Wayne still a minor at the time). But Pocklington was convinced that even more long-term security than this current deal provided protected Gretzky—but also gave Peter Puck the ultimate hockey asset.

Extending Gretzky's contract to an unprecedented 21 years at a total value of $5 million, Pocklington engineered a pact that he hoped would ensure his team's transition to the NHL and, as history would prove, long-term prosperity on the ice too. The signing would pay "The Kid" just over $238,000 a season. Such a sum was a king's ransom to most hockey players back in 1978 and certainly represented a gaudy figure to a humble 17-year-old kid whose father barely made that much in a decade of work himself. Nonetheless, $238,000 a season would seem like chump change just a few years later, once "The Great One" was rewriting the NHL record book seemingly on a weekly basis. No one at the outset imagined just how much money Gretzky would generate not just for his team, but for the sport itself. Nor did they consider how pro sports salaries would explode even more thanks to an increasingly profitable 1980s landscape. Therefore, what No. 99 was originally slated to earn seemed rather excessive and reactionary at the time, as opposed to the positively puny salary that it looked like just half a decade later.

As it was, the contract would receive his John Hancock during a pre-game ceremony at centre ice in front of 12,321 (mostly unsuspecting) Edmonton fans, on Wayne's 18th birthday. Presented with a bottle of baby champagne and two birthday cakes each with the number nine (spelling out 99), Gretzky was surrounded by dignitaries and family alike (his parents, three brothers and sister) when he signed. It was a deal that, in principle, sought to guarantee the Great One remained an Oiler employee until 1999 (which, ironically, proved to be the year he would retire from the game anyway). Alas, for Oilers fans, there was one caveat to the contract no one discussed much. It allowed for the possibility of moving on from Edmonton with an out-clause following year 10. Nobody really batted an eye at this feature, but it suddenly became mighty important when the year 1988 rolled around.

As he signed at centre ice in early 1979, the two key aspects of this contract were that it would bind Gretzky, the next great NHL box-office star, to the Oilers and would become their very strong negotiating ploy in a bid to earn National Hockey League status. Secondly, its personal services stipulations would keep him from having to enter the 1979 draft and be lost to the franchise. The NHL desired Gretzky in its ranks at any price. Standing in the way of that was its policy of not permitting players to enter the ranks until after an age-20 season of play at the amateur level. This stance had gone largely unchallenged but had hurt the league when the WHA began drafting and/or signing up junior stars to one-up its established rival. Twenty years old wouldn't come around for two more years in Gretzky's case, making him potentially 1981's fabled prize. But people couldn't wait that long, and the WHA's impending dissolution made it apparent Gretzky would be an NHLer at age 18, come hell or high water.

The wish that he be the shiny toy dangled as the number one pick in any upcoming entry draft (as the amateur draft was now being called) was stymied by the partnership Pocklington had fashioned with his diamond in the rough. Once the 1978–79 slate ended, the NHL (no fan of the WHA's impact on its overall bottom line during a seven-year rivalry) preferred Gretzky go to the Colorado Rockies with the first pick—even if it meant teenagers were now fair game for drafting. Landing Gretzky certainly would have turned around that troubled franchise—already having undergone a disastrous two-year run in Kansas City as the Scouts—and likely would have brought hockey fever to the Denver area (not quite in the cards yet, as it turned out). Any merger talks would certainly have seen the NHL change its under-20 rules to accommodate its next marquee attraction.

Following a season in which the Oilers made the Avco Cup Final for the first and only time (losing four games to two versus the Gretzky-spurning Jets), merger talks would ramp up in a major way. Four of the remaining

seven WHA teams—Hartford, Edmonton, Quebec City and Winnipeg—
were invited to join the NHL. The Cincinnati Stingers and Birmingham
Bulls, meanwhile, would join the Racers (whose financial insolvency
caused them to fold 25 games into 1978–79) in not making the grade for
inclusion. Despite all the *Sturm und Drang* of this wild merger situation, the
Oilers would pull through largely unscathed thanks to Gretzky's unique
contract situation and his camp's unwillingness to let the NHL void it
through the courts.

It was unusually bold for this normally deferential youth to refuse
entry into the NHL Entry Draft. The humble Gretzky usually catered to
the whims of his superiors in the management and ownership field, deliv-
ering polite if not trite comments and actions in a respectful, small-town
Canadian boy sort of way—even when he progressed to manhood and
then family life. But now this raw newcomer was pushing back against
those same elders.

Yet could anyone really blame him for carrying that mindset in 1979?
After all, the number one overall pick was owned by a sad-sack Rockies
team, one that had just come off a dreadful 15–53–12 last-place overall finish
that made its dreary first two seasons after moving from KC look almost
competitive. In the end, Gretzky and the Oilers won the argument. He
would avoid the rocky Rockies and stay an Oiler while getting to live out
his NHL dream at just 18 years old. Even at that early point in the proceed-
ings, it was thought that the Oilers were the runaway winners in merger
negotiations. The only downside? Once Gretzky's deal with Pocklington
was confirmed, he no longer was considered a rookie and thus was inleigi-
ble to be honoured as NHL's top rookie in 1979–80. This was no big whoop
in the long run, and it was a mere technicality that explained why the
Calder Trophy would be absent from his overstocked trophy case when all
was said and done.

With Gretzky spurning them, the Rockies would not have a shoo-in
saviour to resurrect them. They still had a bushel of options from eligible
players, WHA underage castoffs and trade possibilities if they wanted to
use their top selection to improve immediately. In the end, Colorado would
turn their attention toward their D corps. Settling on Rob Ramage—a
player who wouldn't go down in history as even the third or fourth best

option from that deep draft year—the Rockies made what seemed like the right pick for the situation at the time. Seemingly a man amongst boys during his three-year OHA career with the London Knights, Ramage displayed size, grit, defensive awareness and offensive upside—all aspects teams crave in any prospect, let alone a blueline one. In retrospect, picking the highly promising Ramage was a curious move for the Rockies considering that just two years earlier they had used a second overall pick on a different "franchise" D-man when selecting Barry Beck.

There has long been the theory of going with the "BPA" (best player available) over drafting for need, but subsequent moves made the Ramage selection look even odder. Only a few years after that pick, it appeared to be a misstep and yet another nail in the coffin of the Rockies franchise, whose efforts to avoid relocation were once again unsuccessful. Taking Ramage didn't even work out as well as it had with Beck, a heavy shooter who still holds the record for goals in a season by a rookie defenceman (22 in 1977–78). Upon Ramage coming into the Rockies' fold, he and Beck had folks drooling at the potential of a new dominant blueline duo in the NHL. That fearsome one-two punch was supposed to give the Rockies their very own "Big Three," with Beck's offence and Ramage's two-way abilities put alongside the more defensive-minded John Van Boxmeer—a former Canadiens prospect and future Second All-Star Team member in 1979–80 (albeit for the Sabres).

While all three players had star seasons as NHLers, it never coalesced at the same time, and each would be hastily traded away for quick fixes within four years. No wonder the team's next incarnation, in New Jersey—derided as a "Mickey Mouse organization" by Gretzky himself—struggled to gain its footing and find respectability for a good half-dozen years after landing in the Meadowlands from the Rocky Mountains.

The big day—minus Gretzky—came on August 9 instead of its usual early-to-mid-June date. As mentioned, the delay mainly came about because the NHL board of governors had been hammering out details of who was eligible. The 1979 WHA/NHL merger—and Gretzky's arrival—was a watershed moment that changed the structure of the draft. In its efforts to make Gretzky eligible, the NHL created a larger overall ripple, as it now made available many of the WHA's other under-20 stars while also allowing teams to scour the amateur levels for under-20 kids. As a result, this draft year would be the most fruitful in NHL history.

But the NHL needed time after decreeing it would be lowering the minimum draft age to 18 in time for the following draft in 1980. Only an 18-year-old who had already played in the WHA could be selected in 1979. As it happened, there were only two of them in the WHA's final season. One was the now-untouchable Gretzky. The other was former Stingers winger Mark Messier. Everyone else was free for this draft if born before the determined cut-off date of January 1, 1961. The reduced number of rounds that year was due to the short time between holding the draft in August and the opening of most NHL training camps a few weeks later in September.

Some other alterations to the 1979 format were temporary measures that the merger forced upon the NHL. Others would stick permanently. For instance, teams had previously been allowed to decline a selection in a round when their turn came up. They could also jump back in later, pay the NHL a fee to make extra selections and/or sell picks to other teams if they felt they had no use for them. All of this would no longer be permitted by 1979.

Looking back on these old standards being dropped, the limiting of rounds truly did end up blocking off some of the advantages that the stronger NHL clubs had utilized. Sam Pollock's Canadiens in particular had employed advantageous tactics during their dynasty days by not only making numerous trades to acquire draft picks, but using their ample team budget to stockpile as many picks as possible too. Some years in the 1970s had seen the Habs double the selections made by most other clubs (for instance, a whopping 27 in 1977, right after their commanding 60–8–12 season that saw them claim the second of four consecutive Cup wins). Now, sure, they had a fine system full of very capable players, but the ability to draft so much more in the way of depth had made any of their scouting mistakes or inefficiencies obsolete. With a glut of skilled players in their midst, Montreal could also shuffle their good development pieces to the minor-league level in order to avoid owning more contracts at the pro level than what was permitted. Hence, their affiliate in Nova Scotia was also the dominant team of the decade in the AHL.

At the time of their peak drafting wizardry, the Canadiens enjoyed a distinct revenue edge over most franchises as well. Because they didn't have to share what they made off of corporate sponsorship, they could wield significant financial clout. The major boon to their coffers came in the form of Canada's biggest brewer, Molson, sponsoring them for years and then even assuming majority ownership in 1978. Once these benefits were stripped away, the Canadiens' decline from lording over the league to being just another hopeful contender would begin in earnest.

Another interesting feature of this signature draft year was the option for juniors who went undrafted to sign as free agents or return to junior and try their luck again at the draft table a year later. This provision came with a November 1, 1979, deadline for agreements to be made and resulted in 31 different 19-year-olds being inked—a group that included four-time 50-goal man Tim Kerr and 600-goal power-play specialist Hall of Famer Dino Ciccarelli (a teammate of Ramage's in London, who led that team in scoring at age 19 and would have likely been a 1980 first-rounder but was not drafted in 1979 because of a variety of factors, including height, youth, the number of older options to pick and his reputation for one-way hockey). Not to mention very useful players like five-time Cup champion defender Charlie Huddy and four-time 20-goal scorer Ron Flockhart.

The rare quality of the undrafted free agents who were nabbed a few months after the 1979 draft further proved how impeccable the talent taken that year really was. If so many undrafted names became stars, it says a lot about the quality of the names in the six rounds that did take place. Even though the Great One himself was absent, the unique set-up of 1979 produced gems unearthed every few choices on average. Most franchises would come away from the draft floor that day with a future linchpin of the team for years to come. The ones who didn't would go on to pay dearly for their swing-and-a-miss in such a fertile year. Ironically, the 21-pick first-round selections ran the gamut wildly in terms of quality—another example of how much of a crapshoot the draft was and still is.

That opening round ranged from the legendary (Mike Gartner, Ray Bourque, Michel Goulet) to the excellent (Rick Vaive, Paul Reinhart, Brian Propp, Craig Hartsburg) to the very good (Ramage, Mike Foligno, Tom McCarthy, Mike Ramsey, Kevin Lowe) to the serviceable (Perry Turnbull,

Keith Brown, Laurie Boschman, Duane Sutter, Doug Sulliman, Ray Allison). Truly, 1979 was so excellent that the first round provided only one glaring bust: Jets number 19 overall pick Jimmy Mann—a John Ferguson pet project who was supposed to be the power forward extraordinaire they needed for both scoring and protecting a European-heavy lineup, but instead wound up serving as a one-dimensional enforcer who racked up a mere 10 goals and 30 points with 895 penalty minutes in 293 career NHL games. While he was at first pegged as a modern answer to the fierce and fearless Hab tough guy Ferguson, Mann lacked the offensive skill needed to stick as anything beyond an enforcer. Ferguson, on the other hand, had showed decent hands during his career—aided greatly by playing wing alongside Hall of Fame and All-Star centres like Jean Béliveau and Henri Richard—and would make just as much happen with his stick as with his fists. A lot of the time, most players were too scared to mix it up with "Fergie." Mann would never enjoy that luxury, breaking into the big leagues on a skill-deprived team and yet still proving unable grab a chunk of top ice time despite that.

Craig Button recalls that Mann earned the majority of his offence with the QMJHL's Sherbrooke Castors because of his nasty nature on the ice: "I remember no one ever went near him. It was crazy. Because he was so mean, I think no one wanted to even touch the guy, and because of that, he was able to put up some good scoring numbers." Mann's most famous on-ice moment was not one of heroic scoring or lovely stickhandling, but was a flash of brutal violence. It came when he left the bench during a brawl against the Penguins on January 13, 1982, and delivered a jaw-breaking sucker punch to Paul Gardner—a vicious attack that netted him a 10-game banishment by the NHL and a suspended sentence for assault in a Manitoba court of law. Swing and a miss indeed, Jets.

The rare 1979 draft misses like Mann looked even worse when compared to the many future stars taken after round one, stalwarts such as Pelle Lindbergh, Mats Naslund, Dale Hunter and Neal Broten in round two; Guy Carbonneau, Mark Messier and Keith Crowder in round three; and John Ogrodnick, Glenn Anderson and Anton Stastny in round four. Even the last couple of rounds saw steals in the form of excellent role players like Dirk Graham (number 89 to the Canucks, but flourishing as a two-way stud his late 20s as a Blackhawk following a brief stop with the

North Stars), Thomas Steen (number 103 to the Jets), Doug Crossman (112 to the Black Hawks) and Mike Krushelnyski (120 to the Bruins).

While the talent at teams' disposal was monumental, the draft presentation itself was still a casual undertaking. Compared to the showy TV event it would become, the 1979 draft was fairly basic. Few of the top players travelled to Montreal at the Queen Elizabeth Hotel (where it had been held each of the prior 16 years; this would be its last year there). Out west, the Canadian national team was holding camp at Calgary's Stampede Corral at the same time and picking a roster to represent the country during the 1980 Olympics in Lake Placid (of "Miracle on Ice" fame). The camp could boast draft-eligible attendees such as Laurie Boschman (who eventually went 9th overall to Toronto) and Paul Reinhart (who went 12th overall to Atlanta), not to mention Hockey Hall of Famer Glenn Anderson and future NHL mainstays Kevin Maxwell and Tim Watters. Following a practice on August 9, Boschman showed some curiosity about how exactly the draft—which was not being televised in those days—was going. Eric Duhatschek at the time was a young reporter covering Canada's training camp:

> I remember Boschman asking me if I knew what stage the draft was in. I told him, "Well you know, if you want to come into our newsroom, we can just watch them cover the draft over CP (Canadian Press)." So Laurie Boschman, on the day he was drafted, spent two hours there watching the names come across over the ticker tape with me. I thought it was really unique, but that's what an odd draft it was, coming so late as a result of the WHA merger. That was the first draft I ever covered, too, and I'll never forget it because it wasn't like it is today at all, where the kids are there (in town) often for weeks at a time.

All told, the success rate of 1979 was a staggering one. A whopping 81.7 percent of the selections made that year ended up playing at least one NHL game. The highest rate in a year before that was only 58 percent. That 81.7 percent rate would have been even higher were it not for the glut of 19-year-olds passed over until the junior free-agent period had elapsed.

From this classic crop, the final player to hang up his skates (the 126th taken that year) wouldn't do so until 25 years later. That player was Messier, who concluded his quarter-century NHL career (26 years as a pro, including his lone WHA season) at age 43 following 2003–04. Fittingly, the very last goal scored by "The Moose" would move him into second in career points (1,851) behind his close friend Gretzky, a position he would hold on to until Jaromir Jagr surpassed it 14 years later.

Even though keeping Gretzky out of the draft represented the ultimate coup for Edmonton during 1979, the Oilers had lots more to celebrate that year and beyond. It was in that draft that they picked up defenceman Kevin Lowe from Lachute, Quebec, with the final pick of round one (number 21). Then they scored another success by snapping up Messier in the third (after having dealt away their second-rounder to regain eventual Gretzky wingman and "bodyguard" Dave Semenko, who had been a priority pick by his NHL rights-holders, the North Stars).

Like Gretzky, Messier was a WHA refugee. Unlike his pal, Messier had a ways to go in his development toward stardom, as he had only mustered a goal and 10 assists in 45 games with the Stingers during 1978–79. Fame and fortune wouldn't come as quickly or easily for the Moose, but it did come. Even with his rookie-year struggles, Messier managed to make a favourable impression on Glen Sather by thrashing Oiler Dennis Sobchuk in a fight. "Even as a seventeen-year-old, there was no mistaking it. They talk about Maurice Richard. Well, Mark has the same look," Sather was later to remark to Rick Carpiniello, author of the 1999 book *Messier: Steel on Ice*. Lee Fogolin, a mate of Messier's over his first seven NHL seasons, told Carpiniello that Messier was "as mean and tough as anybody I've ever seen, anybody I'd ever played with or against." But at the time of his drafting, no one exactly was predicting the second coming of Gordie Howe. Any reservations about Gretzky looked tame next to Messier; most observers were only questioning whether Wayne would become the NHL's pre-eminent superstar, like the Orrs and Howes of the world; questions about "Mess" concerned whether he would become anything more than a fourth-line grinder.

Those close to this teenage "raging bull," for whom the league would one day name a leadership award, did not always envision or notice any greatness in him. Future NHL head coach and ESPN hockey commentator

Barry Melrose played defence for those Stingers and noted in Jeff Z. Klein's 2003 book *Messier* that his teammate "didn't have that work ethic he has now . . . He had a lot of physical skills, but he was very young and childish at that time. I don't think anyone would have told you he was going to be a Hall of Famer and win six Stanley Cups and be considered one of the great leaders in hockey."

It's not as if Messier was seen as a home-run pick at the time of his drafting. Experts saw him as far more of a project than Gretzky was, or even more than steady, dependable Lowe, who was noted as one of the top five junior prospects on the blueline that was available in '79. Not helping the assessment of Messier was his 1978–79 pro showing, where he looked more like just a kid out of his element who should have stayed in junior where he would get more seasoning and ice time up against players his own age. He would put up very modest totals between centre and left wing throughout his first two seasons in the NHL ranks, while being noted for his wild, aggressive and untamed ways on the ice (and for similar behaviour as a party animal off of it too). As mentioned in "Of Ice And Men (McFarland Walter & Ross)," Sather had to discipline Messier in his early days. When Messier phoned to say he'd be late for a team flight, Sather directed him to the airport where'd find his plane ticket. But it wasn't to anywhere the Oilers were going. Messier found himself demoted to the Wichita Wind, the Oilers farm team way off in Kansas. A pleading Messier begged for a second chance, but Sather let him stew until the message was clear. "Mess" did indeed tap into his potential soon after, spring-boarding from the team's surprising 1981 playoff success—much like others on the team who took their game to a new level after that breakthrough— to author a 50-goal season in 1981–82. That was followed up by his first 100-plus-point point season in 1982–83 and then another in 1983–84, punctuated by a ferocious two-way showing once he got switched into the Oil's second-line centre spot for the 1984 playoffs.

Messier's next-level ascension in the '84 playoffs garnered Conn Smythe Trophy honours in the Oilers' first of five Cup wins, confirming superstar status for the 23-year old and determining once and for all that Sather and company had hit a true drafting home run back in 1979. After 1984, Mess would stay positioned at centre to give the Oilers likely the greatest one-two punch down the middle in NHL history. Instead of taming his ways, he would remain—albeit in a more measured, controlled way—passionate, mean and borderline predatory with his liberal use of elbows, intimidating with his offensive skills but with physicality as well. Messier channelled his determination and eventually matured into a vaunted leader in the sport. Post-Gretzky's 1988 trade to Los Angeles, he took over as the Oilers' Mr. Everything: its heart, soul, brains—and its captain too.

In spite of the drama of Wayne Gretzky's skipping the whole draft process, 1979 still will go down as the most ridiculously stacked draft in NHL history to date. What made it even more compelling was the fact that Gretzky was the potential carrot waved in front of some lucky downtrodden team's eyes only to be snatched away months before the draft arrived.

As anyone with any familiarity of hockey history knows, Gretzky almost immediately upon joining the NHL began to substantially prove that his performances as a newcomer to the OHA and WHA scenes were no fluke at all but instead were, in fact, a blueprint to what lay ahead. In that rookie NHL campaign of 1979–80, he would drag Edmonton to the last of 16 playoff spots thanks to a mammoth 137-point season that tied Marcel Dionne for the scoring lead but saw him lose out on the scoring title due to a goals tiebreaker—51 to Dionne's 53 (a scenario for the Art Ross Trophy only repeated once since, when Jaromir Jagr edged Eric Lindros for it in 1995; in both of those years, the one who lost out on the tiebreaker received the MVP as a so-called "consolation prize"). Gretzky would be rewarded after that magical debut NHL season, earning the first of his eventual nine Hart Trophies—the first eight coming in his first eight seasons, when the next-longest stretch of consecutive wins is three (Bobby Orr from 1970 to 1972). Rewriting official league records during his second season and hoisting his first ever Stanley Cup by his fifth, Gretzky would shoot down every nitpicking detractor along the way (though there weren't many to begin with, and next to none left by the mid-1980s).

Even now, when you watch his highlights, it's as if someone developed a time machine to drop a modern superstar with all their competitive advantages (equipment, coaching, training, medicine, etc.) into a lower-quality circuit. (The only other such character was probably Bobby Orr, with whom Gretzky, along with Mario Lemieux, is often compared to as a candidate for the "GOAT" in NHL history.) When he was first considered not "tough enough" to win under the grind of playoff hockey, the idolized No. 99 reeled off four Cup wins in five years from 1983 to 1988 while still only in his mid-20s. Even when he had done everything at the NHL level that could be done, some mused that because he hadn't been able to overcome the Soviet powerhouse in the 1981 Canada Cup, maybe he wasn't as much of a top dog as everyone was saying.

And yes, Gretzky, after confirming his greatest in the world status in 1980–81, did see his Team Canada get scorched 8–1 in that Canada Cup Final, with unheralded USSR winger Sergei Shepelev taking tournament MVP—leading the rather vocal sportswriter Dick Beddoes (a precursor to talking heads that argue, complain and give "hot takes" on sports talk shows today) to grumble on a CBC TV interview upon Gretzky's record 1982 contract restructuring that he wasn't the best player in the world simply because Shepelev had supposedly proven that the prior September (a declaration chuckled at by counterpoint guest Peter Gzowski). Hello, recency bias!

With that in mind, Gretzky did what he always did and added a few more notches to his belt of unparalleled achievement by captaining a pair of those tournament victories in 1984 and 1987 and going toe to toe with the best the Eastern bloc had to offer, just as he had done on the NHL stage. Wayne would turn not just the hockey world but the athletic world upside down through unprecedented statistical mastery of a team sport. While Michael Jordan has received a plethora of accolades as the most iconic team sport athlete ever—receiving more honours, praise and money than just about every NHL superstar, including Gretzky, has earned combined—several American sports figures who tend to focus way more on football, baseball and basketball have pointed to the fact that even "Air Jordan" didn't statistically dominate his sport as thoroughly as Wayne did.

A lot of that comes down to hockey's second-class status among pro sports south of the border, not to mention the fact Gretzky did a lot of his greatest work during a decade when Edmonton was the most northerly sports market in North America. Perhaps if Gretzky had been situated in a major media market the whole time that he tore up the NHL—as a King, Ranger or even Blackhawk or Bruin for life—his impact could've been even greater. Either way, when the final story could be written, Gretzky had made his status as the "likely number one prospect" for his intended draft year look like a massive underselling in retrospect. What Gretzky did prove conclusively was that he became the first home-run of the draft since Lafleur in 1971—and he did so without being picked. Had he been draft-available, he arguably would have gone down as the greatest selection in NHL history.

Why do we only say "arguably," in this case? Well, down the road lay another generational junior talent who was set to take the draft by storm for his own unique reasons. While Gretzky was kicking off his first stunning NHL campaign, this other phenom had only just turned 14 but already was being considered a shoo-in to achieve legendary feats himself. The day his name would be called was still five years in the future. This time, no one would undersell his talents as anything but a complete game changer for whatever franchise took him, and their easiest path to championship greatness down the road. By that time, No. 99 had mastered the sport so thoroughly that any mega-prospect to come down the pike would be forever lauded as the "Next One" (since "Next Gretzky" is just too unfair a tag to lay on someone). Mario Lemieux turned hockey—and Gretzky's number—upside down in writing his own legend.

RE-DRAFT OF 1979 FIRST ROUND (TOP 10)

#	PLAYER	TEAM	ORIGINAL	ACTUAL
1	RAY BOURQUE	ROCKIES	#8 (BOS)	ROB RAMAGE
2	MARK MESSIER	BLUES	#48 (EDM)	PERRY TURNBULL
3	MICHEL GOULET	RED WINGS	#20 (QUE)	MIKE FOLIGNO
4	GLENN ANDERSON	CAPITALS	#69 (EDM)	MIKE GARTNER
5	MIKE GARTNER	CANUCK	#4 (WSH)	RICK VAIVE
6	GUY CARBONNEAU	NORTH STARS	#44 (MTL)	CRAIG HARTSBURG
7	DALE HUNTER	BLACK HAWKS	#41 (QUE)	KEITH BROWN
8	BRIAN PROPP	BRUINS	#14 (PHI)	RAY BOURQUE
9	MATS NASLUND	MAPLE LEAFS	#37 (MTL)	LAURIE BOSCHMAN
10	NEAL BROTEN	NORTH STARS	#42 (MNS)	TOM McCARTHY

CHAPTER 3

SUPER MARIO WORLD (1984)

1. Mario Lemieux, Pittsburgh
2. Kirk Muller, New Jersey
3. Eddie Olczyk, Chicago
4. Al Iafrate, Toronto
5. Petr Svoboda, Montreal

6. Craig Redmond, L.A.
7. Shawn Burr, Detroit
8. Shayne Corson, Montreal
9. Doug Bodger, Pittsburgh
10. J.J. Daigneault, Vancouver

THE CITY OF MONTREAL HAS LONG cherished its historical significance not only within Canada but in North America as a whole. Discovered in 1535 and then later established as a town in 1642, Montreal is one of the oldest cities in the "New World" (Quebec City got the jump on it and takes great pride in that themselves). After being settled and populated during its first century of existence by France, it would go on to become a unique, sometimes volatile, mix of English and French enclaves. The Scottish merchants settled downtown at the foot of a former volcano that forms Montreal's distinct mountain. For a long time, the French-Canadian side of the divide was centred in the many working-class areas throughout Quebec's most populous city. One of these areas was a neighbourhood in Montreal's Sud-Ouest (Southwest) borough called Ville-Émard. Predominately Francophone, Ville-Émard came to be known for its heavy industrialization, which provided the majority of employment opportunities for its residents.

Sandwiched between the less rough-hewn Côte-Saint-Paul and Angrignon neighbourhoods, Ville-Émard was fortuitously located between the important commercial hubs of the Lachine Canal and Aqueduct Canal—two huge construction projects of the 19th century that transformed the principal mode of employment in the area from agriculture to hydro power. Subsequently, factories sprang up to meet the growing demand. Job openings would follow in the first half of the 20th century, but by the middle of that century the industries found in Ville-Émard would be greatly reduced when Lachine Canal expansion efforts were deemed too difficult to engineer and were ultimately abandoned.

The completion of the St. Lawrence Seaway in the late 1950s led to the eventual closure of the Lachine Canal to shipping vessels in 1970. Subsequent degradation and devastation to the economic viability of the Sud-Ouest borough loomed large. As was common for workers in Ville-Émard in those latter days of its industrial relevancy, Jean-Guy Lemieux found employment as a construction labourer and engineer. He carved out enough income to support a stay-at-home wife, Pierrette, and their three sons. He also was able to fund their involvement in hockey—an activity not cheap even back then (today it takes a six-figure income to equip and train just a single child in hockey).

Among the trio of Lemieux sons, the eldest, Alain, was the first to show promise in the sport. He would go on to a superb minor pro career that included a few short NHL stints along the way with St. Louis, Quebec and Pittsburgh. However, he stood "only" six feet tall and could not hope to physically dominate like his youngest brother, Mario, who grew to just slightly under six-foot-five. Mario towered over other junior prospects, let alone his brother, in skill as well as in height. Four years his brother's junior, Mario was destined to become the most hyped draft-eligible prospect in hockey since his childhood idol Guy Lafleur over a decade earlier. Mario would grow—literally and figuratively—to become a force in the sport before he was even of legal age to operate a vehicle. And, in contrast to Lafleur and those who came before him, he would understand all the ramifications of that leverage and wield it liberally in the highly productive 1984 NHL draft—a draft that would produce three Calder Trophy winners as well as three Hall of Fame legends in Patrick Roy, Brett Hull and Luc Robitaille.

Unlike Gretzky, Lemieux competed for more than a single season at the major junior level. For that reason, there was a longer buildup toward his NHL arrival and more of a chance to foment a substantial legacy even before his first pro game. Outclassing his peers from 1981 to 1984 moved Mario toward the inevitable top position in the entry draft. He would justify the early number one projections by carving out a mesmerizing major junior career, certainly the greatest seen to date—even with heady challengers such as Eric Lindros, Alexandre Daigle, Joe Thornton, Vincent Lecavalier, Sidney Crosby and Connor McDavid.

While Gretzky was the eldest of his four brothers, one similarity he shared with Lemieux was that both of them grew exponentially by playing with and against much older players during childhood. That started outdoors too. As Wayne's father, Walter, had done with the backyard of his Brantford home, Jean-Guy Lemieux put his construction skills to work by creating a makeshift skating rink on the front lawn of the family house. It came in handy during the winter months, when his boys would be able to practice at all hours of the day. The Lemieux patriarch would even pack snow in the hallways of the house so that skating could be worked on indoors when it became too dark or too cold out front. By the time Mario's adolescence arrived—and the major growth spurts along with it— there was no longer any strong competition for the youngest of the three Lemieux brothers.

After dominance in his peewee career, word of mouth began to spread. Mario concluded his bantam days in 1979–80 with the Montreal Hurricanes, then moved on to torch the Junior A level in 1980–81 by posting 62 goals and 62 assists in only 47 games with Montreal-Concordia of the QMAAA. This allowed Mario to become that rare 15-year-old gem taken first overall in a major junior league draft, when he was chosen by the Laval Voisins (the last-place finisher out of 10 QMJHL teams in 1980–81).

The much-talked-about 16-year-old managed to lead the rebuilding Voisins with 96 points in just 64 games. A year later, as a 17-year-old in the 1982–83 season, he built on that with an incredible 184 points (84 of them goals) in 66 GP to become the most scouted junior in the entire world. Born on October 5—just a few weeks after the September 15, 1965, cutoff for draft eligibility—Lemieux wasn't yet available for NHL teams in the

1983 draft after his brilliant sophomore season in the Q. Nonetheless, the additional year of junior would give him the chance to further enhance his excellent resumé. In that way, his birthday was a blessing in disguise. If Lemieux had set out to make 1984 his argument for the "number one with a bullet" draft evaluation, he would achieve that goal and then some.

His records were, in part, due to the free-for-all offensive game of Quebec junior hockey in those days—as well as his otherworldly skill. Also, Mario was able to complete a full 70-game season at Laval— despite a highly publicized controversy. Forgoing a return to represent Canada in the World Junior Championship tournament, Mario attracted what would not be his last bout of criticism. He had disliked his experience the year before due to head coach Dave King's handling of his ice time (and, in the view of many Quebec hockey figures, the distrust of French-Canadian players). So he took a pass on travelling to Sweden to don the maple leaf.

That stance garnered Lemieux considerable scorn, and the QMJHL threatened to suspend him if he didn't accept Team Canada's invite and report. Rather than acquiesce to the demands, Lemieux and his agents, Gus Badali (Gretzky's early pro representative, you'll recall) and Bob Perno, stood firm. Following a tense standoff in which the Lemieux camp even threatened to sue the QMJHL if any suspension was imposed, the dispute was heard in the law courts. It eventually generated a ruling in favour of the junior superstar, as Quebec Superior Court judge Fraser Martin determined that Lemieux had no legal or contractual obligation to participate in the tournament.

All this legal wrangling seemed to suggest that Lemieux was selfish, unpatriotic and a malcontent. It was also early evidence that he was not a young man who would be so easily swayed by the hockey world's standards and expectations; nor was he afraid to stick to his guns, unlike most predecessors and contemporaries. This character trait would rear its head again when his draft day arrived the following spring. In the 1997 book *Mario Lemieux: The Best There Ever Was*, Perno told the authors that "Mario seemed to have a knack for stirring up controversy. But even at that young age, he was so strong in character. He had an unbelievable maturity. Nothing bothered him. He took the pressure and converted it into success."

Then in his younger days of covering sports on the radio in Montreal, Mitch Melnick saw a few examples of Lemieux's combative nature:

> While I didn't see it a lot, it was noticeable at times. Like when he didn't want to go to the World Juniors. Wherever the theory came from, there was some bullshit going around about Dave King being anti-French or whatever. I didn't buy into that. It was just bull, whether Mario believed it or not. I also recall him claiming to be too sick to play one time, and I saw him sitting in the press box at the Forum with a beer in his hand. I mentioned it on the air, saying "Well if he's feeling so bad why was he in the press box drinking a beer? He couldn't have been *that* sick." People took issue with that. I recall he wasn't very talkative back then too. He was hard to read. Still is, really. Very quiet for the most part.

Unburdened by suspensions, serious injury or international "duties," an undaunted Lemieux authored the single most awe-inspiring campaign from an 18-year-old. Leading Laval to a 54–16–0 mark and a QMJHL championship, Lemieux broke a series of Canadian major junior record marks likely never to be topped: goals (133), points (282), consecutive games with a point (61) and fewest games needed to reach the 50-goal plateau (27). His Laval club was also a formidable scoring powerhouse, recording an outrageous 527 goals in 70 games that year. Even with that lofty total, Lemieux managed to factor in on over half of Laval's goals. His uncanny dominance was illuminated with a season finale in which Les Voisins torched the Longueuil Chevaliers 16–4 while he chipped in points on 11 of the tallies.

But that was nothing compared to another record. Mario had already smashed Pierre Larouche's CHL points record (251, set with the Sorel Black Hawks in 1973–74) a couple of weeks beforehand. With eight games to go, he needed four tallies to break Lafleur's hallowed mark of 130 goals from 1970–71. Lemieux achieved the unthinkable, not only breaking the record but managing three goals more than the Flower. He did it by notching an incredible double hat trick (six-goal) performance in that finale against Longueuil.

Once the playoffs rolled around, Laval pulled off a pair of sweeps before a six-game President's Cup series defeat of Longueuil—a squad that had beaten Laval a year earlier with Jacques Lemaire in his one and only season coaching at the junior level. The Chevaliers had pulled off that massive upset by somehow controlling Mario and negating his teammates (a foreshadowing of Lemaire's expert defensive tactician's ways behind NHL benches). The redemption for Laval in 1984 was finished off with a laughable 17–1 thrashing of Longueuil in the clinching sixth game—an affair that determined once and for all Lemieux's status as the greatest Quebec junior talent yet to be seen.

Though playoff hockey was supposed to be more low-scoring—even in the "shoot 'em up" QMJHL—Lemieux produced at a nearly identical pace in the 1984 post-season, tallying 29 goals and 53 points in a mere 14 games. In fact, the team that "best" held high-powered Laval at bay was their round one victim, the Granby Bisons, who allowed "just" 22 goals in four games thanks to a player born on the same day as Lemieux: an eccentric, acrobatic and highly competitive goaltender named Patrick Roy. Sharpening his NHL readiness by having to regularly turn away 50 to 60 shots a game in his junior career with the porous Bisons, Roy did better than any goalie could have hoped to do against Lemieux's mighty crew. Nonetheless, it was a short series where no Quebec goalie really stood a chance.

Laval's expected wipeout of the QMJHL was followed by a Memorial Cup appearance that didn't go nearly as well. The 1984 Voisins lived up to the unfortunate stereotype of the time that the QMJHL was inferior on the grandest stage against the other Canadian junior powers. With an epic offence held in check, Laval could not hope to rest on a strong defence (since they really didn't have one) and lost all three of their round-robin games. Finishing behind the host Kitchener Rangers, champion Ottawa 67s and Kamloops Junior Oilers, Laval may have faltered as a team, but no one was questioning Lemieux. Even with this tiny blow to his aura of invincibility, there was zero question who was going number one overall. The real mystery throughout 1983–84 was which team would claim the right to grab him. As the conclusion of that NHL regular season approached, the pitiful Pittsburgh Penguins would emerge as the likely suitor for "Mario the Magnificent."

Having been in the NHL for nearly two decidedly mediocre decades by this point, the Pens had been uninspiring on the ice and frequently in the red off of it. Even the franchise's mascot penguin had succumbed to their jinx, dying of pneumonia. It was a team seemingly always headed for either relocation or a repeat of past bankruptcy crises—a recurring issue in nearly all of their first four decades of existence.

Since their birth in 1967, the Penguins had never truly become a big attraction in the Steel City. Often forgotten and far less covered than even the University of Pittsburgh's football and basketball programs, they were the third-ranked pro team in town, behind the Steelers and Pirates. There had been star players throughout the years for the Pens, so it's not as if they didn't own marketable names. The Penguins were known for proficient scorers such as Lowell MacDonald, Pierre Larouche, Jean Pronovost, Syl Apps Jr. and Rick Kehoe—all of whom would, at some point or another, crack the NHL's top 10 for goals and/or points in a season.

But there wasn't much else to crow about, especially on defence, where only Randy Carlyle, Ron Stackhouse and Dave Burrows got any All-Star recognition for Pittsburgh. Meanwhile a glut of goalie mainstays did their best but usually petered out after initial successes (Les Binkley, Gary Inness, Denis Herron, Greg Millen, et al.). Symbolic of the Penguins' bad luck in these tumultuous early years was the tale of super-rookie Michel Brière, who helped the 1969–70 team to the Western Division Final but then was critically injured in an off-season car crash that put the promising youngster into a coma he would not come out of until his death over a year later. This robbed Pittsburgh of a potential star to build around.

By 1974, a few shrewd trades and the drafting of the flashy Pierre Larouche restored some degree of respectability. Following a tremendous sophomore campaign, though, Larouche would get caught up in his newfound fame and tailed off until a transaction would see him shipped to the Canadiens. In true Pens fashion, the dealing of a once-lauded franchise cornerstone only netted them Peter Mahovlich (not as deadly a scorer without his superstar Habs teammates and on the wrong side of 30) plus depth scorer Peter Lee. (To add to the Penguins novelty act, virtually the entire team was, at one point, supposedly represented by agent Alan Eagleson—who controversially doubled as the head of the NHL Players' Association.)

The Penguins' inability to stand prosperity of any kind was best represented by a quarter-final appearance in 1975 where they got up three games to none on the New York Islanders—an organization in just its third NHL season—only to blow it with four straight losses. With that monumental choke, Pittsburgh became just the second team in North American "Big Four" pro sports history to lose a best-of-seven playoff series after leading it 3–0. It would unfortunately be the defining event in their history for the first two decades of NHL existence. Their greatest publicity arguably came in the middle of the 1979–80 season, when they changed from their Arctic blue, white and black colour scheme to the traditional black and gold pattern the Pirates and Steelers wore (and still do). The new look engineered a temporary distraction (and drew the ire of the similarly black-and-gold-adorned Bruins), but the Pens would have stayed mired in mediocrity with or without the change. Poor drafting and scouting and many badly executed trades had begun to catch up to the team on the ice as the decade progressed. Then came a disastrous 1982–83 showing on the heels of three straight hard-fought first round exits in the prior years. Souring the situation even further was the death of GM Baz Bastien in a March 1983 car accident.

Adding to Penguins fans' aggravation, their team at the start of 1982–83 had swapped first-rounders with the Minnesota North Stars. The October trade eventually saw them lose out on the top overall pick which, although it was used to select Brian Lawton, was seen as another missed opportunity to find a superstar to construct around. To top it all off, owner Eddie DeBartolo Jr. described the financial outlook as dire enough that they could either suspend operations or be sold to interests that would move the franchise to Hamilton, Ontario (coincidentally enough, the "Steeltown" of Canada). With these relocation rumours being bandied about—enhanced by the construction of a new arena in Hamilton's downtown core (Copps Coliseum)—the 1983–84 Penguins played with a dark cloud hovering over them.

With truly awful hockey on display, apathetic fans began tuning out in droves too; crowds averaged around 6,800 a game during that fateful season—fewer than the city's indoor soccer team averaged in the very same 16,033-seat Pittsburgh Civic Arena (a.k.a. "The Igloo"). All this came with a paltry season ticket base that numbered barely over 2,000 people.

Ownership and newly minted GM Eddie Johnston—the team's head coach in the prior few seasons, who had since installed his old Black Hawks teammate Lou Angotti behind the bench—decided the team's survival rested on landing the next NHL draft gem in Lemieux. It proved prescient. The Penguins would most likely have gone belly up if they had settled for any other prospect in 1984 or had held on to their 1983 first-rounder (whether to take the bust Lawton or an actual star performer like Sylvain Turgeon, Pat LaFontaine, Tom Barrasso or yes, perhaps even Steve Yzerman). Not to slight prospects like Kirk Muller or Ed Olczyk, but the predicament required a legend—and not simply a garden-variety star NHLer—to resuscitate the organization.

To ensure they'd be in line to select Mario, the Penguins made many questionable moves with their roster in order to "tank" and put themselves dead last in the league standings. They traded away 1981 Norris Trophy winner Randy Carlyle to Winnipeg and later sent their best-performing goalie, Roberto Romano, to the AHL in favour of a sieve-like Vincent Tremblay. Managing to "outlast" the Devils by three points (38 to 41) with a brutal 16–58–6 record at season's end, the Pens succeeded in their quest for salvation via futility. The Devils organization had similar intentions too, of course, but got held back by head coach Tom McVie (he of "Gretzky looked like he'd be killed" fame in our last chapter). Taking over early on in the season for Billy MacMillan, McVie was apparently not amenable to icing the worst possible lineups. He had already been the bench boss of historically wretched Capitals and Jets teams in prior years and had no appetite for living through such professional misery again. With its coach unwilling to endure a third wave of embarrassment behind the bench, New Jersey would prove only slightly less terrible than Pittsburgh. Nevertheless, the Devils still cried foul to the NHL head office about the Penguins' dodgy tanking measures.

The league didn't bother to fully investigate these howls of protest. After all, who wanted to dredge up something that could tarnish their credibility? This epic race to the bottom, and then another tanking battle between the Senators and Sharks in 1993, became the impetus for the creation of the draft lottery in 1995. As it was at the time, the draft order standards benefitted the inept Penguins. They now had the right to land

Mario Lemieux—along with also owning the 9th and 15th picks in the first round (acquired in the Carlyle deal and in that trade that had landed Minnesota the 1983 first overall pick).

Checking almost every box for scouts, Mario came with very few red flags. One of those though, was that in his younger years, Mario the Magnificent was coasting on his supernatural gifts and neglecting to improve his muscle mass and/or stamina. Never one to engage physically or backcheck for much of his pro career, he was even more unwilling to mix it up during his junior days. Lemieux never really had to play a two-way game, though. Trying to do so would likely have detracted from his core strengths—even if he didn't have the greatest "core strength" at the start.

Spending his teenage years in Montreal while his father, Jack, ran the NHL Central Scouting Bureau there, Craig Button attended a game with his dad in Mario's draft year:

> I think Laval lost the game 10–7, but it doesn't really matter what the score was, because Mario was what stood out the most to me. He was truly incredible to watch that night. I think he had five goals and two assists or something to that effect. What I really remember is that we were sitting with these other scouts, and I was hearing some say after the game things like "That fucking Lemieux, did you see how little he tried? His backchecking was non-existent! You can't have that sort of fucking attitude on your team!" I'll never forget it. It was unbelievable, and I couldn't understand it. Driving home afterward, I said to my dad, "Lemieux was so great tonight. He was the only reason Laval was even close! So why were those guys down on him?" He said, "Well, you know, unfortunately some scouts make up their mind before they even see a player that they've read or heard about. Then they watch him and see what they want rather than change their opinion." It just shows how even scouts can have their biases. I mean, Mario that year was so fantastic in the Q. Kirk Muller went number two in that draft and yeah, he had a good career. But in their draft

years, Mario scored more goals than Muller had points. I mean, come on! Who cares about trivial things when a guy can outscore the next best junior like that?

Former Canucks GM/President Mike Gillis concurs. "In many circumstances, drafting today is a big improvement over what I remember it being once. However, yes, I do believe there are still built-in scouting prejudices and confirmational biases that occur." If the imperfect world of scouting is rife with that sort of thinking even in this more enlightened modern age, one can only imagine what permeated through it almost four decades ago, when Lemieux was ascendant.

Once in the NHL, Mario added other facets to his supposedly one-dimensional game. While that took some time, it eventually did arrive; once it did, he began doing things unseen before in hockey. Despite his reluctance to engage physically (unlike what the hulking Eric Lindros would later do), Mario was still not one to be manhandled or pushed around. Sometimes getting into scraps, taking retaliatory penalties or compensating for his lack of defensive prowess with hooks and holds of his own, "Super Mario" was no shrinking violet.

He was not a "turn the other cheek" type à la Mike Bossy—as demonstrated by seasons such as his final one in the Q, when he accumulated 97 penalty minutes. In his NHL career, Mario would rack up numerous seasons averaging over a penalty minute per game. It looks alarming now, but in an era when at least a dozen players could post over 300 penalty minutes in a single NHL season, he was simply a minor offender.

As of 1984, no one thought they were looking at a brittle, injury-plagued commodity. The conventional feeling around Lemieux was that a player of his size would not be beaten down the same way that a five-foot-eight player could be. (And yet a short player like Marcel Dionne managed to carve out an amazingly healthy career compared to several of his larger-bodied peers.) But Mario's conditioning was less than ideal in his early days. Built like a beanpole, he frequently indulged in junk food, smoked cigarettes (a habit he reportedly finally gave up after his cancer scare in the early 1990s), seldom lifted any weights or did extra cardio training. Lemieux's lax approach to fitness, coupled with the routine punishment he endured from opposing players, would lead to back woes that flared up seriously by the end of the '80s. And yet, with his freakish athletic ability and incredible dexterity for a youngster with such a big frame, it hardly seemed to matter. If anything, scouts thought the more punishing pro game would not be a huge imposition on a player of his physical stature (a belief that has been proven wrong several times since, notably by Lindros, who was built like a truck but broke down as often as a Ford Pinto).

Lemieux's arrival in the NHL was akin to that of Jean Béliveau three decades earlier at six-foot-three. In their respective eras, most players of similar height were either stay-at-home defencemen with minimal skating ability or low-ice-time goons, muckers and grinders. (Almost forgotten now is that Béliveau himself led the NHL in penalty minutes early in his career when still trying to prove himself to the competition and when he had less control over his temper.)

Heading into the 1984 draft, Lemieux made it clear that he was going to be his own man. While the French-Canadian media longed for a Canadiens draftee who could inherit "the torch," (in this case from a fading Guy Lafleur), Mario dared to tell the local press that he would never want to take on that enormous pressure of becoming a Hab, irking many in Montreal who thought a great French-Canadian player should jump at the chance to be the next standard-bearer hero of Les Glorieux. (Although the Habs didn't get Mario that year, they still reaped a legendary Quebecker later in that historic draft—along with other parts of a couple more Cup winners). Almost no one before had dared utter such disregard for the major honour of being a Quebec kid playing for the Canadiens, but again, Mario was not one to shy away from being brutally honest if it got his message across.

In the spring of 1984, when it was apparent that Lemieux would be Pittsburgh-bound in a matter of weeks, negotiations began between the two parties. In the past, Pittsburgh had been one of those teams guilty of going for short-term gain. In fact, they had amazingly dealt away top 12 selections in six of the prior nine years. In spite of rumoured massive trade packages, the Pens made clear their intention to hold on to this pick. For once, this wasn't going to be a struggling outfit that didn't appreciate the value of a number one selection—unlike so many others in the past.

Even with reported pitches like the North Stars' promise of all of their draft picks that year and the Nordiques' offer of the three Stastny brothers, Johnston told them all the same thing: "'Stick it in your ear!' I was emphatic I wasn't going to trade him . . . It wasn't really a hard decision," he told the authors of *Best There Ever Was*. The Penguins would indeed stick to their guns while others got trade offers stuck in their ear. In the lead-up to the big day, Johnston quipped to *Montreal Gazette* legendary scribe Red Fisher, "Why would anybody think we wouldn't (take him)? We worked too hard to get him! . . . If the draft starts at precisely 3 P.M., we'll name Lemieux at 3:01."

However, before the draft was set to take place, the franchise's tattered reputation came to the surface again when Mario began to grumble publicly about unproductive contract talks between the Penguins and his negotiating team. Though he was being promised the biggest rookie contract in NHL history, the two sides remained at odds heading into June 9th's official festivities. The impasse prompted Lemieux to openly muse that the struggling organization didn't want him badly enough. There was even talk he might skip the ceremony itself. Lemieux stoked the suspicions by telling reporters the day before the draft that a boycott of the events might make the Pens "agree to make me a better offer, because they'd look pretty stupid if the number one pick in the entire draft isn't there." Strong words, no doubt.

As a result of the stalemate, Lemieux decided to part with tradition. He'd neither don the ceremonial jersey nor greet the management of the team that took him—this in a time when players only went to the team's draft table. (There wasn't a stage on which draftees were presented until 1987.) This refusal was seen by traditionalists as an unacceptable snub. Upon Johnston's bilingual announcement of Lemieux as his top choice, Mario sat wordlessly with a rather nonplussed expression on his face. According to the *Montreal Gazette*, with Mario not moving from his seat, Pittsburgh's Quebec regional scout, Albert Mandanici, attempted to draw Lemieux over to shake hands, pleading with him to "come to the table. There are people waiting for you . . . Do it for us, Mario." Despite the pleas, Mandanici was turned down and reminded by Badali not to force the 18-year-old to go anywhere he didn't want to go.

Lemieux repeated his points of contention to Don Wittman, who served as one of CBC TV's roving reporters on the floor for its first-ever live coverage of an NHL draft. Many—including Red Fisher, the afore-mentioned all-time dean of NHL beat writers—were rather put off by the youngster's brazen (by hockey standards) display. By then in his 30th of a 57-year career covering hockey professionally, Fisher was particularly offended by the charade, writing the day after that it was "the biggest mistake (Lemieux) will ever make . . . The certainty is that the boy was influenced by his agent, Badali, but Lemieux isn't blameless. An 18-year-old with grown-up talent can make up his own mind. It was a tasteless demon-stration of bad manners unmatched by anything I have ever witnessed at events of this kind. This should have been his grand moment, right?"

Years later, Mario would express regret at that approach, lamenting to author Chrys Goyens, "I was advised to do things that way, and was a young guy listening to advice from people who were in charge of my career path. I wish I had done things differently, to spare Eddie the embar-rassment. Still, things turned out pretty good for the both of us, and we're the best of friends today."

"I think Mario has always been his own guy," asserts broadcaster Gord Miller. "He was always going to be his own guy, and he was going to do things his way. And as a result, he probably ruffled some feathers. Maybe people didn't know him well enough or weren't ready for that. But I think Mario, with some of the stances that he took and how he carried himself, for sure helped empower the next generation of players."

Lemieux's actions were amplified because this entry draft was not only on TV but also open to the public, a practice started in 1981, when it was moved from its traditional locale at the Queen Elizabeth Hotel to the Montreal Forum. As expected, a bigger than usual crowd made it to the Forum in 1984—the draft's final year there before it became a travelling event, starting with the 1985 edition at Toronto's Metropolitan Convention Centre in time for the Leafs to use that top overall pick on Wendel Clark. Mario's snub made this TV event all the more intriguing. Even in the for-mal photo sessions after the selections were made, Lemieux remained decked out in his suit and never once put on a piece of Penguins mer-chandise—even in group poses with the next two picks, Kirk Muller and

Ed Olczyk, who beamingly wore their respective Devils and Black Hawks uniforms. "I don't think the controversy was as amplified then as it would have been today," contends Mitch Melnick.

"Even seven years after that, there was huge coverage over Lindros, and the Lemieux thing was minor by comparison. By then, there were sports TV stations and talk shows, but in '84, if there was only one sports-specific show in a market, that was considered enough. So it's not like there was an onslaught of controversy, and it was mostly in print anyway. But Lemieux always had an independent streak in him, for sure. I know a lot of Montrealers were upset because the guy he was showing up was Eddie Johnston, who was born and raised in Montreal and from a notorious family there, actually."

Luckily for the beleaguered Pens, the stalled negotiations finally pushed ahead over the following days. The talks eventually resulted in an official agreement just 10 days following the drama on the draft floor. During this era without rookie signing caps, contracts were not quite as cut-and-dry as today. Even so, Lemieux would come to an agreement with his new club on a three-year deal (the third year being a club option worth $575,000) that came with a $150,000 signing bonus. It was a pact that would be renegotiated in the middle of season two, when it turned into a four-year, $3.5-million agreement.

Given that the 1984 entry draft was in Montreal and a locally developed superstar was going first overall, one would assume that no other story could've approached the enormous level of interest in Lemieux— even if that story happened to be related to the hometown Habs. But then the Canadiens dropped their own bomb with a surprise reveal that shook the hockey scouting world. It came with a pick that, as history proved, helped shape the NHL's European future, even if it didn't shape the Canadiens' future quite as much (nor even as much as other picks that they made that same day).

The NHL had been slow in catching on to the wave of successful European imports outside Scandanavia leading up to 1984. There had been home-run acquisitions such as Borje Salming, Stefan Persson, Tomas Jonsson, Mats Naslund, Jari Kurri and the Stastny brothers—but not a lot else in terms of star power. This was especially meagre compared to how much the World Hockey Association had capitalized on that previously untapped goldmine. The early part of the 1980s had seen a realization that even more potential lay in importing European skill—not just from the traditional Nordic nations but from behind the Iron Curtain too. In those nations however, it was a much higher-stakes venture than finding your average Swede, Finn, Dane, West German, etc.

Scouting missions inside Europe's Communist countries offered far more political peril, and trips within these places often weren't feasible due to the tight grip of government control. As a consequence, most young players from the Eastern bloc were noticed either on video that had been smuggled out, by word of mouth or at international tournaments held in Western nations. To land players from locales such as Czechoslovakia, East Germany or the Soviet Union required not only international diplomacy but secret midnight moves, incognito agreements, bribe money and eventual defections at an embassy.

Again, the WHA had instigated sneaking out highly protected European superstars. The first incident came when the Toronto Toros (later to move to the Deep South, rechristened as the Birmingham Bulls) pilfered future Hockey Hall of Famer Vaclav Nedomansky out of Czechoslovakia in the mid-1970s. It was a calculated move, as the rival Maple Leafs under owner Harold Ballard would never dare undertake such a risky venture. Ballard, who had just gotten back at the helm as Leafs majority owner after spending two years in prison on fraud and embezzlement charges, was notorious for his dislike of European players. In particular, "Pal Hal" carried a serious mistrust and loathing of anyone from any socialist nation and extended that policy to his hockey club as well.

The imprisonment that prevented Ballard from operating Maple Leaf Gardens had actually been the only reason that the 1972 Summit Series even saw a game played in Toronto. He blocked subsequent Canada Cup contests in 1976, 1981, 1984 and 1987 from his arena—a moratorium only lifted by his 1990 death and the subsequent change in Leafs ownership. Due to Ballard's deeply held aversion to showcasing "pinko commie" hockey teams at his rink, the Leafs were largely prevented from raiding Europe for talent until the late 1970s, when he was finally convinced by his management—led by legendary talent assessor and then-team GM

Jim Gregory—that his team badly needed the talent infusion. After all, it had worked very well in 1973, when Ballard was serving his prison sentence and Gregory capitalized by signing Swedish talents Borje Salming and Inge Hammarstrom. While Hammarstrom was ridiculed for his non-physical play, often by Ballard himself (famously labelling him so soft that he could go into the corner with a dozen eggs in his pockets and come out with not a single one of them cracked), Salming would manage to endure the North American game's rigours to become an All-Star and one of the greatest defencemen in Leafs history—not to mention one of the great European blueliners to play in the NHL to this very day.

The WHA Nedomansky signing saw majority owner Johnny F. Bassett, the son of Ballard rival John Bassett, one-up the established Leafs. The senior Bassett had been a substantial figure, no doubt, building his wealth on highly successful media properties. Prior to his son's foray into WHA ownership, Bassett had been part of the "Silver Seven" ownership committee that ran the Leafs in the wake of Conn Smythe's retirement from the day-to-day operations and his selling the majority of his shares in 1961. When Smythe's son Stafford and his close ally Ballard were charged with tax evasion and using Maple Leaf Gardens Ltd. to fund personal expenses in 1969, Bassett had been able to persuade the board to fire the two from their positions of president and executive vice president. Bassett would take over as team president afterward, but that proved brief as he lost a power struggle to Stafford and Ballard, who had not been forced to sell their shares and therefore still controlled half the shares.

In 1973, the junior Bassett would enter the sports-ownership world when he joined a group of 26 investors in purchasing the WHA's Ottawa Nationals. The Nats moved their home base to Toronto late in the 1972–73 season and were dubbed the Ontario Nationals in an effort to give them both local and provincial appeal. Keeping them in Toronto with the new Toros moniker, Bassett Jr. would decide to go head-to-head with the Maple Leafs and play in Varsity Arena that first year (making waves by almost signing away young Leafs centre Darryl Sittler while coercing former All-Star Leaf defenceman Carl Brewer out of retirement). The Toros would, for both alliterative and competitive reasons, be known as a Toronto team, as the Ontario naming experiment proved short-lived.

A year later, the Toronto Toros landed Nedomansky following his July 1974 defection during a family vacation in Switzerland. (This cloak-and-dagger addition came in the same summer that the Toros also inked former Buds Frank Mahovlich and Paul Henderson—the latter coming straight from the Leafs roster after not being offered the pay he felt he deserved from the team's then-stingy ownership). While Nedomansky being lured to T.O. may have just been a public-relations coup and/or affront to the Leafs' hegemony, it did point a way to the future talent influx that would transform first the WHA and then later the NHL. For the Toros, it would not help them out as much financially as they'd hoped. Even though they moved out of the outdated and tiny Varsity Arena into the Gardens in time for 1974–75, matters didn't exactly improve. Ballard was none too pleased to have his WHA rival in his very own arena—a predicament that arose thanks to an agreement his son Bill had made while acting in his imprisoned father's place.

To curtail the new competition, Ballard used some classic passive-aggressive techniques. The gruff owner made demands of the Toros in regards to rent, use of dressing rooms and even the arena lights as well as the cushions for the home team bench. Any pushback from the Toros would likely have been met with "let's resolve this in court," costing them time and money they didn't have. All of this hampered the Toros despite respectable fan interest at the outset. A drop in the standings and in attendance for 1975–76 saw financial difficulties start to arise.

The rocky experience of trying to co-exist with the standard-bearer Leafs convinced the younger Bassett to move the team to Birmingham, Alabama. Two years later, the financial realities of trying to make hockey work in the Deep South while paying exorbitant salaries led the Bulls to make a rare inter-league trade that transferred Nedomansky to the NHL in November 1977 as they would deal the Czech star to the Red Wings. Once signed on to Detroit, "Big Ned" wouldn't quite put up the same solid numbers as he had enjoyed in the WHA, where he counted three straight seasons of 35-plus goals, including 56 in 1975–76. Still, the six-foot-two,

200-plus-pound winger proved more than competent at the NHL level—a fact not lost on hockey scouts.

Nedomansky's journey to North America was an early demonstration that players within Czechoslovakia were much more willing to turn their backs on the rigid political system of their country, perhaps emboldened by the fresh memories of Soviet tanks invading to suppress attempted democratic measures in 1968. Though they had political regimes in common, Czech players after the so-called Prague Spring became even fiercer rivals with Soviet teams on the international stage—a rivalry that probably outdid any in terms of bitterness and made Canada versus USSR, Canada versus USA and Sweden versus Finland look tame by comparison.

Post-WHA/NHL merger, another major victory for North American pro hockey was the dynamic Stastny brothers, Peter and Anton, being snuck out of an international tournament to defect to Canada and sign with the Quebec Nordiques in 1980. The elder Stastny brother, Marian, would follow a year later. By then, Czechoslovakia's hockey federation had seen the writing on the wall and began to ease up on the restrictions, provided they could get compensation for the lost players and beef up their own shaky finances in the process. Growing tired of losing its main attractions, the Czechoslovakian hockey federation began to take a different approach.

Figuring they'd let the older stars seek their fame but hold on to the younger or prime-era stars, the Czech powers-that-be decided in 1981 to make several of their established figures—many already in their late 20s to early 30s and exiting their prime—available to any NHL clubs interested and willing to compensate them. While tight-fistedness over hockey properties continued in the USSR throughout the 1980s, the Czechoslovakians played it more diplomatically and pragmatically. Some NHL teams balked at the demands, but others—namely those on the lower end of the spectrum that were starving for elite players—would gladly pounce on some of the newly available foreign talent.

For instance, the Canucks, mired in mediocrity since day one of their NHL existence, used the fire sale opportunity to grab scoring whiz Ivan Hlinka as well as defender Jiri Bubla (later infamous for being imprisoned as part of a heroin-smuggling ring). They wouldn't radically transform

Vancouver's luck, but they did add depth that served them well the next few years.

If the Czech hockey body at the time believed this new openness on older players would placate NHL interest, they were proven wrong. NHL teams desperate to have coveted names strategized creative new ways to land them. Defections increased from over the following years. Clubs that had seen the merits of these players began to use higher and higher selections to secure their rights as well. The 1982 entry draft saw the selection of several Czechs and Slovaks. Before the 1984 draft, several such picks were used on other players, but most were not granted permission to leave and/or their NHL rights-holders were unable to organize defections. This came after the NHL, increasingly worried about competition that would drive up the bargaining prices (the horror!), ruled that a number of the players could not be signed as free agents. Though the 1981 talent raid and the subsequent next few drafts may have only resulted in a few minor long-term successes on the NHL stage, the Czechoslovakian selections of the 1980s still paid off much quicker than any of the long shots for Soviets—many of whom never arrived to the NHL or didn't come until much later, with the initiation of glasnost in 1989 (but more on that in our next chapter).

Various clubs sampled the forbidden hockey fruit. Strangely enough, 1982 found the typically regressive and bumbling Maple Leafs rolling the dice on Czechoslovakian players more than any NHL team. GM Gerry McNamara and his perennially under-equipped scouting staff would secure the elder of the Ihnacak brothers (Peter) in that draft. Peter turned into a mainstay of the Leafs during their lean 1980s years and outshone young Miroslav, who didn't pan out once signed by the Leafs in 1985 (infamously, team ownership permitted Mirko to take the No. 27 once worn by Frank Mahovlich and Darryl Sittler). The 1982 draft saw notable USSR-based picks in Vyacheslav Fetisov (taken by the Devils when the Canadiens' rights from 1978 lapsed), Sergei Makarov and Alexei Kasatonov—all of whom would arrive in North America but not until several seasons later. Led by GM Lou Nanne, the Minnesota North Stars were also willing and able to take a chance on some foreign hidden assets in 1983. While their draft that year was defined by their disastrous number one overall selection of U.S. high school phenom Brian Lawton, their effort did pay off thanks to second-rounder Frantisek Musil (at number 38 overall).

A standout rearguard in his homeland, Musil would fulfill his military obligations, refuse to sign any long-term contracts and learn to speak English in secret over the next three years as part of his plot to eventually defect to the West. He would do that in the summer of 1986 while holidaying in Yugoslavia. This defection came about after several of his teammates had shown the way for Musil to do the same. Through a mutual contact in Czech player Miroslav Maly, Edmonton-based agent Ritch Winter began a dialogue with Musil in the early part of 1986. Maly had already defected before being accepted as the first hockey client of University of Alberta law graduate Winter, who had always been eager to get into representing pro hockey players and hoped taking on these European defectors would lead to greener pastures.

A 1984 North Stars fourth-rounder, Maly went back to Europe after a short stint in the AHL with the Springfield Indians and Baltimore Skipjacks during the 1984–85 season. Playing in Germany in 1985–86, Maly ran into Musil at a tournament and was approached by the surprisingly candid Czech youngster with the idea of defecting. He informed Musil that his agent could help and would go on to later deliver a letter from Winter outlining just how he could do so. Recalling the events in 2020, Winter described the frenetic situation that got Musil to North America—a prime example of the cloak-and-dagger operations that were common in getting big-name players out from behind the Iron Curtain in the 1980s:

> I was a young guy at the time, and so I didn't have a lot of room on my credit card. Therefore, I asked my mom if she could put my flight on hers. I did a little bit of research and figured out that I needed a visa to Yugoslavia, where Frank was at the time. I had previously talked to Lou Nanne to let him know I was going to get Musil. He kind of laughed it off, saying "Yeah, you and everybody else. I've heard this story before." I didn't really know what to say to that, other than "Well, Lou, I don't know what other people did, but I am leaving for Umag, Yugoslavia (now Croatia), and I'm

going to pick him up, and I wanted you to be aware of that."
I was prepared to do this thing all on my own. But as I flew
from Munich to Trieste, Italy, I noticed Lou was on the same
plane as me! He had decided that I was actually going, so
he went to connect with me. None of us had cellphones at
this stage, don't forget. I had no idea what he was thinking,
and meanwhile he has this camera crew with him. I was
thinking, "Hmm, I don't know much about this defecting
business, but my thinking is you should be trying to kind of
slide it under the radar a little better than this."

After I walked off the plane in Trieste, I got to the train
station and found out there was a train not leaving until well
after the time Frank and I were supposed to meet up. Again,
there's no cellphones, so we have got to meet at that appointed
time. I go hail a cab and kept saying, "Umag, Umag" because the
(cabbie) kept replying, "Umago, yeah, no, no, no, it's okay."
I'm like, "'I hope there's not an Umago, Italy!" But it sounds
like they knew where I wanted to be going.

Winter finally made it to Umag and had his planned meeting with Frank:

I'd never seen a picture of him, but it was pretty obvious
who this guy in this short-sleeve shirt—looking to be in very
good condition—was. I rented a car, and we started driving
towards Zagreb, where there was a consulate. It was the closest American consulate to Umag. I was going to use my best
persuasive skills at that point to see if I could get him into
the United States. Thinking back, I wonder what was I thinking? Did I think I was going to show them my Mastercard?
We just never really thought it through properly. In Zagreb,
they told us to try at the American Embassy in Belgrade, so
we drove there just in time to get to the embassy before it
closed. There, they told us they couldn't help either and suggested we go to the United Nations High Commissioner for
Refugees, which we also did. Once there, we started sharing

his story in the lobby at the reception area. From that point, we were quickly whisked to the high commissioner, who told us to keep our story to ourselves because among athletes of Frank's profile, the last one they had seen come through had never been seen or heard from again. At that stage, Frank understood enough English that he started getting pretty nervous about what was happening. We went back to a hotel that I booked and decided we'd give Lou a call. At this point I wasn't having any success. I really had no idea what to do.

Lou advised me that he was in Zagreb and was making very good progress putting in place the steps necessary to secure Frank a visa, with the help of a U.S. senator from Minnesota. We thought, okay, that sounded really good, but there were no flights back to Zagreb. So we had to drive. But strangely enough, our car broke down. Frank and I had to push it back two kilometres to the closest hotel and car-rental place. We ended up getting a replacement, getting up to Zagreb, where Lou was already. He wasn't having any luck with the councilor there, though—that is, until the cameras turned on and started recording their conversation. When that happened, the head of the consulate felt a little bit more pressure, and, with the support of U.S. Government officials overseas, made an agreement to grant Frank a visa. Lou arranged to fly us all back to the U.S. through London. Once we got on the plane, Frank embraced me in a way where I thought he was going to crush me! He was pretty excited once we left. We didn't have the internet then obviously too, so I personally didn't really know how good these Czech National Team players were. It became the door-opener for me, though, because Frank turned out to be very close friends with (future client) Dominik Hasek.

This incredible escape would bring Musil to Minnesota and the start of an NHL journey that stretched over a decade and a half (further extended when his son David was drafted years later by the Oilers). Though his career never peaked to the level originally expected, Musil's tricky defection had a clear impact. Even though it wasn't quite the equal of the escape made by a Red Wings' pick in the fifth round that year.

Petr Klima was a mercurial, goal-happy fellow who also enjoyed the party life. Due to some disciplinary issues (i.e., a propensity to go on all-night drinking escapades with teammates such as Bob Probert) and a more one-dimensional style of play, Klima never quite materialized into an NHL superstar despite his initial promise. That said, he still racked up several 30-goal seasons, hitting exactly 40 with the Oilers in 1990–91. He would also become one of the first Czech players who proved himself to be a highly capable performer at that elite level of pro hockey.

What made Klima's defection unique was that he was still only 20 at the time, risking nearly everything to make his riches on the big stage. Before Klima, only Anton Stastny at age 22 had been considered a fairly young and developing player when he escaped from the Iron Curtain. Bolting from a training camp in Nussdorf, West Germany, in 1985, Klima had prearranged a rendezvous with Wings president Jim Lites and assistant GM Nick Polano. This came on the heels of a two-year process that had begun when Klima first expressed his desire to defect at a secret meeting during the 1984 World Junior Championships in Sweden. He then confirmed that interest by inking a multi-year contract with Detroit—shuttled to him under the Czech authorities' noses during a national team stop in Vancouver for games during the 1984 Canada Cup. After a complex web of diplomatic string-pulling got Klima and his girlfriend their freedom to enter the United States, the Wings had not only their man, but also one of the most expertly achieved defections ever in the hockey world. Making his Detroit debut in time for 1985–86, Klima would remind himself and others of this escape to the West by wearing No. 85 for the rest of his career—much as countryman Jaromir Jagr would wear No. 68 to honour the freedom fighters of the Prague Spring uprising against the USSR in 1968.

But all these daring events owed their inspiration to 18-year-old defenceman Petr Svoboda, who had defected from Team Czechoslovakia in the spring of 1984 during the IIHF World Hockey Championships. Svoboda's sudden exit to the West was not immediately reported, resulting in a surprise selection at number five overall by the Canadiens—a pick that proved to be the first example of a prized teenaged player from the Iron Curtain being not only smuggled out but drafted at the same time.

Svoboda was a whole new model for acquiring Iron Curtain assets. Prior to 1984, defections had usually happened after a player was drafted or (as with Peter Ihnacak) when he was already well into the prime of his career. Sneaking away from a national junior team tournament in Munich, Germany, Svoboda was able to make contact with the hockey world via telephone. "The procedure started right away," Svoboda recalled later to Tal Pinchevsky in his 2012 book *Breakaway*. "In those three months (living in Munich), there were a lot of general managers flying in to have interviews with me. So I knew I was going to be drafted." Canadiens GM Serge Savard caught wind of his gambit before almost anyone else and pressed hard to make the youngster his team's next franchise defenceman, arranging for the teenaged blueliner to be flown to Montreal just before the historic June 9 draft. "They brought me to Montreal about five days before the draft. Basically, they hid me in the Ritz-Carlton. They claimed they hadn't heard from me and then drafted me fifth overall," Svoboda recalled.

Savard's crafty machinations would have made his old boss Sam Pollock proud. Svoboda's draft announcement in the Forum that day came to the bewilderment of fans, scouts and reporters alike. Merely a rumour before that point, the reveal was a shock to some as TV cameras focused on the newest big defector donning a Canadiens jersey in the Forum's arena entryway. Unlike Mario minutes earlier, Svoboda happily walked out to greet team personnel. According to Mitch Melnick, who covered the event, "That was quite a splash. I remember people being impressed just by the sheer drama of it. Even though he was relatively new into his job as GM, Serge Savard had so much respect here from people that they thought, 'This kid must be really, really good for Savard to do that.'"

Most "experts" had slotted the Habs to nab Shayne Corson with their fifth overall selection spot—a position acquired thanks to a deal in December 1981, when Pierre Larouche had been sent to the Hartford Whalers (then-GM Irving Grundman's attempt at a Pollock-esque swindle to bag Lemieux?).

But after the Svoboda reveal at number five, Savard was not finished wheeling and dealing. He swapped second-rounders with the Blues while also giving them goalie Rick Wamsley and the second-rounder acquired from Hartford in the Larouche deal—plus the Habs' third-round pick (number 53 overall). Coming back to Montreal with the second-rounder was the Blues' first-round pick—the eighth overall selection, to be exact. Savard used that to snag Corson after all, giving the Canadiens the youngster that most were anticipating they'd get—plus a European surprise a few spots earlier. The deal never would have materialized without Svoboda, though. Savard was planning on Corson at fifth overall if he couldn't guarantee Svoboda making it to Montreal without incident. Telling Red Fisher about his dilemma, Savard claimed, "We had called the airlines the day before to see if he was on the plane from West Germany, and we were told he wasn't. We called back an hour later, and that time we were told he *was* on the plane. If he hadn't been on there, the deal with St. Louis probably wouldn't have been made."

While Svoboda and Corson would turn into quality NHLers at their career peaks, it was with post-first-round choices that Savard built the true foundation for the Canadiens' consistent run of Stanley Cup contending seasons from 1985–86 to 1992–93. They would first do that by utilizing the number 29 pick from St. Louis to take the franchise's last 50-goal scorer to date in Stéphane Richer, a speedy, hard-shooting winger who would score 50 in both 1987–88 and 1989–90. (In a later 1991 transaction with the Devils, Richer was parlayed into fellow 1984 draftee and eventual 1993 Cup hero Kirk Muller).

More pivotal in shaping the future of Les Glorieux, however, was a 1983–84 trade that was consummated before the draft with John Ferguson, Savard's former teammate in Montreal and also his boss when he suited up for the Jets over his last two seasons as a player. The transaction saw defenceman Robert Picard shipped to the Jets for what turned into goalie Patrick Roy, a third-round pick who paid huge dividends as perhaps the greatest big-game goalie in modern NHL history.

It's a very fine line between triumph and failure at a draft table, and that was never more evident than in 1984. Roy was actually the third goalie chosen that year. Career backups Craig Billington and Daryl Reaugh (later to become the witty colour analyst for the Dallas Stars) were snapped up by the Devils and Oilers respectively prior to "Saint Patrick" going to the

Habs. Despite NHL's Central Scouting Bureau designating him as merely the fourth-best Quebec goalie and 14th-best goalie available overall, Roy was reportedly tickled just to be considered for drafting at all. But one-time NHL goalie Charlie Hodge, by this time a scout, was enamoured with the youngster. The Canadiens' former starter back in the 1960s later said, "We had also put Patrick's name on our list because, in my eyes, he was the best junior in Canada during the 1983–84 season. This young man will have an excellent career. He is quick as a cat and never goes down needlessly. I think he is the greatest junior I have watched since Grant Fuhr."

In his 2007 biography of his own son, *Patrick Roy: Winning, Nothing Else*, Michel Roy acknowledged, "Now we know that Hodge had it right, but this enthusiasm seemed a little excessive at the time, given Patrick's unimpressive outing on the previous day to his comments" (a 7–2 preseason whipping by the Jets in September 1984).

Clearly overlooked after toiling away with a weak supporting cast in Granby, Roy began to demonstrate that was worth the Habs draft gamble when he joined their AHL affiliate in Sherbrooke after his final QMJHL season in 1984–85. Once established as a "Baby Hab" team member, Roy pitched in on a 1985 Calder Cup championship run—a very significant AHL title conquest too, as the journey came with seven other teammates who would just a year later contribute to the 23rd and, perhaps, most unlikely Canadiens Stanley Cup team ever. That 1986 Cup conquest saw the 20-year-old Roy become arguably the most surprising Conn Smythe Trophy winner to date, as well. Based on his track record (a promising yet inconsistent rookie campaign during the 1985–86 regular season), it was unforeseen that Roy would lead his underdog Habs throughout the spring of 1986.

Much like Mark Messier, Patrick Roy was not one of those raw talents being routinely praised as a future legend. Even his rookie season didn't convince people of that. Mitch Melnick admits:

> Anybody who tells you that they knew when he was drafted
> or even when he debuted in the NHL that he was going to
> be *that* good is full of shit. At that point, there was no chance
> that I thought he was going to be what he became. I know

maybe he got overlooked because of his inflated numbers and because there were a ton of goals scored in the Q. He was routinely facing 50 to 60 shots a night, but unless you saw the game in person you didn't realize how much of a competitor he actually was. You can't look at a guy's goals against average and make any kind of judgment a lot of the time, I've discovered. But unless you were an expert on that league or you were a scout, you glanced at this kid's stats and the fact that he looked like if you blew on him he'd fall over, and you didn't think big things were in store at all. Patrick was just so skinny in his rookie season. Even towards the end of that 1985–86 year, there was no indication that he was going to do what he ended up doing. The Habs were in turmoil late that year as well. There were a lot of serious issues between Jean Perron and the players. They were ones that got him canned a couple of years later, as it turns out.

People forget the Habs were in danger of missing the Adams Division playoffs altogether and were going through a six-game losing streak in March that nearly did them in. As it was, they managed to finish second in the division, but they were only seven points up on Buffalo, who was fifth and last, and that margin was a lot closer with a couple weeks left too. They kept having to have all these team meetings and whatnot. It was basically the leadership core that kept things together. And then, of course, Roy became that one performer to rally around. Going with him kind of was a process of elimination too. First off, we had seen the best of (goalie) Steve Penney and that was long gone with no magic left. The league just figured him out, plus he was hurt by the end of that season anyway. Doug Soetaert had the better numbers of all the Habs goalies that year, but he was doing it in a backup role and there was no way they were going all the way with him. The attitude in Montreal was simply, "Oh well, it happened before with Dryden, so let's give it a shot here with this Roy youngster." I know I couldn't remember the defining moment where it turned around for Lafleur, but to me the Roy mystique was born in the playoffs, and namely that one game in New York (Game 3 of the Wales Conference Final) when he made like 13, 14 saves in overtime, and (Claude) Lemieux scored the winner. I was like, "Holy shit" while I was watching that. That performance started the legend.

Given his draft position at the time, Roy is arguably the savviest draft selection in Canadiens history. And Savard, on the job for only a year at the time, was the key ingredient. On that late spring day in his team's home city, Savard got the better of former Habs assistant GM and head of scouting Ron Caron—now St. Louis's GM. Caron was a victim of the Canadiens' post-dynasty purge when they cleaned house after 1982–83, leaving Savard as the replacement for GM Irving Grundman. The poor playoff results of the Canadiens' post-dynasty malaise from 1979–83 had prompted newly minted team president Ronald Corey to dismiss Grundman and most of his staff as well as head coach Bob Berry (who got a final chance under Savard before being canned late in 1983–84). It also didn't help that former Habs executive Bill Torrey had built a four-time Cup winner with the New York Islanders and another ex-Hab product, Glen Sather, was building an even greater dynasty with Gretzky in Edmonton.

Craig Button, for one, feels that Grundman was in deep trouble from the start due to his lack of real hockey experience and the impossible expectations he had to live up to:

> Unfortunately for Irving, he just didn't have the background of a Sam Pollock. He didn't scout, he didn't know players, and he didn't know development. I know Sam was very, very strong on a manager's job being as much about business as it was about hockey. And sometimes that becomes a misunderstanding too, like, "Oh let's get Irving Grundman, he's a really good businessman, and we'll run it like that."
>
> That isn't a total criticism of Irving, though. He came into an almost impossible scenario. It's that saying: "You don't want

to replace the legend, you want to replace the guy that *replaced* the legend." That was the benefit for Serge. You know, Serge is a very measured person, very calm. He's not knee-jerk, and he's not going to do things just because he feels compelled to do them. Obviously, that comes with the pedigree and credibility he had as a Hall of Fame player too. Irving really didn't have that. He didn't have the same *gravitas*.

Savard's main strengths going into the job were a sterling playing career and several off-ice business dealings, principally through owning race horses (a passion he shared with Jets GM and former teammate Ferguson). But could the former player judge talent? On that day in 1984, he showed his skill as a judge of hockey flesh with the massive Blues deal returning two future key pieces. It's no wonder the Habs won a pair of Cups in the subsequent decade under Savard's guidance, while Caron's Blues only advanced beyond the second round once (1986, when his Bluenotes came a win away from clashing with Savard's Habs in the Cup Final) before dismissal for the "The Professor" finally came in 1994.

Buoyed by late Pollock/Grundman-era draft gems, plus Savard's own home-run selections from 1984, the Canadiens were a model organization during a period from 1985 to 1993 that saw them routinely finish top five in the NHL standings and go deep into the post-season as well. To that end, Montreal would finish as high as second overall (115 points in 1988–89) and no worse than seventh overall (87 in 1985–86), with both years seeing them in the Cup Final. In fact, only one franchise won more playoff games (the multiple-championship Oilers, with 104) between 1984 and 1994 than the Canadiens' 94. It was a good 38 more than the third-best club in this period of time, their hated rivals the Bruins.

In retrospect, it's intriguing how third-rounder Roy turned out to be such a gem considering all the hoops and barrels gone through in securing the number five overall pick. With the Svoboda selection, Serge Savard was certainly banking on the idea that he'd found the Canadiens' next, well, Serge Savard. Instead, Svoboda ended up more like the next Terry Harper or Brian Engblom—a solid defender with some All-Star stretches of play here and there and a small offensive upside, but not the slam-dunk cornerstone that many had expected when Svoboda made the jump to the West.

Savard would go on to make some ill-advised trades in the 1990s and falter at the draft table after that too, but his handiwork early in his tenure set the table for several deep playoff runs. There is a misguided historical view of the '80s Habs as a weak shadow of their former selves, a franchise that failed to meet the unattainable expectations they had set by winning 15 Stanley Cups between 1956 and 1979. While it's true that the Habs would slow down their runaway mastery of the rest of the league, they were still almost the same regular season powerhouse from 1979 to 1983, when their grasp on elite talent was far less ironclad than before.

Grundman's tenure is now seen in a negative light, but that's largely in relation to what came before and what came just after. The regimes of Réjean Houle, Pierre Gauthier and Marc Bergevin look downright ugly by comparison to Grundman's record, and it's not as if he left a disaster in his wake that Montreal couldn't recover from for years. The Canadiens of his era may have struck out on first-rounders, but they did dig up diamonds in the rough such as Chris Chelios, Mats Naslund and Guy Carbonneau during that period. Although 1983 did provide arguably the most pessimistic environment a Canadiens team had faced since the ushering in of Dick Irvin as head coach after the most disastrous year in franchise history (a 1939–40 showing of 10–33–7), the scenario would be repeated again and again as the franchise became accustomed to dashed expectations and lowered standards of excellence (for example, house-cleanings of 1995, 2000, 2003, 2012 and 2018).

Compared to what passes for achievement in Montreal these days, the tenure of "The Senator" Savard was a true success. Even if it was a step down from the dynasty years, that was just the reality sinking in that the Canadiens' supposed birthright to the Stanley Cup had finally disappeared.

Meanwhile, adjusting to the drastic change of going from his native Czechoslovakia to North America, Svoboda became a fine two-way presence by the end of the '80s despite being somewhat injury prone. To his credit, Svoboda often played through his many ailments. "Even though he never became the kind of superstar player that you'd think somebody of that stature would have been, I think Svoboda is constantly overlooked for the career he had," insists Mitch Melnick:

> I mean, he skated beautifully, he was a great passer, he had a head for the game, he was tough, and he was very durable for a thin, lanky kid. The poor guy was constantly abused, especially every time the Habs played the Bruins. Cam Neely would just plaster Svoboda into the glass behind the Canadiens net all the time. But he never backed down. He stood up to the grind of it all. In my opinion, he's one of the most underrated players who ever played for the Canadiens during my lifetime. He was really good, he just wasn't Hall of Fame–calibre good, which I think some people might've thought initially because of how he arrived here. Nonetheless, he was an excellent defenceman for a long time, and not just in Montreal

Things ultimately soured for Svoboda in Montreal when he began to clash with fiery head coach Pat Burns. It finally came to a head with a trade to the Sabres partway through the 1991–92 season. By then, Svoboda's personal life was relatively normal again, as he was allowed to travel back to his homeland after the fall of Communism throughout Eastern Europe. As well, he was able to complete internationally as a member of the Czech Republic. His crowning achievement came when, as a member of this national club, he scored the only goal needed in a 1–0 win over Russia in the gold medal game at the 1998 Nagano Winter Olympics.

Svoboda's pro career was almost done when he popped that monumental tally, but when he retired in 2001, he had logged a respectable decade-and-a-half-plus of NHL service. Hoping to help players deal with the changes and difficulties that pro hockey brings (like those he experienced in his transition as a teenager to a completely different continent, country, language and culture), he would go into the player agent business post-retirement. While he wasn't ultimately the franchise player he was originally hailed as in 1984, several top-five overall picks have fared far, far worse than Petr Svoboda.

The 1984 draft didn't just set up future championship successes for the Penguins and Canadiens, but also saw late-round gems galore. The 1986 rookie of the year, Gary Suter, and the 1987 winner of that award, Luc Robitaille, were steals in the eighth round by the Flames and Kings respectively. Robitaille was an oversight indeed, a smart and opportunistic winger who had put up monstrous numbers in the QMJHL but slid due to the preconceived notion that offensive stars from Quebec were ill-suited to the more physical NHL. The consensus also suggested that Robitaille lacked the finesse and speed needed to take his scoring touch to the next level.

That assessment proved mistaken on many levels in a career that made him the top point-scoring left winger in NHL history to date and, until Alex Ovechkin, the top goal-scoring left winger too. Even the Kings were in no hurry to call his name, selecting college hockey star Tom Glavine, a future Baseball Hall of Fame pitcher, in the fourth round—well ahead of their future Hockey Hall of Famer "Lucky Luc."

Stealing Robitaille in the eighth round didn't lead to a Stanley Cup for the beleaguered Kings franchise, but the Flames draft handiwork in 1984 would help bring them Cup glory five years later. That's no surprise considering their haul: before plucking the U.S. college defenceman Suter, they had already made a slam-dunk first-round pick in Gary Roberts and then got Brett Hull (still dismissively known as "Bobby's son") out of the BCHL in round six. All three would have star-studded careers, but especially the "Golden Brett," who fought out of the obscurity of his draft selection to dominate in a college career at the University of Minnesota Duluth before excelling as one of the purest shooters ever seen in hockey (albeit most of that for the Blues, after Calgary dealt him in 1988 for Rob Ramage and Rick Wamsley). While the Flames may have gotten components for their 1989 Cup win with a top-four defender in Ramage and a high-quality backup goalie in Wamsley, many believe keeping Hull would have possibly led to more Cup contention down the road. But Hull's testy relationship with Terry Crisp, Calgary's head coach at the pro level from 1987 to 1990, casts doubt on the idea that he'd rack up 50-goal seasons one after another in Cowtown.

Still, the Flames under Pollock protegé Cliff Fletcher deserved credit for finding such an overlooked talent when they did. After all, the over-aged

Hull had been draft-eligible for two years by this point but was not on the radar, after playing local rec hockey until joining the BCHL's Penticton Knights in 1982–83. After a 48-goal, 104-point year in 50 games as a Junior A rookie, Hull set a record for the province of British Columbia at that level when he poured in 105 goals in just 57 games during 1983–84. With that output came a scholarship to play under Mike Sertich at Minnesota Duluth (alongside future NHLers Bill Watson, Norm Maciver and Jim Johnson) plus some notice from NHL scouts. As Hull portrayed it in his 2003 autobiography, "I really wasn't all that excited about being drafted. When the NHL's Central Scouting Service sent me questionnaires, I would send them back unanswered. As a 20-year-old, it was my last year to be drafted. And someone had told me that I would be better off as a free agent. That was true enough. (Brian Burke) told me that had I gone undiscovered in Penticton, passed over completely in the draft, I probably would have been asking for a $1.4- to $1.8-million package. That's what Burkie got the Red Wings to pay Ray Staszak of Illinois-Chicago that summer when he was a free agent."

Eric Duhatschek recalls how a future Hall of Fame goal-scoring phenom escaped till so late in his draft year. "Well, commitment was considered an issue there. His weight was too. I remember talking to his junior coach, and he said his nickname was 'Pickles' because he had a bulbous kind of body. I mean, he was practically out of hockey for a period of time when he was 15 or 16. Scouts knew that he was a happy-go-lucky guy, but they just didn't know how the skating weakness or the scoring that he produced at that B.C. Tier II junior level would translate into the NHL." History proved those concerns minor. It also proved 1984 to be a goldmine draft for the Flames, and not only for the Suter and Hull picks. They struck gold so often that it set them up for the next decade and contributed to their 1989 Stanley Cup in a significant way.

Mario's sulky selection was the obvious headline in 1984. But Savard's drafting triumphs showed that a few successful swings for the fences are all it takes for a general manager to build his reputation. Sometimes, it can happen all in one year. In the end, Savard would survive for over 12 years as Montreal's GM before the axe finally fell in a messy early 1995–96 bloodletting—not a fitting finale for the last GM to guide Montreal to the ultimate prize. Serge largely lasted that long based on the fine performance that his scouting and management team put forth in 1984—a year in which his biggest coup of all, Petr Svoboda, helped change the hockey universe.

RE-DRAFT OF 1984 FIRST ROUND (TOP 10)

#	PLAYER	TEAM	ORIGINAL	ACTUAL
1	MARIO LEMIEUX	PENGUINS	#1 (PIT)	SAME
2	PATRICK ROY	DEVILS	#54 (MTL)	KIRK MULLER
3	BRETT HULL	BLACK HAWKS	#117 (CGY)	ED OLCZYK
4	LUC ROBITAILLE	MAPLE LEAFS	#171 (LAK)	AL IAFRATE
5	GARY SUTER	CANADIENS	#180 (CGY)	PETR SVOBODA
6	GARY ROBERTS	KINGS	#12 (CGY)	CRAIG REDMOND
7	KIRK MULLER	RED WINGS	#2 (NJD)	SHAWN BURR
8	STÉPHANE RICHER	CANADIENS	#29 (MTL)	SHAYNE CORSON
9	KIRK McLEAN	PENGUINS	#107 (NJD)	DOUG BODGER
10	JEFF BROWN	CANUCKS	#36 (QUE)	J.J. DAIGNEAULT

CHAPTER 4

RED DAWN RISING (1989)

1. Mats Sundin, Quebec
2. Dave Chyzowski, NY Islanders
3. Scott Thornton, Toronto
4. Stu Barnes, Winnipeg
5. Bill Guerin, NY Islanders
6. Adam Bennett, Chicago
7. Doug Zmolek, Minnesota
8. Jason Herter, Vancouver
9. Jason Marshall, St. Louis
10. Bobby Holik, Hartford

CONVERGING ON BLOOMINGTON, MINNESOTA, on an early summer's day in 1989, few hockey reporters and fans were focused on exactly what the perennially underachieving Detroit Red Wings would do with their draft picks, let alone considering if they would dive into the European talent pool. Members of "Leafs Nation," for instance, were focused on hot-button issues such as what their beleaguered favourite team could do to with their three first-round picks (spoiler alert: they didn't do much, selecting a somewhat lamentable trio from the OHL's Belleville Bulls in Scott Thornton, Rob Pearson and Steve Bancroft). Other fans and media were speculating on whether Mats Sundin would live up to the hype and become the first European to go in the top draft position to the Quebec Nordiques.

Buried beneath these headline stories, however, the Wings were indeed on the verge of a revolution in drafting and scouting. Their first two selections that year were standard enough, plucked from tried-and-true North American sources in junior. First, at 11th overall, they picked journeyman

Mike Sillinger from the WHL's Regina Pats. Following that choice would be rugged Sault Ste. Marie Greyhounds defender (and future NHL bench boss) Bob Boughner, who was snapped up in the second round at number 32. By the prevailing standards of that NHL draft, these two picks seemed in line with conventional wisdom. Both went on to have respectable careers, which is more than a lot of draftees could say, even those taken as high as the first round. But neither player was the kind you'd build a franchise around, which is what the Red Wings truly needed as of 1989.

In most draft years, North Americans start to tune out as the names become unfamiliar, especially as they don't sound like they played in major junior or college hockey. That typically is the case following the second round, when the highly scouted names have been taken off the board. Most draftees are already out of the building, celebrating their good fortune. But this was precisely the time when the Wings pounced to stock their cupboard with future greats. The unconventional path made 1989 a watershed year in NHL history.

As mentioned before, a desire to comb through Europe for talent was non-existent in the pre-1967 NHL expansion world, when the competition for roster spots was fierce and job security very scarce. It was deemed not to be cost effective for the powers-that-be to even try and pluck these talents out of Europe, what with so many hungry competitors battling away in the AHL or even lower levels of North American hockey. Notable European-born players in the NHL before the mid-'70s almost exclusively had moved to Canada in childhood (Russian-born Dave "Sweeney" Schriner, Ukrainian-born Johnny Gottselig, Finnish-born Pentti Lund, Swedish-born Bob Nystrom, Czechoslovakian-born Stan Mikita). While interest was brewing in Europe, hockey was still considered nearly exclusively a part of the Canadian idiom.

Even the trickle of U.S.-born players—a noticeable presence in the league before World War II—had dried up for the most part by the 1950s, as the league was comprised of well over 95 percent Canadian content at the height of the Original Six "golden age." Until Carl Brewer ventured to Finland to play professionally in 1967, few North American stars had ever found their way into the supposedly inferior domain of European club hockey either. Despite Brewer's endorsement of the skilled players that he found in Finland (and their lightweight KOHO hockey sticks), few paid any attention. But then, Brewer was always a few steps ahead of the crowd.

The doubling of the league in time for 1967–68 didn't initially lead to an explosion in talent importation. Instead of looking overseas for answers, many expansion franchises opted for personnel who would have been toiling in the AHL or an even lower-level league just a half decade earlier. Many of those expansion teams floundered and were forced to scrape the bottom of the talent barrel as a result. Today, one has to keep in mind how scouting in Europe was also a costly endeavour. Owners of newer franchises that could barely survive day-to-day operations without going deep into the red on razor-thin revenue margins.

But by the time the 1990s were done, Detroit had bucked the conventional wisdom that said championship teams could not be built on a base of European talent—specifically Russians, who were accused of being selfish, robotic and lacking the toughness for the more aggressive North American game. Yet it was with the impact of European 1989 draftees—in particular Nicklas Lidstrom, Sergei Fedorov and Vladimir Konstantinov (joined later by picks such as Vyacheslav Kozlov and trade acquisitions like Igor Larionov and Slava Fetisov)—that helped the Red Wings bust that myth.

To call 1989 a momentous year in world history is an understatement: the fall of the Iron Curtain, the end of apartheid in South Africa, the Tiananmen Square massacre, even the opening of the first McDonald's in Moscow. It also proved pivotal in hockey history. A key component of that change came from extraordinary talent finally arriving from the collapsing USSR—an influx that became a deluge after Soviet premier Mikhail Gorbachev began to open the institutions of Russian politics in a thawing of relations with the West. The seismic shift of glasnost set the stage for the top hockey superstars from behind the Iron Curtain to migrate West in the 1989 NHL draft. It was an upside-down draft of sorts, known today not for its first round (outside of maybe Mats Sundin and Bobby Holik) but for the river of talent that flowed in the middle rounds—a river exploited by the daring, inventive Red Wings. Contrasting that was the futility of old-line thinking that led Toronto to use all three first-rounders they possessed on players out of Belleville.

Held in the Minneapolis–St. Paul suburbs, at the Met Center—home of the North Stars until their departure for Dallas four years later—this particular draft, more than any other, helped usher in the sea change of an NHL Russian invasion. There were, of course, many nationalities to tap into with the political tension fading, and NHL scouts and management figures were now eagerly anticipating finding the inside track to beefing up their squads. But there was still doubt about the viability of selecting players from the USSR.

While Czechs were a regular feature by this time, questions persisted about how soon star Soviet players such as Pavel Bure, Igor Larionov and Sergei Makarov—could be available for big-league service in North America, if ever. Edmonton head scout Barry Fraser summed up the mixed feelings of many teams: "From what I've seen of him, Bure can play on any team in the NHL right now . . . he's quick, real quick, small and very exciting. He may be the top player in this year's draft, but because he is from the Soviet Union, we don't analyze him the same way as a kid from the West . . . I don't expect him to go really early because it is still too much of a gamble to hope he will defect."

While, as Fraser predicted, the 1989 draft didn't see Soviet stars selected early, it was a step up over the environment of just a few years earlier, when teams typically didn't risk picks on a Soviet star any earlier than rounds 6 through 12 (back when the draft wasn't limited to 7). Considering the empty promises that such late-round gambles wound up generating, one couldn't really blame the pro hockey community for hesitating to use picks on players locked down by Communist states. The reality was that Soviet players were unlikely ever to make the jump. The USSR was a harsher climate than elsewhere in the Communist bloc, however. In one bizarre episode during the USSR's early years as a hockey-playing nation, Joseph Stalin had his unpredictable, alcoholic son Vasily run the national hockey team, only to see them all die in an airplane crash in 1950 when he insisted that they fly to a tournament in terrible weather. Diplomats at the sporting level in Russia were a different breed, high-ranking party officials known to keep a very tight wrap on their star names. If a player did escape, there could be serious repercussions for his family left behind the Iron Curtain.

Considering how icy a relationship the Cold War had fostered, a significant thaw was needed to start the flows of talent. A decades-long political, cultural and military standoff known for its proxy battles instead of the traditional direct combat, the Cold War from 1945 to 1991 naturally extended to the sports realm as well. And it was hockey that would see the most gripping sports examples in this fierce battle of ideologies. Many significant names in sports were known to the public only when the high-profile Olympic athletic events such as track and field, rowing and swimming showcased "must-watch" showdowns of East versus West. What really got folks interested was team competitions. The Cold War's effect on sports was highlighted as much by diplomatic issues off the playing surface, such as the widespread boycott against the 1980 Olympics in Moscow due to the Soviet invasion of Afghanistan, or the Soviets doing likewise for the 1984 Games in Los Angeles. The Winter Games, however, remained the ideal ground for the most viable "Cold War" showdowns. That proved especially true with hockey: both Canada and the USA saw their greatest moments against the Soviets come at the rink.

While it may sound a tad hyperbolic today, hockey's version of the Cold War certainly bore all the same tense hallmarks of the real thing. By the 1960s, the seeds had been sown for decades of international puck conflict. Though ice skating was a common winter activity, the Soviet Union still took several decades after the introduction of hockey to turn its national program into arguably its most prized sports asset; still today, it rivals soccer for interest in Russia.

Like most aspects of living under the ruthless dictatorship of Stalin and his predecessors, growth in sports was hindered by the constant flood of arrests, banishments and purges of high-level executives. These chilling measures were intended to clear out any subversion and maintain Stalin's firm grip on power, but they stood in the way of any advancement of the national hockey program to the level of Canada's. Shortly after Stalin's 1953 death, things started to slowly improve for daily Soviet sport. By the mid-1950s, the national squad—comprised mainly of Russians but also of Ukrainians, Byelorussians, Latvians and Lithuanians—began to challenge for supremacy on the international stage, with some startling breakthroughs engineered by master coach Anatoly Tarasov.

First came a Gold Medal showing at 1954's IIHF (International Ice Hockey Federation) World Hockey Championships. Then came an even more important salvo fired at the hockey community at large, when the Soviets took home the gold at the 1956 Olympic Games in Cortina D'Ampezzo, Italy. Prior to that, Canada had typically waltzed through these major international tournaments, sending amateur senior clubs like the Trail Smoke Eaters, the Whitby Dunlops and the Winnipeg Monarchs to face the best any other nation had to offer.

Subsequent triumphs for the Soviets put to bed the idea that 1956 was a fluke. Between 1963 and 1990, the USSR would rack up 18 of a possible 23 gold medals at the World Championships (a tournament twinned with the Olympics every four years, but also held separately in Olympic years during 1972 and 1976). To show they could do it on the grandest stage of athletics, they also claimed six of a possible seven mens hockey golds at the Olympics in this time period. The Soviets' growing international excellence led to the Canadian Amateur Hockey Association (the predecessor of today's Hockey Canada) deciding it was best to field an All-Star amateur team in the hopes of securing victory. This began in 1964 via the formation of a national squad under the tutelage of Father David Bauer.

Any foolhardy notion that this would put this team of "Reds" in their place proved false, as multiple Olympic and IIHF World golds would follow the prodigious national team that wore the iconic "CCCP" on their jerseys. Meantime, the CAHA would continually challenge the idea that the USSR players deserved to retain amateur status, pointing to a roster comprised of Red Army soldiers who were players 11 months of the year and military members for just one in order to meet service requirements. Essentially, Canada claimed the Soviet players were amateur in name only, and in reality were fully trained, equipped and funded professionals—employees of sorts, who didn't need another job as long as they were members of the national squad. The best players that Canada could cobble together had to have jobs outside of hockey in order to earn a living. The IIHF—run by gruff Irishman Bunny Ahearne—countered that, unlike Canada's top hockey names, these Soviets were amateurs simply because they were not paid to compete.

Though the hated "Russkies" were unquestionably a worthy rival on the hockey stage by the 1960s, naysayers in Canada dismissed their success because of the loopholes that let them continually send their greatest while Canada was forced to send inferior amateur teams. For a time in the late '60s and early '70s, Canada actually withdrew from IIHF play in protest of the numerous breaks handed to Soviet bloc teams. Around this time, Canada's role as hockey's greatest nation was being called into question if not outright dismissed by a growing minority of voices. In the frustration, a new idea came to fruition. It was to be called a "Summit Series" and offered up an eight-game showdown in September 1972—a clash to supposedly "settle" the question of international hockey supremacy.

Going in, many in Canada's hockey media ignored the warnings that the Soviets, with their year-round conditioning, were not to be taken lightly against a Canadian team that had been taking it easy for a few months. Originally predicted as a showcase of Canadian superiority with the nation's true hockey might at its disposal (minus an injured Bobby Orr, and with Bobby Hull excluded as punishment for his recent desertion to the WHA), the series certainly didn't begin that way. Soviet wizardry in the first five contests (three Soviet wins, one loss and a tie) finally woke many up to the stunning reality at hand. These dazzling USSR players with their whirlwind skating and intricate passing could no longer be called a hidden secret. No longer would the Soviet national club be labelled a sleeping giant, a fraud or a bunch of cheaters either.

This superiority early in the Summit Series caused a veritable crisis of confidence in the birthplace of the sport. Media that had once extolled Canada's virtues compared to the supposedly "villainous and sneaky" Russians now were firm believers in their coach Anatoly Tarasov and his methods. In the end, Team Canada of 1972 redeemed its early struggles. Despite the stacked odds of having to win three of four games in Moscow, they pulled off a comeback capped by Paul Henderson's famous winner late in the eighth game. With its high level of entertainment and gripping drama that captured the hearts and minds of Canadians alike, the 1972 Summit Series ushered in a new era of respect for international hockey—not only for the USSR but also Czechoslovakia, Sweden and Finland. The Canada Cup was created in 1976 to capitalize on this. This wasn't just a two-nation event; other strong hockey countries were invited to get involved. The NHL would try to cash in on the craze as well, organizing the 1979 Challenge Cup and Rendez-vous '87 (both substitutions for the normal All-Star Game).

The NHL also welcomed travelling Communist-bloc teams to play exhibition matches against its clubs. It didn't always produce brilliance, except when the Central Red Army—a club that made up of the core of the Soviet national team itself—battled the Montreal Canadiens to a thrilling 3–3 tie on New Year's Eve 1975, a tilt still declared the greatest hockey game ever by several who saw it. Canada Cups garnered plenty of attention, but 1987 stoked interest back to a fever pitch. Without the same political importance as 1972 but arguably surpassing that in entertainment level, 1987 presented the strongest rosters yet for all nations involved—and a preview of professional hockey's future makeup.

It featured Canada and the USSR playing their last significant battles before Communism's fall in Eastern Europe. The eventual Canadian win proved as closely fought on the ice as any showdown in the long history of the Canada–USSR/Russia rivalry. Not long after the 1988 Olympic Games, the détente between the global powers became a peaceful co-existence when Mikhail Gorbachev's glasnost policy introduced previously taboo concepts to the Soviet public. Intended to allow more freedom of speech, freedom of the press and openness than the majority of citizens had ever seen in their entire lives, this about-face was meant to boost the Soviet Union's declining economic fortunes and bring it into the modern world once and for all. Ultimately, though, Gorbachev's efforts did not prevent the downfall of the Communist system.

Flames radio broadcaster Peter Loubardias remembers the mood surrounding the 1989 draft and the end of the USSR:

> It would have been so interesting to see what the NHL in particular would have been like had we been able to have those guys during their prime. Yet we still got to focus on rare and fascinating displays of hockey on the international stage instead. Not a bad alternative. My favourite thing in sports is country versus country. So, I have more vivid

memories of world championships than most people. I especially do for the Olympics going all the way back to 1980. All the under-18s, all the World Juniors too. I'm probably more surprised that the European invasion didn't happen sooner rather than later. But I think we as Canadians still struggle with the fact that other countries are good at this game too. We're not the only ones who are pretty good at it.

On the hockey side, glasnost was akin to opening Pandora's box. Suddenly, it didn't seem so far-fetched that brokering a series of talent transfers with the Soviets could be on the horizon for NHL teams. What aided in that outcome was the frustration of Soviet players with their bosses and their willingness to be vocal about it. Receiving the brunt of the antagonism was drill-sergeant Viktor Tikhonov, the Soviet team head coach who instilled a more defensive system while going even more hardcore with the training and conditioning regimen first instituted under his predecessor, Tarasov. Talking to Tal Pinchevsky in 2012, Lou Vairo—a long-time USA national team coach who was also good friends with Tarasov—recounted that "at that time, the average Soviet player, between training and games year-round, I believe (logged) 1,000 to 1,200 hours a year . . . (Tarasov said) the Canadians had a big head start on us and the only way we had to catch up to them is if we work three to four times harder. What's wrong with an eight-hour workday? Everyone in the Soviet Union works eight hours a day. Why shouldn't our hockey players?"

The firm control by the Soviet hockey governing body over its players was nearing its end by the time everyone gathered in Bloomington on June 17, 1989. Whatever chafing Soviet players had been feeling under Tarasov and later Tikhonov, North American clubs were still not entirely convinced that there was any hope of landing a great star from the USSR. That left the door open for Detroit to became that first organization determined to dig up gems not only among the Soviets, but throughout the proliferation of skill Europe now was developing.

It's easy for most hockey fans today, who witnessed their championship glories, to forget, but the Red Wings carried a tattered reputation during the late '80s. Still smarting from years of mismanagement and embarrassment that had them derisively called the Dead Things, Detroit was undergoing its long-haul road back to respectability. Once viewed as the jewel of the four American clubs during the Original Six era, the Wings by 1986 had become a team not only distant from title contention but barely ever challenging even for a playoff spot.

The majority of this chaos happened under the watch of owner Bruce Norris, who had inherited the team from his father, James Norris. After taking over full control by replacing his sister Marguerite as team president and CEO in 1955, the younger Norris struggled mightily to recreate the greatness his father had carved out in his days running the once-iconic franchise. By the early 1960s, the Wings were still coasting on farm system talent developed in the early to mid-'50s before general manager Jack Adams began forcing out popular veterans such as Ted Lindsay, Terry Sawchuk and Red Kelly while prematurely trading future legends like Johnny Bucyk and Glenn Hall in the name of short-term fixes. In 1963, former on-ice hero Sid Abel, Gordie Howe's centre on the Production Line, replaced Adams in the front office, and the team got a short-lived boost over the next few seasons. Howe would guide the Winged Wheel to four Cup Final appearances in a six-season span between 1960 and 1966, a bittersweet accomplishment though, as Detroit lost every one of them.

Following its defeat in the 1966 finals to the Habs, Detroit endured a ghastly stretch of 15 playoff misses in 17 seasons (for perspective, when the Florida Panthers of 2000–19 saw 16 playoff misses in 18 seasons, almost half the league's 30 teams missed the playoffs, instead of the five to seven clubs that did between 1974 and 1986). Supposed saviours could not live up to the high expectations saddled on them. Amongst their Original Six brethren, no one came near this level of ineptitude until the Leafs joined the Wings in ignominy in the early 1980s.

Eventually, the fatigue of perpetual losing and his health issues led Norris to sell the Red Wings to Little Caesars pizza magnate Mike Ilitch in 1982. A local product, Ilitch's Little Caesar's hockey programs had been long associated with minor hockey in the Detroit region leading up to this sale. The infusion of a genuinely enthusiastic owner was the badly needed turning point for a franchise that had trouble drawing fans despite its hockey-mad market. Starting with the ownership transaction, the Ilitches began to remove the accumulated rot as they tried to return the Wings to a first-class operation from top to bottom. But it took over a decade to reach the top.

A year after the purchase, the Wings struck it big with Steve Yzerman, taken fourth overall in the 1983 draft. But even a superstar talent like Yzerman needed a supporting cast, and unfortunately, "Stevie Y" played a solo act for years afterward. Nothing highlighted this more than 1988–89, when he posted the best single-season point total in NHL history for a player not named Gretzky or Lemieux (155), yet saw his club still finish right at .500 with 80 points in 80 games (good enough for first in the mediocre Norris Division, but the prelude to a first-round letdown against the 66-point Hawks).

Drafting remained as spotty as it had been in the Norris era, with first-round failures such as Brent Fedyk, (1986 top overall pick) Joe Murphy, Yves Racine and Kory Kocur. The costly signings of free-agent NCAA players Tim Friday, Ray Staszak and Adam Oates backfired when Friday and Staszak flamed out and future Hall of Famer Oates was traded just as he blossoming into one of the great passing centres in NHL history. While Jim Devellano, who became the GM after the Ilitches' purchase of the team, had been striking out on players at the draft (disappointing fans who had expected that almost overnight he would turn the Wings into the same kind of Islanders dynasty from which he had been pried away), he had been acquiring a splendid scouting staff along the way.

Containing names such as Neil Smith, Ken Holland, Christer Rockstrom and Doug MacLean, Detroit in the mid- to late 1980s boasted several innovative hockey minds on its staff. In response to its inability to raise the franchise to the next level via the conventional route, the Wings scouting team reinvented itself. They began to look for hidden gems throughout the hockey world rather than focusing on combing the depths of junior hockey in Canada with the odd visit to the U.S. college ranks. It was an approach that eventually paid off . . . with four Stanley Cups, no less.

This shift to a focus on international talent was overseen by Devellano, whose crack scouting staff at the time was headed by future Cup-winning Rangers GM Smith. Just 33 at this point, Smith's roots with Devellano stretched back to when he had been a prospect of the Islanders in the mid- to late 1970s. The Isles were the gold standard in NHL drafting when Devellano was employed as their head of scouting and director of player personnel (under Sam Pollock alum Bill Torrey). Smith became a part of that system first as a player then as a scout. His journey to key figure in American hockey history kicked off with a playing stint at Western Michigan University that led to his becoming the program's first ever NHL draftee in 1975, when the Isles took him in the 13th round (204th overall).

As a testament to the Islanders' superb drafting abilities in those days, Smith was followed by future star defenceman Stefan Persson in round 14, at number 214. Persson defied the odds by having a very solid run in the top four of the Isles' dynasty defence corps during a nine-year NHL career. Smith would never get that far. His playing career worked through the minors until he retired in 1980 at 25 years of age. He would remain in hockey, turning toward scouting and cutting his teeth with the Islanders' Central Hockey League affiliate, the Indianapolis Checkers, before moving on to Detroit with Devellano in 1982. Excelling first as the GM of Detroit's AHL affiliate in Adirondack (highlighted by 1986 and 1989 Calder Cup wins), Smith earned more titles and promotions, eventually becoming head of scouting and assistant GM to Devellano. His reputation was confirmed when the Rangers later hired him to replace Phil Esposito as their GM exactly a month after the draft, on July 17, 1989.

Perhaps Smith's greatest discovery was not even a player. In 1986, Smith had been sent on a mission to find a full-time European scout for Detroit. Visiting Sweden, he encountered Christer Rockstrom. Smith was already somewhat acquainted with this scouting whiz, because Christer had been the cab driver who would take him to and from games he was scouting. Realizing he was dealing with a hardcore but perceptive fan who knew the players inside and out, Smith persuaded the Wings to give the Swede some scouting employment on a part-time basis, and then promoted him to the full-time European scout role a couple years after. It was a partnership that paid huge dividends.

The results of the organization's new dedication to searching deeply into Europe was never more evident than with their third-rounder in the 1989 draft. That pick (number 53) may just be the best mid-round steal in NHL draft history. Rockstrom had put in tremendous diligence to find him, alerting his higher-ups to this thin, wiry kid playing for VIK Västerås HK of the Swedish Elitserien. A teenaged defenceman who had drawn into only 20 games in 1988–89 with just two assists to show for it, this player didn't get much ice time when he actually did find his way into the lineup. Nonetheless, he happened to catch Rockstrom's eye. That D-man was none other than Nicklas Lidstrom.

At the time, NHL draft rules stipulated that a 17- or 18-year-old from Europe was required to have played at least two seasons in a European First Division, with a minimum of 11 or more games on their senior team as well. Not doing so made them ineligible to be selected in all but the first three rounds. Fearing Lidstrom would be lost to them in the 1990 draft, when he'd likely be considered a first round-worthy prospect, Detroit pounced a year in advance. Rockstrom convinced the Wings brass to use their last possible chance to grab Lidstrom—a potential gem whom he believed would turn into a top pairing defender. Wary that someone could spill the beans to other teams, only four members of the organization—Devellano, Smith, Holland and Rockstrom—knew the secret until the day of his selection.

It worked like a charm. Lidstrom was still available come round three and was taken by the Wings—to the confusion of many in attendance. Even the NHL's Central Scouting Bureau had very little info on what was considered quite an off-the-board choice (or "project," as it's often dubbed today). Lidstrom proved to be a true diamond in the rough—a perfect example of the rare finds that have become increasingly harder to hide in this day and age. In today's NHL, there's so much more coverage, and every team sends its people to all the tournaments.

According to Eric Duhatschek, "Scouts are constantly going to Russia to scout the KHL and those junior teams, so the number of eyeballs on these players around the world is just so different. The net effect of that, to me, is that you just don't have nearly as many misses as you once did. I remember about 10, 12, 13 years ago, I was doing a draft preview. It might have been when I was talking with Kenny Holland. He had all his draft documents out on the table, and he said, 'For Christ's sake, look at this! We're even looking at a player from Denmark.' And this was the draft where Frans Nielsen was taken. Now, how many Danes are in the league? Like 8 or 10, right? But it wasn't that long ago when experienced general managers were shaking their heads, because that's how far spread the scouting world had become."

As the league scrambled to figure out the Lidstrom pick on the draft floor in Minnesota, the Wings were thinking even further to the east for other delightful discoveries. Once the spring of 1989 rolled around, Soviet authorities had finally begun actively marketing some of their established stars to interested buyers in North America. While the Flames had taken 25-year-old Sergei Pryakhin with their final 1988 pick, it was still believed that the Soviets would want to hang on to their elite younger talent for several years to come. This mindset warded off many teams from wanting to "waste" a pick on such an arduous scenario. The Wings were not so easily scared in 1989. Having already passed on grabbing Sergei Fedorov when they had the chance in 1988, they used their fourth-round pick, number 74 overall, to select him the following year.

Devellano certainly wasn't planning to miss out on Fedorov on this particular occasion. As he told NHL.com in 2015, "My thinking was, 'Let's call a spade a spade; how many fourth-round picks who are North American make it big?' Very few . . . So what I said to myself was, 'This is the best 19-year-old in the world, and I'm going to pass on him (again) to probably take a minor-league player?' Forget about that, he's coming on the Red Wings' list, and we'll worry about it in the future." A star centre with Moscow CSKA, Fedorov internationally and domestically was featured as the playmaking, defensively responsible force on a line with fellow teen-aged phenoms Alexander Mogilny and Pavel Bure—a ridiculously potent grouping that was the equivalent of a 2004 Russian squad icing a line with Evgeni Malkin between Alex Ovechkin and Ilya Kovalchuk.

This magnificent Soviet troika of Fedorov-Bure-Mogilny had also torn it up at several international tournaments, right up to the IIHF World Junior level in 1988. It was seen as Russia's next version of the famed KLM line (Vladimir Krutov, Igor Larionov, Sergei Makarov) from the prior decade, a dominant unit that had snagged them so many medals at various World Championship and Olympic Games in the 1980s. Mogilny himself had been secured by the Sabres with the 89th overall pick a year earlier, but scouts were salivating that perhaps Bure or Fedorov could be available the next year as well.

Fedorov had even been offered the chance to jump ship with Mogilny earlier. Before becoming the first Soviet player to successfully defect, Mogilny revealed his intentions to close friend Fedorov in a Stockholm hotel room they shared. Fedorov rejected the offer to join him, however, figuring it was a lark, prank or some sort of joke that was never supposed to be acted upon. But within 48 hours of the chat, Mogilny bolted the premises in an elaborate escape where he gained contact with the Sabres and the parties enacted a covert flight plan into the USA. While Fedorov stayed put for the meantime, the Wings were undeterred in taking him, even if it made the Soviet authorities keep even stricter surveillance on their prized pupils.

One round after they got "Feds," there was a chance that the Red Wings were going to secure another third of the USSR's top junior line by selecting Bure. However, there was a significant uncertainty that Bure could only be had in within the first three rounds in 1989 due to the service rules for international 18-year-olds. It wasn't a matter of making it strike three times to get Bure to come, it was simply a matter of whether he would even be eligible now that round four had passed. At his team's drafting table that day, Devellano reportedly promised Smith that they could go after at least one more Russian before the day was over. Fedorov was the prize pick of the lot to many, as many whispered he might just have been the best on that line because of his uncanny ability to handle the duties of a two-way centre while the explosive Mogilny and Bure were freed up to earn the glory of scoring most of the goals. Devellano would make his reasoning clear down the road by stating, "As was the case with Petr Klima, my strategy was simple. We would draft the best players, and if they happened to be behind the Iron Curtain, we would use our owner-ship resources to find a way to get them out." Such boldness confirms the theory that quality ownership is perhaps the most important element in forging a perennially successful sports club.

Indeed, the Ilitches—who also own the Detroit Tigers—were the polar opposite of what Wings ownership had been under Bruce Norris. Their willingness to use their big dollars, trust their personnel and treat their employees with a degree of loyalty and compassion certainly gave the franchise some incredible mileage in their eventual reign as the model

NHL organization from the mid-1990s to the early 2010s. The drafting wizardry of 1989 didn't necessarily begin and end with the Wings, though. And it could've been even richer. While Wings personnel in later years claimed they were ready to grab Fedorov's linemate Bure with their sixth-round pick and deal with any questions of his eligibility later, they never got the chance to add him. Another team's plans got in the way.

Detroit's management group had apparently mused about grabbing Bure in the fifth round after already having secured Fedorov. As Holland told the *Toronto Star*'s Bob McKenzie in 1995:

> We (were) at the draft table and Christer tells Neil, "Now we should take Bure" . . . Neil said he didn't think Bure had played enough games to be eligible. So Neil goes and checks with (NHL vice-president) Gil Stein, and Stein tells Neil that Bure has only played seven games and it has to be eleven (sanctioned games) to be an eligible pick. Neil comes back and tells us that, and Christer says "No, that's not right. He played eleven. I know he played eleven." Neil goes back to Stein and tells him our European scout said Bure should be eligible.
>
> Stein still said no. The NHL's records showed just five games played in 1987–88—figures Rockstrom believed were erroneous. So Neil comes back to the table and it's coming to our turn. We didn't think Bure was eligible, so we took someone else (Shawn McCosh) . . . Finally, Neil said we were going to take Bure with our next pick no matter what and let the league settle the eligibility thing later. We were just about to pick him when the Canucks announced his name.

It was Canucks GM Pat Quinn who swooped in on Bure during that sixth round (overruling his second-in-command, Brian Burke, who at the time thought Bure was too small for the big leagues of North America). Thankfully for the Canucks, their head scout, Mike Penny, agreed with Rockstrom's assertion that Bure had made the required number of appearances and convinced his boss to turn in the card with Bure's name on it.

With whispers that the Oilers were looking to nab him too, the Canucks stepped up to make "The Russian Rocket" their own at number 113, and did so only three spots ahead of where the Wings ultimately took Dallas Drake—perhaps Detroit's most successful North American pick that year, but a far cry from a future Hall of Famer like "The Russian Rocket" became.

Jack Button, once the head of the Central Scouting Bureau and by this point the Washington Capitals director of player personnel, later conceded that, if it had been conventional knowledge, "everybody would have taken him earlier. We assumed he was not eligible . . . You've got to give the Canucks credit for doing their homework." The legality of Bure's selection wasn't so clear-cut right away, though. Like the Wings, the Canucks came into this draft with the reputation of being a perennial doormat in desperate need of talent. Detroit at least had Steve Yzerman to brag about; the Canucks franchise as of 1989 had never been able to boast a genuine superstar. Richard Brodeur's clutch 1982 playoff goaltending was the nearest any Canuck had gotten to that level of superb play, and a few hot stretches from names such as Bobby Schmautz, Thomas Gradin, Stan Smyl, Tony Tanti and Petri Skriko had given way, and they had evened out into merely good players.

Prior to Bure being taken, history hadn't been very kind to Vancouver in its first two decades of existence. While 1988's number two overall pick, Trevor Linden, would become an instant fan favourite for his complete game and leadership abilities, he never came close to the level of an Yzerman. Unlike Detroit, Vancouver didn't have former Stanley Cup glory to hang its hat on. Over the franchise's first 21 seasons in the NHL, it had managed a winning record just twice (back-to-back from 1974 to 1976). Constant retools and rebuilds failed, drafts netted consistently lousy results, and few trades shook down as well as anticipated.

In spite of frequent losing records, the Canucks managed to register several post-season appearances between the 1974–75 and 1983–84 seasons, though they rarely owned home-ice advantage in any series. These came mostly as a result of the NHL's very generous divisional playoff formula that saw as few as five teams out of 21 eliminated each year.

Vancouver's one reprieve amidst the mediocrity was their surprise trip to 1982's Stanley Cup Final—an unexpected development that, at least temporarily, reignited a fan base that had become all too accustomed to disappointment. But even when they made that unlikely run, the Canucks had finished at three games below .500 in the regular season and had only caught fire in the spring after assistant coach Roger Neilson took over for head coach and GM Harry Neale, who was suspended for a stick-swinging incident with a fan in Quebec. Thanks to Neilson's magic touch, Neale decided not to go back behind the bench. The 'Nucks also took advantage of playing three playoff teams with even worse records in the mediocre Campbell Conference of 1981–82. It ended in a sweep at the hands of the vastly superior Islanders. But that proved to be the end of any progress the franchise had made over the previous few years, as the glory proved all too fleeting and the organization soon reverted to futility. After the excitement of '82, it would be nine seasons without winning so much as a single playoff series or finishing above .500, (Vancouver ended up missing the post-season outright in four of those nine seasons).

All of this alienated an already fickle B.C. West Coast market; fans in the province's eastern portion, understandably so, gravitated toward either the vastly superior Oilers or Flames. In Game 3 of their 1986 Smythe Division semifinal against Edmonton, this apathy was made clear when fewer than 8,000 fans were in attendance at the Pacific Coliseum to see their 59-point Canucks become lambs to the slaughter versus a 119-point Oilers juggernaut—a team most were positive was en route to its third straight Cup title. Desperate for that true number one centre that off-season, the Canucks decided to deal future Hall of Famer Cam Neely and their 1987 first rounder (an eventual number three overall pick used on star defenceman Glen Wesley) in exchange for a former local junior legend with the Victoria Cougars, Barry Pederson.

Once a highly productive centreman with the Bruins, Pederson had endured many serious issues with his shoulder and was no longer the same elite player of his first four seasons. Shipped out of Boston, where he had enjoyed the comfort of a better supporting cast (Rick Middleton, Ray Bourque, Peter McNab, Steve Kasper), Pederson never found his superstar touch again and proved to be yet another Canucks trading dud that was erroneously pegged as the long overdue game-breaking saviour.

Rubbing salt in the wound of the failed Pederson experiment, Neely would form into the perfect (albeit oft-injured) power forward. Notching three 50-goal seasons (and four others where he missed many games but maintained a 50-plus-goal pace), hundreds of penalty minutes and dozens of fights in 10 years on the B's, Neely would be the ideal Bruin while Pederson would not prove to be the answer for the Canucks. Looking to go in a fresh new direction, the Canucks turned to Pat Quinn, a coach who had once guided the Flyers to the 1980 Cup Final in a season that included an NHL record 35-game unbeaten streak. Quinn had also helped the Kings record their only winning season between 1981–82 and 1987–88 (82 points in 1984–85).

Taking a franchise short on both established talent and quality prospects, Quinn finished his first year as GM in 1987–88 with yet another Canucks non-playoff finish. But a year later, Vancouver recorded its best point total in six seasons (74) and came within an OT goal of a massive first-round upset over the eventual Cup winners from Calgary. It was still clear that they needed a much better youth movement if they wanted to ascend the NHL's ladder (as demonstrated by two more losing campaigns in 1989–90 and 1990–91—the former a last-place Smythe Division finish and the latter a first-round exit at the hands of the Kings).

The larcenous selection of Bure certainly went a long way toward changing this woeful status in Van City. Bringing a young phenom to a team that was badly overdue for one, the pick may be the most vital draft-day move in franchise history to date—more than taking Linden in 1988 and perhaps even taking the Sedin twins in 1999. After all, those players were highly touted and the Canucks got to select them with high picks. Bure, meanwhile, was a sixth-rounder who dwarfed every high Canucks pick that had come before, and most that have come since, in franchise history.

The three selections the Canucks made before Bure in 1989 were a gauntlet of ordinary prospects: Jason Herter at 8th overall, Rob Woodward in the second round at 29th overall and Brett Hauer in the fourth round at number 74 overall. Herter would stick around in the NCAA for three more seasons before finally signing with Vancouver but never advanced beyond the team's AHL level and played a single NHL game in December 1995, but not even as a Canuck. Forgettable prospects like Herter were a common result for first-rounders during Quinn's 1987–98 stint as GM—an era marked by on-ice successes built mainly off the backs of great trades. Because the Canucks consistently failed to hit home runs on draft day under Quinn, the calculated risk of the Bure pick was all the more crucial toward creating the first true period of sustained competence in franchise history (1991–96).

The Canucks boasted a front office with experience fighting legal battles too, which would help the campaign to establish Bure's eligibility. Quinn had earned a law degree following his career as Flyers head coach, while Burke, his director of hockey operations at the time, had also studied law. With the recommendations of Penny, and rumours running rampant that the Oilers were hoping to snag the Russian wunderkind before Vancouver did, Quinn used his team's 113th overall pick on a winger and a prayer. Penny claimed to have seen Bure play in Finland on Christmas Day 1988 in a remote part of the USSR and came away with glowing reviews. Quinn was suspicious, though, and warned Penny and Burke that he'd be mighty perturbed if the information about Bure's eligibility was wrong. Even with that, he still allowed the decision.

Quinn also hedged his bets that the pick would be deemed legal by league authorities. As mentioned earlier in this chapter, for a player aged 18 or younger to get selected after the third round in 1989, they had to have played at least 11 games in each of at least two seasons in a recognized/ sanctioned league. No problem came from 1988–89, where Bure took part in 32 games with the Central Red Army team. But the second season? Penny would deny the existence of a secret informant when interviewed by Kerry Banks for his 1999 book *Pavel Bure: The Riddle of the Russian Rocket*, claiming his scouting trips made him aware of four extra Central Red Army games and that he had actually witnessed two games in Finland between the Finnish national team and the USSR—both of which involved Bure. He believed that, although those were not Central Red Army games, they were IIHF-sanctioned and therefore should have counted toward Bure's official total.

Huddled at his team's draft table on the day of reckoning, Penny pushed for his prize prospect. He would explain to Banks his line of thinking: "What was the risk? If someone challenged the pick and it was denied, then we'd lose a sixth-round pick. But if we were right, we get a hell of a player." He also claims Quinn at first stared at him, then growled, "Jesus Christ, I hope you're right on this one." After NHL vice-president Brian O'Neill uttered the name Bure, it was commotion on the normally docile drafting floor. Specifically, the way Burke remembers it, "The other teams were tossing expletives at me and everyone else on the Canucks."

Most believed that, based on publicized comments pledging to remain playing in the Soviet Union for the foreseeable future, Bure would not be coming to the NHL anytime soon. However, no one at the time of those remarks foresaw that the USSR would cease to exist by the end of 1991. The play-by-play voice of the WHL's Regina Pats at the time, Peter Loubardias, attended that 1989 draft as part of the club's ownership group (an entourage that travelled to Bloomington from Regina in a rented mobile home):

> My memories of that year are just so vivid. I'd already watched Pavel on television. If I'm not mistaken, it was in the '89 World Juniors, in Anchorage. So I understood then that, oh my God, does this guy ever do things on his skates that I'm not sure I'd seen a lot of or that anyone had done when you really think about it. But because of the political situation, the world was just so different at the time. Until the climate really changed after 1991, you could only talk about things that you would have loved to have experienced in some way, shape or form.

Bure's immense abilities and Vancouver's new information emboldened the Canucks' fight for their bold choice, a fight that became even fiercer when John Ziegler declared on March 17, 1990, that it was an illegal pick. Given his curmudgeonly and outspoken nature even back then as a younger man still in his 30s, Burke sounded off, telling reporters he was "astounded by the decision. I'm outraged. There are some hard questions to be asked about the people we pay to tell us whether a player is eligible or not." Armed with substantial evidence that included corroborated testimonials and authenticated game box scores (some even handwritten in Russian Cyrillic script) collected with help from Russian sportswriter Igor Kuperman and Vancouver's 1989 off-season signing Igor Larionov, the Canucks were confident that they could substantially prove Bure had indeed played the necessary 11 games.

On the eve of that 1990 draft—coincidentally held at Vancouver's B.C. Place—Ziegler reversed his decision and declared that Bure was indeed the Canucks property after all. Though the Canucks had determined they would take Bure with either their number 2 pick or their number 18 pick that year (eventually used on Petr Nedved and Shawn Antoski, respectively), they won a huge measure of redemption with the ruling. The blowback from the league office's about-face was strong. Teams grew even angrier at the reversal when a 1992 Tony Gallagher newspaper story cited an anonymous owner and GM alleging that Ziegler had agreed to the reversal in exchange for Quinn dropping his long-standing lawsuit against the league for suspending him when he had agreed to take over the Canucks GM and president positions while still employed as the Kings' head coach.

In that dispute, Quinn used his law degree to his advantage by claiming that the Los Angeles organization had failed to meet the deadline for negotiating the option in his contract. Hired by L.A. in 1984, Quinn had supposedly been promised by Rogie Vachon that he would eventually receive the GM role. But when that hadn't occurred by 1986–87, he began to plot his exit. The imposing Irishman out of Hamilton, Ontario, did eventually depart the Kings after noticing that his contract contained an escape clause in which he would be free to seek employment elsewhere if his deal wasn't renewed by September 30, 1986. He also discovered that his pact hadn't even been registered with the league, so therefore tampering charges couldn't be applied either.

When the struggling Canucks entered the picture and offered the suddenly freelancing coach both the GM and bench boss roles, the wheels were set in motion. Quinn agreed in principle on December 11, signed a deal with Vancouver on December 24 and then received a $100,000 signing bonus from ownership on January 2, 1987. Quinn was set to take over in time to start 1987–88. However, Ziegler attempted to have team owner Arthur Griffiths cancel the deal, so that word wouldn't leak out to the public too far ahead of the official starting date. His efforts were rebuffed, leading to fines against the Canucks for not initially reporting the agreement and fines for every game Quinn had coached for the Kings up until January 30. The punishment called for a banishment of Quinn from the league for this undercover defection to one club while still acting as coach for another.

As a result, Quinn was replaced as Kings coach by Mike Murphy and forced to observe the rest of the season from the sidelines since the league didn't want the embarrassment of a pending GM/coach for one team still working behind the bench of another (let alone a division rival). A subsequent investigation exonerated Quinn, and he was reinstated in the Vancouver GM job by the summer of 1987, with the condition that he not coach anywhere in the NHL until 1990–91. Further legal battles reduced the fines the Canucks had been ordered to pay but still upheld the coaching suspension.

Due to more court dealings—this time with the Soviet Hockey Federation—it would be more than a month into 1991–92 before Bure could make his anticipated arrival on the Pacific Coast. Once there, he justified the fanfare by going on to win the Calder Trophy with a highly impressive 34 goals in 65 games. The Russian Rocket scored 50-plus goals three more times before an acrimonious departure to Florida in 1999. It's a scary thought (for non-Detroit fans, anyway) that the Red Wings' landmark 1989 draft came agonizingly close to claiming Bure as part of its haul. With the right winger on Fedorov's famed line now taken on draft day 1989, the Wings would wait until the 11th round to grab another diamond-in-the-rough Russian. They found it with a far more bruising player than either Fedorov or Bure ever was, "settling" for fearsome defender Vladimir Konstantinov.

The discovery of Konstantinov again came about because of Smith's innate trust in taxi-driver-turned-scout Rockstrom, who had seen plenty of action from perhaps the most defensively adept but physically punishing blueliner Russia had produced yet—one of the notable participants in the controversial bench-clearing brawl in the USSR–Canada matchup at the 1987 World Junior Championships, a.k.a. the "Punch-up at Piestany." Neil Smith recalled to NHL.com in 2015 that he "used to turn to Christer in the late rounds and said, 'OK, it's your pick, who do you want me to take? . . . Anybody that was left and from North America, there was no chance (he'd want them) . . . He says, 'Konstantinov, we should take him.' So, we did."

Konstantinov turned out to be a key contributor to the 1997 Stanley Cup victory, Detroit's first since 1955. Tragically, he was paralyzed just days later in a limo crash that also injured Fetisov, although not nearly as badly. It cut short a steady progression into the NHL's hierarchy of defencemen for "Vlad The Impaler" and possibly robbed the game of yet another Hall of Fame name drafted and developed by the Wings machine.

A year after receiving his first NHL GM job and achieving an impressive draft as his swan song in Detroit, Smith would make Rockstrom his director of scouting with the Rangers. By the time of his departure to New York, Rockstrom had left a significant mark on the Wings, but he furthered his legacy in the franchise's history by recommending Hakan Andersson to take up his position once he left. That particular hiring would result in the Wings scooping up even more elite European talent—far more than any other franchise over the following decade plus.

The hits would keep on coming in Motown beyond Smith's tenure. A year later, in 1990, the Wings would make Vyacheslav Kozlov their newest Russian investment with a number 45 pick in the third round. Owning the rights to these players was one thing, but the crafty defections orchestrated to get Fedorov, Konstantinov and Kozlov was another. Over a two-year period, the Red Wings would indeed find creative ways to get all three over to the U.S. The most long-lasting and impactful of the three, Fedorov, would escape thanks to the aid of a Soviet contact named Michel Ponomarev who tracked down Fedorov on the Wings' behalf.

The team's first meeting with Fedorov came when the Red Army team visited Chicago for an exhibition game on January 3, 1990. There, team president Jim Lites, armed with a briefcase containing $10,000, tried coercing his draftee to defect. But with his commitments to the military still intact, Fedorov demurred. Once that duty had been completed though, he would finally feel comfortable enough to escape from the Soviet team following a 1990 Goodwill Games match played in Portland, Oregon. The next day, Fedorov had landed in Detroit, having suddenly inked an NHL contract and defected from his native land. Even more brazen would be the defection of Konstantinov a year after that. Various bribes would earn the hulking defender a reprieve from his Russian hockey duties when a phony cancer diagnosis was drummed up as the cover for his absence and subsequent disappearance.

Not long after this third heist by the Red Wings, defections and cloak-and-dagger operations to bring Iron Curtain stars to North America would dry up. It's a totally different playing field nowadays, though that's not to say agents, GMs and scouts don't still need a degree of ingenuity to find what they want. The bigger the star, the tougher the extrication sometimes. As his agent, J.P. Barry, recalls, Evgeni Malkin's 2006 arrival to Pittsburgh may not have been a defection but had many of the hallmarks of one:

> Malkin technically didn't have to defect, but in reality, he did because there was . . . hmmm . . . what would you call it? Not just pressure, but he was actually being held outside of his will. They simply just refused to let him go. Every time we would terminate the contract and think he was freed up, they would come up with some excuse not to let him leave. It was a defection from pressure, really. From inordinate pressure. The Malkin escape was scarier than some defections of the past, because those were political adventures where sometimes they just kind of put a guy in the trunk, they got through, and nothing really happened. We actually had the Magnitogorsk team sending people to find us for a week when we were trying to get Geno his Visa. It was termed as the team's "people," but they were practically mafia figures, right? After it all, the team GM even told me there was a silver bullet waiting for me in Magnitogorsk. Apparently, he was joking, but who knows whether or not it was lost in translation. Either way, I wasn't about to go visit Magnitogorsk any time soon after that.

Strengthened by "risky" draft choices and their arrivals on American soil, the Wings would bounce back from a disappointing 1989–90 to make the franchise's first of a remarkable 25 consecutive playoff appearances in the 1990–91 campaign. Fedorov would put forth a Calder Trophy finalist season and for the next year, the Wings would add both Konstantinov and Lidstrom to the blueline as they would finish atop the Norris Division with 98 points (11 more than second-place Chicago, a team that later defeated them in a Norris Division Final sweep that foreshadowed Detroit's high-profile playoff "chokes" to come over the next five years). The 1991–92 season also turned out to be the first of 24 straight campaigns in which the Wings posted a winning record, but at that point it was only Detroit's fifth such season in a 25-year period (alongside 1968–69, 1969–70, 1972–73 and 1987–88).

The Red Wings' impressive draft haul from 1989 made a rapid impact in the early 1990s by immediately propelling the franchise to Cup contender status. It would only grow in stature from there, as their three franchise-altering selections would go on to far outshine the team's top two selections from 1989. Each one also topped Detroit's much heralded number three overall 1990 pick, Keith Primeau, too. While a hulking power forward who, partly due to concussion issues, saw his career prematurely ended in 2006, he never quite became the Mark Messier prototype he was supposed to be even before all that went down.

While the Wings would swing and miss on most first-rounders in the 1990s—exceptions being 1991's Martin Lapointe and 2000's Niklas Kronwall—it would hardly matter thanks to all their savvy late-round steals. Owing to the "pay it forward" legacies of Devellano, Smith and Rockstrom, Hakan Andersson became the organization's newest secret weapon, and he would make up for the Wings' ho-hum first round track record and wholly average fortunes with North American prospects by coming up with incredible finds out of Europe—luminaries that sustained the years of excellence in Motown. Peter Loubardias concurs that the Red Wings were so powerful in the '90s and 2000s due to being so far ahead of the curve in the late '80s:

> Where others were still learning or not in tune with how to improve, Detroit obviously was on the precipice of this European and Soviet revolution back then. The fascinating thing about the NHL draft to me, now more than ever, is that developing is equally as important as drafting. I think

the one thing that doesn't get talked about enough is that when players go into the right culture, it helps them grow exponentially. Even going back to my early days of watching the sport, it seemed like every time somebody went to Montreal from their AHL farm club in Halifax, it was like they had somehow just found a new star. Well, was that just because of their scouting or was that because of the kind of culture and expectation of winning? My philosophy is that it's the hardest thing to get, but when you find it, it can almost be a plug-and-play situation. In a lot of different sports and levels, whether you're talking about the New England Patriots or other really strong organizations, what is it about them? Do they scout things differently? Or is it that their players have a different culture and expectation they get brought into? I don't think you can forget about development and the kind of organizations that allow certain players to flourish where maybe they wouldn't have had they been picked by other teams and been in other not-so-conducive situations. Under the Ilitch family, the Wings were certainly becoming that organization, and the draft they had in '89 definitely clinched that status in my estimation.

It was certainly the raid on the European talent pool that made the 1989 draft momentous. Had Detroit gotten Bure and had Konstantinov continued his ascent as a player, Detroit might've gotten four Hall of Fame players in one draft—something never achieved before or since. But it was another Euro prospect who made top billing in the 1989 draft.

Even with all the progression made by overseas prospects in impacting the NHL, it wasn't until 1989 that a European player ended up as the NHL draft's top-ranked prospect. The Quebec Nordiques would be the ones to make that important number one pick: a rangy Swede named Mats Sundin. A giant yet graceful and skilled centreman with a wicked backhander, Sundin was a less otherworldly Mario Lemieux type at six-foot-five instead of the type that people had come to expecting from Swedish players—finesse forwards like Anders Hedberg, Ulf Nilsson, Kent Nilsson, Jorgen

Pettersson and Mats Naslund. Sundin was the one prospect many pinned their hopes on in dismantling the stereotype of the "Chicken Swede."

When Sundin took the stage upon his drafting that June day and donned a trucker-style hat adorned with the Nords logo, few were surprised he'd earned that position. With an imposing body to go along with his elite abilities, it made sense that the scouting brain trust would "roll the dice" on him. That the Nordiques owned the pick and got to take Sundin seemed fitting, as they had once given the Stastny brothers—not to mention several other Europeans, such as Bo Berglund, Tommy Albelin and Sergei Mylnikov—chances at NHL respectability. Sundin was the first of many tremendous European picks the Nordiques made who would flourish and provide the basis for future championships success—albeit in Denver, Colorado, and not in Quebec. Players from Europe seemed to enjoy their stints with Quebec too, often making efforts to learn both English and French.

Whereas Europeans, specifically undersized ones, were often praised for their abilities to survive a rough-and-tumble 1980s NHL, Sundin had both the blessing and the curse of having so much higher an expectation level. Owning a finesse player's skillset with a stay-at-home defenceman's body meant Sundin was actually more vulnerable to the "chicken Swede" accusations than smaller players would be. A player like Sundin is "supposed" to use his physicality to get his way on the ice and is not supposed to show hesitance to indulge in the game's physical side, right?

Though today lionized by many as the best Toronto Maple Leaf since 1967, Sundin would frequently be called out during his career for being supposedly an uncaring, lackadaisical big man. Suiting up for the Nordiques, he took a lashing from some hockey insiders for not mixing it up—evidenced by Nords head coach Pierre Pagé singling out Sundin with an infuriated tirade during Game 6 of their 1993 Adams Division Semifinal series with the Canadiens (a very public display, with TV cameras focused on it for more than just the usual brief glimpse).

Scorn from Pagé aside, Sundin showed an admirable perseverance given the constant mudslinging toward him, exhibiting trademark Swedish stoicism amidst the nitpickers. When he went to Toronto, he drew the ire of impatient media types there—principally self-professed Leaf fan and

Canadian hockey celebrity Don Cherry. Sundin indeed received his share of flak when, as the Leafs' leading superstar and its first-ever European captain, he was unable to bring his club to a Stanley Cup Final. In reality, Sundin's consistent 70- to 80-point output from seasons 5 through 10 of his 13-season tenure in Toronto lifted a flawed contender to greater heights than it perhaps deserved. He excelled to the point that he became a first-ballot Hall of Famer.

Looking back, it seems perverse that teams were hesitant to venture into European talent even by 1989. A lawyer turned player agent in the 1990s before his stint as the GM and president of the Canucks from 2008 to 2014, Mike Gillis has seen it all when it comes to overseas players, as he's represented, drafted, traded for and signed his share in his three and a half decades since retiring from the game as a player. He played for Cherry in Colorado, represented Pavel Bure and employed Sundin and the Sedins in Vancouver during his stint there. Gillis chalks up this bias to being "most likely caused by an unwillingness to change from old-time hockey guys, combined with a bit of racism or xenophobia thrown in to the mix too."

Peter Loubardias concurs with the perception that hockey culture has been allergic to rapid change, though he also insists it's not unique to hockey:

> We here in North America just weren't quite ready to look at it the same way. The way I would put it is that people here saw it as separate realms that international events were kind of for amateurs and the NHL was for professionals. Even when you could see some great things from these so-called international guys, I think it was still hard to wrap your head around it. Financially, it took a different way (of) employing scouts and spending money. In our world, there's also a lot of old boys' clubs. All these institutions are no different. Change is hard for most people to take, and sometimes you have to be willing to change in order to get to a greater level of achievement in your given field. You have to be able to see it and think it differently. A lot of people make some pretty

great strides in life because they have the courage and the conviction to think and do it differently.

Ultimately, it says a lot about the depth and top-end talent of the 1989 draft that, as the years went by, Sundin's trail-breaking story became an afterthought given the tremendous late-draft finds of Detroit and Vancouver that set about revolutionizing the global scope of the pro hockey world and overturning what scouting had been prior to that watershed year.

RE-DRAFT OF 1989 FIRST ROUND (TOP 10)

#	PLAYER	TEAM	ORIGINAL	ACTUAL
1	NICKLAS LIDSTROM	NORDIQUES	#53 (DET)	MATS SUNDIN
2	SERGEI FEDOROV	ISLANDERS	#74 (DET)	DAVE CHYZOWSKI
3	PAVEL BURE	LEAFS	#113 (VAN)	SCOTT THORNTON
4	MATS SUNDIN	JETS	#1 (QUE)	STU BARNES
5	VLADIMIR KONSTANTINOV	DEVILS	#117 (DET)	BILL GUERIN
6	OLAF KOLZIG	BLACKHAWKS	#19 (WSH)	ADAM BENNETT
7	BOBBY HOLIK	NORTH STARS	#10 (HFD)	DOUG ZMOLEK
8	ROBERT REICHEL	CANUCKS	#70 (CGY	JASON HERTER
9	BILL GUERIN	BLUES	#5 (NJD)	JASON MARSHALL
10	ADAM FOOTE	WHALERS	#22 (QUE)	BOBBY HOLIK

CHAPTER 5

THE GREAT REFUSAL (1991)

1. Eric Lindros, Quebec
2. Pat Falloon, San Jose
3. Scott Niedermayer, New Jersey
4. Scott Lachance, NY Islanders
5. Aaron Ward, Winnipeg
6. Peter Forsberg, Philadelphia
7. Alek Stojanov, Vancouver
8. Richard Matvichuk, Minnesota
9. Patrick Poulin, Hartford
10. Martin Lapointe, Detroit

IF ANYONE IN 1991 THOUGHT THAT Mario Lemieux's path to draft day in 1984 was marked by insubordinate attitude, they were about to experience a whole new level of independent thinking. Eric Lindros would be dubbed "The Next One"—a play on Gretzky's "The Great One" moniker. The difference was that, while he may have seemed mild-mannered and soft-spoken at first, he was not the "yes sir, no sir" youngster that hockey bigwigs were used to. He would be arguably the first junior superstar to call the shots himself and tell the game's decision-makers that his career would be dictated on his own terms instead of on theirs. Controversies of the past suddenly seemed tame by comparison. Lindros made a resounding impact, declaring that he would not play for the club that drafted his rights in 1991 and throwing a total wrench into the process of the NHL trotting out its latest saviour. Like Mario the Magnificent, this young man would be very much his own person. Even the prime minister, Brian Mulroney, would weigh in on the kid.

While every team holding the first overall pick in the NHL hopes they'll draft a generational talent, it doesn't always work out. Sometimes, a future cornerstone is more like a millstone—witness names such as Doug Wickenheiser, Patrik Stefan, Brian Lawton and Alexandre Daigle. Even when a player receives lofty attributes from the scouting world, it doesn't guarantee glory in the pro ranks or even success. Billy Harris, Greg Joly, Mel Bridgman, Rick Green, Gord Kluzak, Chris Phillips, Rick DiPietro, Erik Johnson, Ryan Nugent-Hopkins and Nail Yakupov are testaments to that. Wishing didn't make them legends.

But occasionally, that unique individual lives up to the hype. In the mid-1960s, before the universal draft era, Bobby Orr came into the NHL amidst great hoopla at just 18 years old. Generating anticipation not seen for a teenage talent since Bobby Hull almost a decade earlier in 1957, Orr would mark the first in a long line of media-driven hype trains—increasingly celebrated due to growth in social media over the years.

Following Orr's exalted arrival—more than justified thanks to a brief but phenomenal playing career—Guy Lafleur, Wayne Gretzky and Mario Lemieux saw similar hype from hockey scouts and scribes. Each of those first-ballot Hall of Fame members came with widespread press throughout the sporting world. Seven years after Lemieux's ascendance to superstardom, the time was ripe for a new generational figure on the scene. What made this newest gem so special? Well, there were zero concerns about the physical makeup of the man-child Lindros *on* the ice, that's for certain. Here was a punishing presence when playing his sport of choice, not as dirty or nasty as Mark Messier but so big that he usually didn't have to go the extra mile to intimidate opponents. Lindros was just as bullish, fierce and terrorizing a physical force as "the Moose" was in his prime. Like legends such as Gordie Howe before him, Lindros let his play do the talking on the ice. Going into the 1991 NHL Entry Draft, the assumption was that any team would be blessed indeed to select this force of nature, one who could fuse the skilled grittiness of a Messier with the offensive wizardry of a Wayne Gretzky . . . but in a body more suitable for an NFL linebacker.

The hockey world might have been anticipating a flawless player prototype, but instead it was confronted with an unprecedented hardline stance and more negative attention than any prime prospect had ever received. As with Lemieux in 1984, the worrying signs that Lindros and his omnipresent family could be a handful were everywhere from an early age. This trend harkened back to various hockey leagues at the grassroots stage and a starring role with the St. Michael's Buzzers at the Junior B level when he was just 15 years old. Following his Junior B wizardry, Lindros was the consensus first overall choice in the Ontario Hockey League bantam draft of 1989. The team that had the honour of taking his rights? The Sault Ste. Marie Greyhounds. Much like Wayne Gretzky had done back in 1978, Lindros refused to play in the northern outpost of the OHL, several hundred kilometres from his Southern Ontario home. While the Great One was eventually coerced into changing his mind, the Next One and his parents wouldn't budge.

The issues that the Gretzky camp had brought up in 1978—articulated by Wayne's dad, Walter, acting on his 16-year-old son's behalf—were not unlike those that Lindros's omnipresent parents, Carl and Bonnie, would raise only 11 years later. The difference was that the young Lindros had an even more sheltering support system. Right or wrong, it was a family unit far more vigilant than most other hockey parents were in that day and age. They stood up for each other and didn't suffer fools gladly, often getting accused of going way too far to prove their cohesiveness and protective nature. Eric was often bolstered by the hard-nosed support of his folks, especially his mother, who took a highly vocal interest in her son's life and career, thinking nothing of dressing down reporters that she thought had done her family wrong.

Clearly, Lindros in 1989 was no ordinary teen who could be convinced to "do the right thing" for the sake of the sport. Many speculated this stemmed not only from the pressures he faced as an athlete under the microscope but also from the control exerted over his career by those parental influences. When the Greyhounds made their interest in selecting Eric well known, Bonnie Lindros would inform team founder and long-time GM Angelo Bumbacco that, for a variety of reasons, Sault Ste. Marie was just not the right fit for her boy.

Talking to ESPN's Adrian Wojnarowski (years before his status as the most trusted basketball inside around, dropping "Woj bombs" on Twitter with his NBA breaking news trade / signing reports) in the wake of

Lindros's contentious trade from the Flyers to the Rangers in the summer of 2001, Bumbacco remembered visiting the Lindros household in Toronto and finding only frustration when he attempted to talk the sheltered teenager into the idea of playing in the Soo. He claimed that, exasperated at how the conversation was taken over by the parents, he asked, "Can the boy talk for himself?"

"Looking back, the greatest thing that could ever have happened to Eric Lindros was coming to play in Sault Ste. Marie, just to get the hell away from those parents . . . I'll tell you: that kid has never grown up," an agitated Bumbacco lamented. "(Bonnie) tells me she's going to decide where her son plays. I told her, 'I learned a long time ago, you go where you're wanted.' So, she gives me a tongue-lashing, the brother (Brett) gives me a tongue-lashing, Eric gives me a tongue-lashing, and I left the house." Even with this obviously contentious visit, Bumbacco's Greyhounds decided to select the apparently reluctant prodigy anyway. Even after this testy clash of wills, management rightly figured that they could use him as a bargaining chip should he remain steadfast in his position that he would never join them. It foreshadowed the many battles the Lindroses were to engage in with journalists, hockey personnel and coaches alike.

While rebuffing the Greyhounds, they continually claimed their stance was not at all a grudge against the actual organization nor the city of Sault Ste. Marie itself. "We had nothing against the Soo. We were interested mainly in Eric's education. We also didn't want him on a bus traveling all the time. We told everyone that Eric would play no more than two hours from home," Bonnie later insisted to Jeff Savage in his 1998 book *Eric Lindros: High-Flying Center.*

The Lindroses still preferred the OHL when it came to Eric's career development, but not at the expense of his other interests. For example, the family had wanted to keep open the possibility of him one day being recruited by the University of Michigan Wolverines. Hurting that aspiration was the fact that playing in a single OHL game would lock in his rights to that circuit and make it unlikely he could play NCAA hockey unless litigation was pursued. If the Lindros camp was at all worried about his being handcuffed, it didn't show when they looked across the border for his development to start off 1989–90.

Competing for the Detroit Compuware Ambassadors of the NAHL, Lindros was able to focus on a high school education while simultaneously torching the opposition (albeit at a lower level of competition than the O would provide) to the tune of 23 goals and 52 points in only 14 games. Aside from his Detroit obligation, the "Big E" moonlighted with the Canadian national team for a few games and made his first of three consecutive appearances for Canada at the World Junior Championships during the holiday season.

Shortly before his first showing at the WJC, Lindros concluded his stalemate with the Soo. Newly minted Greyhounds GM Sherwood "Sherry" Bassin cooked up a deal that sent the disgruntled teenaged wunderkind's rights to the Oshawa Generals—a team Bassin had actually recently resigned from in order to take the Sault Ste. Marie job. Crucial to the trade was that Oshawa was one of the closest possible spots to Toronto for the hot prospect to land. In exchange for a large package of players, picks and cash (if anyone's asking: Mike DeCoff, Jason Denomme, Mike Lenarduzzi, Oshawa's second-round choices in the 1990 and 1991 priority drafts plus $80,000), Lindros became Generals property and finally got to report for service in the OHL.

Despite the tardy beginning to his major junior career, Lindros wouldn't miss a step. Playing the final 25 games of the regular season, he recorded impressive numbers (36 points off 17 goals and 19 assists) before slaughtering his foes in the playoffs with 18 goals and 18 assists in only 17 games. As their leading scorer, Lindros greatly aided the Gennies in their J. Ross Robertson Cup championship drive. It earned them an appearance in that year's Memorial Cup where, on the back of more dominant play from Lindros, the Generals ended up taking it all in dramatic fashion over Kitchener with a 4–3 double-OT win. Needless to say, this moved Lindros's projected first-overall status as close to a sure thing as any player since Mario Lemieux. (From 1985 to 1990, the top overall pick hadn't been so clear-cut, with no eventual top selections emerging as runaway favourites from the start of their draft years often not even until the day of reckoning itself.) The blowback on the big trade finally came in the next season's OHL Championship, when his Generals went up against the Ted Nolan–coached Greyhounds. In the series, Lindros experienced vociferous jeering from the Sault Ste. Marie crowds.

Not since Marcel Dionne's controversial junior playoff series in Quebec had there been such focused hostility directed toward a junior star. Every time Lindros touched the puck during the road games of the matchup, he heard it from local supporters who still felt disrespected by this entitled big city "mama's boy." Whether Lindros's slight from two years prior truly galvanized the Greyhounds players or not, they were able to upset the powerful Generals in six games and advance to the Memorial Cup. Nonetheless, Lindros in the spring of 1991 was even more dominant than in his playoff push of a year before, as he recorded 38 points (18 goals, 20 assists) in only 16 games and was named the recipient of the Red Tilson Trophy for MVP as well as CHL player of the year overall.

Lindros's conquest of the OHL was complemented by his international play. Midway through an epochal 1990–91 season came another stint with Team Canada at the World Juniors, which turned out to be a second consecutive gold-medal performance. Where he had four goals in seven games as a 16-year-old in 1990, Lindros took over the top role with this Canadian edition. Easily handling any opposition thrown his way, Lindros earned a gaudy 17 points (6 goals, 11 assists) in seven games and unanimous top forward honours for the tournament. Even with this lengthy time off in the middle of the 70-game junior schedule, the dominant power centre still managed to post OHL highs in goals (71) and points (149) that season. Adding to his burgeoning image of indestructability, Lindros would avoid any notable injuries in 1990–91 and appeared capable of handling the attention that came with being both a scorer of the highest magnitude and a luminous physical presence.

That said, the seeds for future health troubles were sown in the wear and tear of becoming a primary target for every other team. Perhaps fearing being labelled soft if he didn't stand his ground, Lindros often dished out punishment to intimidate anyone thinking of messing with him. In order to demonstrate that he wouldn't back down, "The Big E" accrued an inflated 189 penalty minutes in 1990–91 and frequently showed he was not one to shy away from rougher stuff. Where some junior heroes of yore had been immensely skilled but easy to hound physically, Lindros was so devastating in his bodychecks and brute strength that only the truly huge and freakish sized opposing players stood any chance at neutralizing him.

Standing six-foot-four and weighing 240 pounds during the peak of his playing career, Lindros's physical superiority perhaps also led to poor habits such as skating with his head down or crossing the ice laterally through a danger zone. Despite all his gifts of power and skill, Lindros was not in the Lemieux or Gretzky category when it came to spatial awareness on the ice. (No one's perfect, after all; witness the magnificent Lemieux's shoddy health and backchecking, Gretzky's unspectacular speed and low level of physicality.) In his days as a prized mega-prospect, Lindros was at a much lower risk of being run over by any checker. The junior level might not have legitimately posed threats to Lindros's hulking physique, but the big leagues would be a different story as it offered up defencemen like Chris Pronger, Derian Hatcher and Scott Stevens—all of whom who were able to stagger him with positional awareness and precisely timed, thundering checks—a scenario best perfected by Stevens when he knocked out Lindros with a skull-rattling open ice hit in Game 7 of the 2000 Eastern Conference Final (the sad, early denouement of what was supposed to be a career in the stratosphere of the all-time greats).

The final junior season for the Big E, in 1990–91, was a tour de force that had scouts salivating, a season the likes of which had never been achieved by a player of his size, and still hasn't. The only parallel stretched back decades to when Gordie Howe was emerging in the mid-1940s as a Red Wings property playing for their sponsored "Junior A" team in Galt, Ontario. But most of that attention came from fan hype, small town hockey scribes' reports and general word of mouth. Throughout his career, Lindros showed he wasn't opposed to making hard choices. Many of these brought him a media firestorm of scorn too, something that Gordie never experienced.

Meanwhile, in 1991, an NHL team zeroing in on another finish in the league's basement would become the latest squad to experience Team Lindros and getting caught in the crosshairs of his destiny. Every team entering the draft would have been more than willing to overlook the supposed warning signs of the "outspoken" nature Eric had demonstrated. After all, Mario Lemieux had been labelled a malcontent by some critics in 1984, but he proceeded to rescue the Penguins franchise and then romp over the competition. Just a month before the 1991 draft day, Mario raised the

Stanley Cup and Conn Smythe Trophy for the first time in Pittsburgh—a double feat he would repeat a year later.

Such rewards were predicted for the team that added Lindros. Prognostications of a dynasty were even more prevalent when people realized Lindros could be added to the already promising and youthful Quebec Nordiques. This being the pre-draft-lottery days, only the worst teams in the NHL heading into 1990–91 realistically had Lindros on their mind. Quebec was one of those lower-rung clubs . . . and then some. While some middling squads would need to weigh the benefits of striving for playoff revenues—not tough to achieve when 16 teams out of only 21 got in—against the lucrative benefits of a purposefully terrible season, others had no qualms about losing just for a chance at a franchise saviour.

Though the expansion San Jose Sharks were set to join the fray in 1991–92, the NHL still decreed that the last-place 1990–91 team would receive the vaunted "Lindros pick" at numero uno. Offering a generational player to a franchise right off the bat was a hot potato nobody in the NHL's front office wanted to have to handle.

As of 1991, small-market Quebec was an on-ice calamity and a franchise hurting financially. Struggling to stop from hemorrhaging cash amidst rising salaries, high provincial taxes and a slumping Canadian dollar, Les Nordiques were desperately in need of a new arena to help stem the tide. Anything less would likely kill them off in the provincial capital and force them to move the team out of town (a scenario that proved inevitable, sadly enough). By the time the 1991 draft hit, the Nordiques organization was in dire straits in many ways, having not made the playoffs since 1987 and having finished in the league's cellar for three straight seasons (tied for the fewest points with the Islanders in 1988–89, but owning the tiebreaker for the first overall pick by virtue of fewer wins). The middle of those three ugly campaigns saw them win a pathetic 12 of 80 games before being victorious just 16 times a season later. The humiliating 1989–90 campaign represented the true implosion of the Nordiques—once, shortly after their transition from the WHA, a successful and inspiring underdog story, not to mention the first legitimate threat to the Canadiens' provincial monopoly since the Montreal Maroons folded in the 1930s.

Not only did 1989–90 see on-ice incompetence, but it also saw serious financial issues lead to the trading of the franchise's two genuine superstars during its NHL existence: Michel Goulet to Chicago and Peter Stastny to New Jersey. Hampering things down the road was the pedestrian haul of players that those two trades earned Quebec. Of that group—Mario Doyon, Everett Sanipass, Dan Vincelette, Craig Wolanin, Randy Velischek—defenceman Wolanin was the only quality NHLer, as it turned out. He would last with the franchise until their 1996 Cup win in Denver but along the way was never a huge impact contributor and was reduced to spare part by the time his team hoisted the holy grail of hockey. So much for turning strong assets into future success there. The deconstruction and "tank job" in Quebec truly appeared 100 percent underway after these twin-teardown moves.

If Nords fans thought the rebuild was already painful to watch after these trades, the next few years upped the ante of misery. That said, it was the necessary tonic to improve the franchise's sagging fortunes and revive a team that just a few years before had been considered the hip new favourite among young hockey fans across the province. The rebuild would putter along with a hodgepodge of draft misses, washed-up veterans, borderline NHLers, lifetime AHLers and ineffective free-agent signings. 1989–90 would represent the nadir of this regrettable era, standing as perhaps the worst season by a non-expansion franchise in NHL history. No Nordique during this fallow period would better exemplify being surrounded by scraps yet rising above the deficit than Joe Sakic. The promising centre, a second 1987 first rounder following the Nords' selection of Bryan Fogarty at seventh overall, would persevere through the dreck to record consecutive 100-plus-point seasons at ages 20 and 21, even though his club went a cumulative 28–111–21 during those two seasons.

This anemic stretch included a record of 11–62–7 away from home and a historic 38-game road winless streak (0–28–11) that began on March 14, 1991. Even when Quebec was able to grit out a tie away from home during this ugly run, it usually needed some sort of miraculous individual effort, like when Ron Tugnutt stopped 70 shots in a 3–3 draw with the Bruins at the Boston Garden mere days after the streak began—a skid that didn't stop until March 5, 1992, thanks to an individual bonanza of Mats Sundin potting five goals in a 10–4 win at Hartford.

With all this ineptitude, most did notice some raw talent on display and became confident that things could turn around. Those first two poor years supplied the franchise with the top draft selections in Sundin and Owen Nolan, who both made the jump right away (not a shock considering the minor-league talent comprising most of the Nordiques lineup at the time). Premiering in 1990–91, Sundin managed to top 20 goals and 50 points despite a shuffling cast of weak linemates, while power-forward winger Nolan struggled mightily, lighting the lamp just three times in 59 contests. Sundin and Nolan would break out soon enough, though, with Mats becoming a 114-point scorer just two years later while Nolan upped his measly rookie goal output by 39 in a fantastic 42-goal sophomore year in 1991–92.

If Lindros could be the next prized addition to this expanding stable of impressive youth, it was firmly believed that the Nordiques would be Cup contenders for years to come. And Lindros might even help them get that elusive new rink built. History would prove these forecasts only partially correct. The glory would come, but not with Lindros as the main attraction and not with Quebec City as the home base. Lindros would indeed help build a new hockey palace—but it would be in Philadelphia, and to the benefit of the Flyers. Other than that, things worked out perfectly for the franchise . . . once it transferred operations to Colorado.

Heading into his draft year, Lindros had made no bones about his lack of desire to play for the Nordiques—for many of the reasons explored in the last few pages. It was shaping up to be a stance of "hell, no, I won't go," and people wondered if tensions would ease or just accelerate. This time, Lindros's refusal didn't just annoy a small Northern Ontario city but actually upset people across Canada. Most vitriolic were French Canadians, who reacted far worse than they had when Marcel Dionne abandoned them for junior hockey in Ontario. The ruckus started on June 22, 1991, at Buffalo's Memorial Auditorium, a.k.a. "The Aud." This particular NHL draft was billed as must-watch TV thanks to the controversy over whether Lindros would commit to being a Nordique.

The Lindros side of the equation asked, why he should join the Nordiques simply because NHL protocol (and the league's collective agreement with the players) said so. Sure, it was great for the Nordiques. And sure, the NHL liked helping a failing franchise. But why exactly was it a good move for the kid, let alone the best move he could make? When the day of reckoning came, the Nordiques adopted the same strategy that the Greyhounds had taken two years earlier by making him their first over-all choice: "Grab the asset first, deal with the consequences after." Time proved it to be the right mindset, given the massive bargaining chip Quebec had just gained. But it was to be a long and tumultuous time before the pieces finally fell into place. This would not be a repeat of Mario signing within the week, that's for sure.

On that fateful evening in 1991, Quebec's GM, Pierre Pagé, and direc-tor of player personnel, Pierre Gauthier, came to the stage and announced the expected Lindros pick for all to see. Ordinarily, that should have prompted the newest addition to pose onstage and do a scheduled TV interview afterward. But, like Lemieux, Eric declined to put on the jersey handed him by a team official. Looking back, Eric would admit to Mark Stewart, author of *Eric Lindros: Power Player*, that "I took a lot of flak for not putting the Nordiques sweater on. But I think wearing the sweater would have been a false statement. I didn't want to misguide people as to my true feelings." Despite his hardline stance, the teenager did at least make acquaintances at the Nordiques' draft table, and he didn't dish out any harsh words when asked by TSN reporter Paul Romanuk about the touchy subject of his playing status.

To an increasingly annoyed hockey community, this charade seemed bad enough, prompting howls of "Who does he think he is!?" But the tim-ing of Lindros's refusal couldn't have been worse in terms of Canadian politics either. Coming smack dab in the middle of federal constitutional amendment efforts, the cold shoulder given to the Nordiques was per-ceived as a cold shoulder to all of Quebec, and francophones in general. Prime minister Brian Mulroney's 1991 Meech Lake Accord, named after the Newfoundland location where it was negotiated, was meant to bring about a more defined Canadian constitution. Instead, the project fell apart amidst provincial disharmony. Quebec's demands to be recognized as a "nation within a nation" only served to irk other provinces, who felt special status should not be granted to Quebec and, if it was, should that leave Quebec as the only province to receive added benefits. Some of the provincial delegations—especially Manitoba, with its blend of First Nations, Métis and immigrant Canadians—felt they too represented unique tapestries within Canada.

Mulroney's attempts to satisfy these demands got foiled at every turn, sounding the death knell for his Progressive Conservative party by upsetting its small-but-loyal voter base in Eastern Canada while alienating its prairie support, some of which formed the new, independent Reform Party of Preston Manning. This drama provided a potent backdrop for the anger over Lindros's perceived "disrespect" toward a team in the city long considered the historic jewel of French-speaking Canada. Politicians, media pundits and all sorts of non-hockey figures were soon weighing in.

Everybody was suddenly an expert, whether they knew anything about the hockey business or not. Most Nordiques fans claimed this "spoiled" teenaged jock was just another anglophone exhibiting his cultural antagonism to the francophone world. Mulroney (himself a Quebecker) publicly stated that he thought Lindros should put aside his concerns, do the right thing and wear the *fleur de lys* in the end. He added that the Lindros/Nordiques spat represented everything wrong with Canada at that moment. Even if Lindros claimed otherwise, most didn't really believe— or perhaps want to believe—his side of the story. He was caught up in a whirlwind that was out of his control and proved to be a case of "wrong place, wrong time."

The Lindros family would insist for years to come that the heart of the matter was distrust of and dissatisfaction with Eric's potential boss in Quebec, Marcel Aubut. The player himself would reiterate this stance; in a 2016 ESPN interview, Lindros said, "I was not going to play for that individual—period." The family didn't trust Aubut to build a competitive team, nor did they want their brother/son to play for him. (In 2015, Aubut was forced to stand down as president of the Canadian Olympic Committee after sexual harassment charges from employees.) Gazing back at this powder keg, Mitch Melnick describes how he saw it from Lindros's point of view:

> I was in the minority on the issue, but I was doing a late-night sports show at that time and was constantly defending him.

What bothered me is that the language issue here in Quebec during the '90s, especially leading up to the (sovereignty) referendum, was so divisive. You couldn't look at somebody the wrong way and not be accused of being either anti-French or anti-English, so it was really polarizing stuff. That's when the market started to grow in terms of talk shows and cable and all of that, and I know the prevailing feeling was that it was about a big, spoiled rotten baby from Ontario who was anti-Quebec, anti-French and the attitude was all "How dare he?" I mean, this wasn't just a John Elway scenario (Elway was drafted by the Baltimore Colts first overall in the 1983 NFL draft but declared he'd play baseball for the Yankees instead unless his rights were traded). It was much bigger and more heated than that.

People rushed to judgment, thinking that it was all about disliking the Quebecois and the French language, etc. That was all a knee-jerk reaction based on the kid refusing to go to Quebec City. I think history has shown that he figured out the guy that he was dealing with in Quebec. He figured out what he was about and, whether his parents were involved or pushed him, it doesn't matter. Today, look where Eric Lindros is and look where Marcel Aubut is. Who's the more respected and admired of those two? Lindros would've played for the Canadiens, and I think he said that, so it wasn't about Quebec, it wasn't about French people, it's just he was stubborn and didn't trust the owner.

By the time Lindros came down the pipeline, Aubut had long been the Nordiques president, at first representing the team's corporate ownership (the Carling O'Keefe Brewery) since its days in the WHA. When an impending merger of Carling O'Keefe and Molson forced a $15 million sale of the team in 1988, Aubut also became a shareholder alongside the Quebec Labour Federation pension fund, insurance company La Mutuelle, the Daishowa Paper company and the Metro Richelieu grocery store chain. Given his experience as a hockey executive, Aubut was deemed the natural fit to become the club's chief operating officer. Due to what Lindros perceived as a lack of "winning spirit" and a questionable desire to succeed, he flatly refused to become a part of Aubut's organization. To his credit (even if it became to his detriment), the young Big E refused to waver from that position, no matter the financial figures thrown his way.

"I understand why they have a draft and why 95 to 98 percent of the people are completely on board with it. But I think if anybody actually challenged the legality of a draft system, it'd be hard to keep it together," posits Mitch Melnick.

> You have to accommodate the rare athlete who says, "No, I don't want to go just because a team wants me. I have no say in this, why shouldn't I have a say in it? I want to test this." Just about everybody who has wanted to test it, they've ended up accommodating, correct? Even in football, think of Eli Manning and Philip Rivers and Elway and Bo Jackson. For Lindros, it came down to what he didn't like about Aubut. The fact that his team ended up trading him to two different clubs is something (where) you look back on and go, "Of *course* Marcel Aubut did that." But in the moment, it was more like, "What's wrong with this Lindros kid? How could he do this?" Now it makes a little more sense in retrospect, when Aubut's whole sordid life is out there. I never spoke to Eric's parents, but I just remember the prevailing feeling about it, and I thought it was unfair. I thought so because he was bucking the system, whether he was helped or pushed or aided, or whatever you want to describe it and whether by his parents or not. Either way, he was still doing it, and I thought it took a lot of guts. And it ultimately it worked for him. Then one day, go figure, that supposedly anti-French hockey player ends up marrying a French woman after he retires. It's amazing how things played out.

Echoing the Sault Ste. Marie stalemate of two years prior, Bonnie in 1991 would claim, "We don't have anything against Quebec. It's a fine place for a lot of people. It's just not the place for Eric. It's not the environment we want for him." If language supposedly had little to do with the decision, Eric's strong-minded and fiercely protective mom would still stoke the fires, quipping to the media, "Life's hard enough for a teenager without being sent somewhere they speak a different language. He may be six-foot-five and 225 pounds, but he's still 18 and vulnerable." Other whispers were that the Lindros family also disliked the limited opportunities for marketing and sponsorship that would hurt his "brand" if he committed to Quebec. Unlike those in mixed-language Montreal, athletic stars in Quebec City were thought to primarily draw corporate incentives from French-language companies and would struggle to gain a foothold with nationally distributed groups as a result.

The public relations war was ultimately won by the Nordiques. Future attempts to quell the unfavourable media portrayal of Lindros and frame him as an honourable, upstanding athlete would fail to remove the tarnish around his name. To many across Canada, even if they weren't pro-Quebec, Eric Lindros was considered nothing more than a petulant whiner who didn't appreciate his privileged status in life. Fair or unfair, this damaged reputation followed him his whole career and most definitely would not be helped by later quarrels with some of the other NHL clubs he played for.

As accusations that his parents were too involved grew stronger with each passing year, Bonnie dismissively griped to Jeff Savage, "How ridiculous. Eric's been speaking for himself since he was 10 years old. Everybody believes it was my fault that Eric didn't go to Quebec. What a joke. If Eric wanted to go there, he'd go there." Sensing the legal battles to come following the 1991 draft, the Lindroses hired the services of noted sports and entertainment lawyer Gord Kirke. It proved a wise decision, given all the obstacles their son was to face throughout his pro career.

Inclined to wait until a solution could be found, Lindros sat out the entire 1991–92 NHL season. No matter how hard the Nordiques pushed to convince Lindros to join the fold, talks would inevitably break down; even a reported 10-year, $55 million offer was rebuffed. "The owner told me that if I went to Quebec, I'd be a God. To be quite honest with you, I don't care to be a God," Lindros would quip to Savage. While sitting out,

Lindros suited up in various hockey tournaments and leagues to keep himself sharp.

In late August 1991, with NHL training camps not far off, he received an invite to Team Canada's camp for the 1991 Canada Cup tournament. Thanks to his combination of scoring and ruggedness, Lindros made the final roster and skated very capably among and against the game's very best pros. Contributing five points (three goals, two assists) in eight games despite limited ice time (having to defer to the more proven team members), Lindros was a juicy storyline on a tournament-winning Canadian squad. This tantalizing appearance was parlayed into a long run with the Canadian national team during its lead-up to the 1992 Winter Olympic Games in February at Albertville, France.

Once again thriving against grown men despite being days shy of turning 19, Lindros posted 11 points (five goals, six assists) in eight tournament games—good for a tie for fourth in Olympic scoring. His incredible abilities played a big role in Canada getting as far as the gold medal game, where they lost to a Unified Team of former Soviet states. Once that experience was over, Lindros returned for 13 more games with the Generals before he missed their (albeit short) playoff run due to injury.

Throughout this lost potential NHL rookie season, Eric's crew of confidantes (mainly comprised of Carl, Bonnie, Kirke and agent Rick Curran) gave no indication that an agreement could ever be reached with Quebec. The Lindros side was willing to sit tight and call the Nordiques' bluff. For months, the Nords front office repeatedly denied that he would be traded and insisted that they too would be willing to wait out this contretemps. That resolve began to fade as Lindros showed no signs of caving.

The on-ice product might have had a hand in Quebec's decision, as the 1991–92 season (expected to provide another leap in fortunes after the promise the youngster showed in 1990–91) was barely an upgrade on the one before. There were signs of improvement on the horizon with the now-established stardom of Sakic and Nolan. Sundin went from 21 goals and 51 points to 33 and 76 as a sophomore. On top of that, Quebec had made wise forays into the previously forbidden Soviet talent pool and brought over a pair of shrewd 1988 selections in 25-year-old Russian winger Valeri Kamensky and fellow countryman Alexei Gusarov, a defenceman. As of late June 1992, when the entry draft was looming large, the Nordiques possessed several future NHLers in their system, including Adam Foote, Andrei Kovalenko, Garth Snow, Stéphane Fiset, Alexander Karpovtsev and Dave Karpa. Still, it was a dreary season that, in a way, supported Lindros's claims that the Nordiques were just a small-budget train wreck going nowhere and that he might just be wasting his time trying to make lemonade out of lemons if he did join the roster.

And so, the prevailing Quebec wisdom shifted from retaining Lindros to shopping his rights around the league. Dragging toward the finish line of a season in which they would win a mere 20 of 80 games and avoid the league cellar only thanks to the expansion San Jose Sharks (39-point finishers versus Quebec's 52), something needed to be done. Hearing the trade returns bandied in the media, why not stock the cupboard even more if that mega-star player wasn't going to show? By the time the season was over, the Nordiques also recognized the potential risk of him getting hurt while playing/training elsewhere and reducing the value of their investment.

A few months after the regular season ended, the 1992 draft provided the impetus for Lindros's rights to finally be dealt. The trade watch began in earnest on draft day in Montreal—and it was vintage Aubut. The problem for Lindros, the NHL and the teams involved was that a *pair* of trades were made. The first would be with the Flyers—a transaction contingent on GM Russ Farwell finding out if the two sides could come to a financial agreement and determining that the situation was amenable to both parties.

But then Aubut independently took charge, proving the Lindroses' point that ownership in Quebec was a "gong show." In search of a bigger offer, Aubut had decided to court teams even while his own GM was doing so separately. He accepted a rival offer from the Rangers only hours after Flyers management had come to an agreement with Quebec GM Pierre Pagé.

What ensued was mass confusion over who exactly owned the rights to Lindros, as the Flyers and Rangers were each under the impression that their trade package was the officially accepted one. The matter was finally handed over to a Toronto-based arbitrator named Larry Bertuzzi (great-uncle of future All-Star power forward NHLer Todd Bertuzzi), who announced his decision on June 30, 1992. Bertuzzi decreed the Flyers' offer to be the official transaction, chiefly because the Nordiques provided Farwell the contact information for Lindros. In Bertuzzi's opinion, this constituted confirmation of an agreement and thus nullified the Rangers claim that followed.

With this decision, the standoff had finally ended just over a year after the events of the 1991 NHL Entry Draft. The Nordiques received a massive return from Philadelphia for the 19-year-old, receiving Ron Hextall, Steve Duchesne, Kerry Huffman, Mike Ricci, Peter Forsberg, Chris Simon, two first-round picks and $15 million. It was a transaction that shaped the NHL's balance of power over the next decade in a major way. While the Flyers would frequently contend, and Lindros's arrival helped them construct a new arena and move out of the aging Spectrum in time for 1995–96, they never did win the famed silver chalice. Philly only once reached a Finals series at all, falling in a 1997 sweep at the hands of the Red Wings. They would cough up their next-best chance to get there in the 2000 East Final when they blew a 3–1 series lead to the Devils.

The Flyers also got their own chance to play hardball with Team Lindros over his contract. As documented in the book *Money Players*, it ultimately took the personal intervention of Flyers owner Ed Snider to get the six-year, $18 million (plus a $2.5 million signing bonus) contract completed. At one point in the acrimonious negotiations, GM Farwell asked agent Curran how he could justify an equivalent contract to superstar Mark Messier's. "Me justify it?" asked Curran. "You're the ones who just traded six players and $15 million. You're the ones who say how valuable he is." Game, set, match.

In the wake of the historic transaction, Quebec fans at long last saw an upswing on the ice after five years of the dregs. The Nordiques put together quality seasons in both 1992–93 (jumping to 104 points—double the total of 1991–92) and 1994–95 (an Eastern Conference–high 61 points in a lockout-shortened 48-game schedule) while an off year in between was mostly the result of some players having fallbacks from career years and key injury absences (Kovalenko, Simon, Foote and Nolan—lost for all but six games due to a serious shoulder injury).

While the two superb seasons saw first-round playoff exits, the hockey future finally seemed to have arrived and looked promising indeed. But it was unfortunately brief for Nordiques fans. The return to winning only made the franchise a more attractive asset to outside interests. As of 1995, the organization was still in the red financially and still stuck with an outdated arena in a city that featured a small, mostly French-speaking population base. Quebec could not hope to rake in the necessary revenue streams of TV, advertising and luxury boxes that most reasonably healthy organizations were enjoying by this point— while paying salaries in a powerful U.S. dollar.

Earning revenues in the weakened Canadian dollar, they were unable to compete without losing significant money. The increasingly high operating costs in a non-salary-capped NHL spelled doom for small-revenue clubs such as Quebec, the Winnipeg Jets and the Hartford Whalers—all of whom would be in new locations by 1997. As the Nords on the ice were on their way to banner seasons, Aubut began threatening to sell the team to other cities. The scenario would come true a few months after 1994–95 ended, when he and his partners sold the Nords to the COMSAT Entertainment Group, which transferred the franchise to Denver.

A quarter century later, NHL hockey has yet to make a comeback to Quebec City and may never do so if relocation of an eastern-based franchise doesn't become a viable possibility. With NHL commissioner Gary Bettman's zeal to secure owners who will keep teams in existing markets even if they are struggling (as with the Coyotes, Ducks, Hurricanes, Panthers, Devils and Islanders), it seems like a distant possibility. Perhaps the economic fallout over the COVID-19 pandemic will force the issue, but it remains to be seen. It has been argued that Lindros's rejection of the Nordiques sowed the seeds of their departure. But that's debatable. Not many at the time of the "Trade of the Decade" realized just how great a player Joe Sakic would turn out to be, let alone Peter Forsberg. Lindros carried name recognition that neither Sakic nor Forsberg had in the early part of their NHL stints, but frequent injuries left him less effective over the course of his career than the highly consistent and dazzling Sakic, while Forsberg, dogged by health issues himself, would nonetheless deliver greater playoff glory than Lindros on both a team and individual level.

At the same time, any criticism of the Flyers counts as armchair quarterbacking, considering Forsberg wasn't nearly as prominent on the radar as much as Lindros was. "The bottom line is: you built a building around Eric Lindros, but you couldn't build a building around Peter Forsberg," contends Gord Miller. "As great as Forsberg was, the Flyers weren't constructing an arena around him, let's be honest. Lindros was the biggest name in the game then. And rightfully so. Those who saw what he was capable of at the time would all have said the same thing."

Lindros's flat refusal to join Quebec dragged his name through the mud but also showed that a player could buck the system and still come out with his pro career unscathed. NHLPA executive director Bob Goodenow recognized it in 2004 in the book *Money Players*: "There's no question that the Lindros contract showed what the value could be for a fresh product coming into the NHL. Eric was unique, an instant impact player." Adds agent J.P. Barry, "I think it turned the eyes of a lot of players who had been performing in the league for four or five years." Yet, Lindros's approach hasn't really been attempted by such a top prospect since 1991. What if a repeat scenario ever occurred?

"I don't think the league would exert any formal pressure on a player or a team if they couldn't sign a top draftee," says Eric Duhatschek, "because I think that you could get into some legal issues if you did do that. But I do think they certainly wouldn't want to establish a precedent of that happening either. I just think that agents now understand that it's a bad idea to fight that, because the draft is the collectively bargained system that's in place, and if you want to play in the NHL, you have to abide by the rule. Right now in this climate? It's hard for me to imagine that something like the Lindros saga could possibly happen again."

But Barry, who with Pat Brisson started up CAA's hockey agency—representing some of the NHL's cream of the crop, including names like Evgeni Malkin and David Pastrnak—in 2020 contended that a scenario like Lindros's could be repeated:

I think it's still a possibility in this day and age of pro sports. I do think it's something that could happen again in the NHL. Obviously, being the number one pick is a little different than a lot of other picks. There's a lot of possibilities that go with it, like being the franchise player on a desirable team. In the future, if you had a team that was a really poorly managed— or at least perceived as such—and you had a generational player coming up, I do see the possibility of that being a problem. For me, it's all hypothetical, but the reality is that if it's one of those teams that have just shown a consistent, long-term inability to perform and compete, then that could be an issue that comes up.

Or what if you have a team, that already has a really top-level player but hasn't been able to perform around him? And he's been stuck there. Now you're the next one up in terms of future superstars and you'll be stuck behind that guy? I don't want to throw darts, but lately there's at least one Canadian team in that group and there's a few U.S. teams, right?

Recent departures by stars requesting trades (e.g., Pierre-Luc Dubois from Columbus to Winnipeg for equally disgruntled Patrik Laine) have shown that certain young players are willing to reject teams. What is for certain is that Quebec's fans, who showered Lindros with baby powder and soothers upon his first NHL visit to Le Colisée, were the most cheated by the dispute. For a second time already in his young hockey career, Lindros heard the derision of the crowd in an opposing arena. Not only in Quebec City would he get that treatment, but also in Montreal, even though it was the local team's arch-enemies that he had slighted: Montreal francophones (and even some anglos) were offended by the Big E giving what they saw as a proverbial middle finger to their culture.

By the time of the Nords' departure to Denver, most of the return for Lindros had been moved out of the organization's system. But the benefits were still deeply felt during the debut season in Colorado, as one of those first-rounders received from Philly was used on a goalie, 1993 pick Jocelyn Thibault, who became part of the Avalanche's critical trade to snag Patrick Roy from the Canadiens. Even parts of the deal that didn't stick around for very long reaped rewards, such as when reluctant Nordique Ron Hextall was sent to the Islanders before 1993–94 in a deal that netted a first-rounder used on corward Adam Deadmarsh (himself later swapped to the Kings as part of a 2001 deal that brought in All-Star defenceman Rob Blake, en route to the Avs' second championship).

Forsberg, Ricci and Simon were the remaining holdovers from the Lindros trade who played varying roles in helping the Avs to their unexpected Cup triumph in 1996. Ricci would be gone soon after, though, getting shipped to San Jose in 1997 for a first-rounder that Colorado used on left winger in Alex Tanguay. In other words, the Lindros deal was the gift that kept on giving to the Nordiques/Avalanche. The gargantuan trade pulled off in 1992 helped Colorado thrive for several years, while the Lindros timeline ended for the Flyers by 2008, when Sami Kapanen was the last remaining piece from a trade sending Pavel Brendl (part of the Flyers' 2001 trade package for Lindros from the Rangers) to the Hurricanes.

Lindros's own tale in the City of Brotherly Love ended when he was dispatched to New York following a lengthy period of being at odds with the organization. Upset at how Flyers management and medical staff were handling his mounting health issues (namely his concussions and an undiagnosed collapsed lung in 1999–2000), Lindros again sat out an entire season. Taking off 2000–01, Lindros for a second time in his pro career decided to forgo a year until a trade could be negotiated. Lending to the belief that history repeats itself, Lindros ended up burning his bridges in Philadelphia with a series of clashes (mainly orchestrated by Bonnie) versus GM Bobby Clarke.

The feud simmered until finally the Flyers were glad to be rid of him and the city's hockey fan base—already legendary as a ruthless, uncouth and cynical group—had turned on its once-lauded hero. While the bittersweet parting of ways would be patched up years later with Lindros's Hall of Fame induction and admission back into the Flyers fold, 2001 was another example of Lindros appearing to be a volatile personality.

Lindros may not have brought a prized elusive third Cup back to Philadelphia, but he did alter the NHL landscape in many other ways. As Barry puts it:

> When Eric Lindros got drafted, that might have been the
> start of the younger player being able to step into the league

and have a huge effect very quickly. Until that time, almost everyone thought that very few 18 or 19 year-olds could enter the league and dominate right away. Wayne and Mario had done that, but not many others were superstars upon arrival while still teenagers. Right around '89 or '90 is when you got larger numbers that were prepared to start entering the league. To me, that is what led the league to want a rookie cap. They wanted to stop those guys from being able to earn money in their first contract, and largely because that was what Lindros had been able to negotiate. After him, guys wanted to immediately be compensated because of their impact—or at least their predicted impact.

When Lindros was able to ask for more money than Wayne Gretzky was making, that put a lot into perspective. The NHL doesn't mind paying stars so much, but what was happening was the signing bonuses all the way through the first round, even to the second round, had grown so large. Many first-round picks were getting close to million-dollar signing bonuses, and many of those were not panning out. Any mega-rookie since has been significantly impacted in their ability to obtain signing bonuses, and they have had to do performance-bonus-based deals.

In the end, the Lindros era in Philly ended not with a bang but a whimper. He had not been healthy enough to sustain his rightful place as the game's pre-eminent superstar and, most importantly, there were none of the expected championships out of his tenure either. Nonetheless, the presence of the phenomenal No. 88 on the Flyers initiated a revival in the franchise's fortunes. Putting up consistently superb regular seasons from 1994–95 through 2005–06, with no playoff misses to be found, the Flyers may not have won any Cups during this renaissance, but it was their best period of sustained excellence since the Broad Street Bullies era.

The Flyers—once a model of how to turn an expansion team into a perennial winner—had been stuck in purgatory before the arrival of Lindros. Weak drafting, badly executed trades (e.g., Brad McCrimmon to the Flames) and the decline of star players—sometimes due to chronic injuries, as with Tim Kerr and Mark Howe—had led a once-powerful franchise to crater into a mediocre also-ran from 1987–88 to 1993–94, missing the playoffs in the last five of those seasons.

It wasn't until Lindros was at the peak of his powers in the mid-1990s that the Flyers were considered contenders again. Despite all its drama and intrigue, Lindros's controversial snubbing of Quebec on draft day wasn't the only compelling storyline that developed over the subsequent years. One of the other big stories to form served as a "what if" in a variety of ways, mainly regarding which players a marquee NHL franchise—one that's made misstep after misstep in five plus decades of championship drought—might have lost out on.

While only a few Hall of Fame names aside from Lindros were taken in that 1991 draft, one clear slam-dunk candidate turned out to be defence-man Scott Niedermayer. (And one certain loser? The Toronto Maple Leafs.) Taken with a number three overall pick acquired by the Devils in 1989, Niedermayer was a fluid, majestic skater with smooth, deft stickhandling. Not necessarily a flashy offensive player, Niedermayer sacrificed the 70-to-90-point Brian Leetch–type seasons he was capable of in order to play within New Jersey's lockdown defensive system of play. Winning was the mindset for Niedermayer 24/7, and statistical elitism was far from his mind even if he was aware that such things could sweeten the pot in contract earnings. Part of that approach came from his humble nature, but another part was in the "win first, ask questions later" system that GM Lou Lamoriello constantly stressed in Jersey.

The fact that Niedermayer put forth respectable numbers on offence was particularly awe-inspiring given that that he served a predominately defensive Devils franchise for most of his prime, especially under coaches Jacques Lemaire, Kevin Constantine and Pat Burns. Niedermayer's round-about route to becoming a Devil came via a trade by a Canadian NHL franchise once considered the jewel of the pro hockey world. That franchise? Who else but the Maple Leafs.

As a miserable decade for the Leafs was nearing its end, they still had many needs (even after routinely drafting within the top five selections throughout their lost decade). Because of their lucrative market, they were never close to financial ruin despite the years of mismanagement, poor results and lousy PR—all insulting to a loyal fan base that hoped against hope that things could turn around.

But they needed impact players. In 1989, a high-scoring blueliner was deemed first among the critical elements needed in Toronto. Not since the days of Borje Salming and Ian Turnbull had they possessed defencemen who could put up elite offence on a consistent basis. Draft and development failures had seen a litany of blueline prospects come and go without ever reaching expectations, whether in a blue and white uniform or at all in their NHL journeys (such as Craig Muni, Bob McGill, Fred Boimistruck, Jim Benning, Gary Nylund, Darryl Shannon and Luke Richardson). Throughout this ugly period—marked by the increasingly erratic and frequently embarrassing conduct of elderly owner Harold Ballard—only Al Iafrate proved worth the investment. And even "The Freighter" was a streaky player who struggled to string together the quality seasons he was capable of.

Early on in the first of his two seasons as the team's general manager, Floyd Smith—a Leafs front office loyalist since the late 1970s (and a role player during the late '60s involved in the Frank Mahovlich deal with Detroit)—decided to take action by pulling the trigger on finding Iafrate a viable partner on power plays. He figured he had accomplished this by bringing Tom Kurvers over from New Jersey in October of 1989. In return, the Devils received the Leafs' first-round pick for 1991.

Many pundits at the time felt it was a worthy gamble, considering Kurvers was still in his prime at age 27 and already an established NHL defenceman who could help out on the offensive end. Leafs draft picks often flamed out in those days anyway, so why not cut to the chase and get a proven commodity? Plus, the Buds were coming off using three first-rounders in 1989, so perhaps draft picks were a rather cheap commodity in Smith's eyes (or more likely Ballard's). Of course, this is just a typical rationalization people make when there are much deeper issues within a team—ones whereby even fans and the media have lost so much faith in the ability to cultivate talent that they begin to actually prefer short-term moves instead (repeated many times in Leafs history, such as when Phil Kessel was acquired in 2011 at the expense of what turned out to be drafting Tyler Seguin second overall the next spring).

Most approvals of the trade ignored the fact that Kurvers had already been dealt twice in his five NHL seasons and was exchanged for lesser draft picks each time (Montreal sending him to Buffalo for a second-rounder in 1986, while the Sabres sent him to the Devils for a third-rounder a year later). But such was the desperation to find any landmark move in Toronto at the time. Though the U.S.-born Kurvers wasn't the primary reason, the Leafs of 1989–90 actually turned out to be an improved club.

For whatever reason, things clicked more than in any other post–Lanny McDonald, pre–Doug Gilmour era of futility (which isn't saying much). In retrospect, it was just a perfect storm of the accumulated offensive talent connecting all at once. For all that, though, it was only sufficient for a .500 season. The 1989–90 Leafs primarily "turned things around" by lighting it up in the scoring department. The influence of new head coach Doug Carpenter and the maturation of several promising young guns was credited as the Leafs churned out 337 goals—good for third-highest in the NHL that season.

The fact that the Leafs were still a tire fire on the back end (358 goals against—fourth-most in the NHL) went a tad overlooked, because the offensive breakthrough accounted for the franchise's best regular season between 1979–80 and 1991–92. Kurvers contributed 15 goals and 52 points in 70 games to this offensive arsenal, pairing nicely on man advantages with Iafrate, who enjoyed 21 goals and 63 points in his own right.

As opposed to inferior clubs from 1985 to 1987 that elevated their play when the Norris Division playoff bracket rolled around, this up-and-down Leaf team ended things on an anti-climactic note when they were quickly outclassed in a five-game division semifinal series loss to the Blues. Despite the setback, optimism was high going into the next season. To the types who saw change at the top as a chance for renewal, the passing of Ballard at age 86 (during that very same series loss to St. Louis) on April 11, 1990, offered a progressive new direction for a team in dire need of one. As often had happened in that era, whenever things seemed to show a glimmer of hope, the Leafs went right back down the tubes instead. Despite the suddenly uplifting hoopla around them, 1990–91 was a total nightmare right from the very start.

The encouraging 1989–90 developments, such as Kurvers's production, a heady 94 points from 22-year-old Vincent Damphousse (Toronto's first-rounder at sixth overall in 1986), an unexpected 51-goal showing by winger Gary Leeman and 39 goals in just 68 games out of sophomore sniper Daniel Marois, all proved to be fleeting. (Damphousse still led the team with his regression to 73 points, though his reward would be a pre-season move in October 1991 to Edmonton so that the Leafs could bring in veteran help in the way of Grant Fuhr and Glenn Anderson).

Reality set in almost immediately for this edition of the Leafs thanks to the worst opening to a campaign in franchise history. A truly awful slide put them at an embarrassing 2–16–1 by November 11, just over a month into the season. Over the course of the season, their offence would slip by 96 goals to a mediocre 241 (18th of 21 teams that year).

Their improvement of 40 in the goals-allowed department was more than nullified by the drop in scoring. This trip back to the gutter never snuck up slowly on them; it became a brutal reality immediately. It was an unstable time at the front office level too, as the ownership structure had changed following Ballard's death. The maladies of the Leafs' scouting, drafting, development and minor-league system were so deeply engrained in the franchise's fabric that it was inevitable that the promise turned into yet more failure.

The new-look Leafs ownership/management hierarchy started the purge by, somewhat unfairly, pinning that failure on their once-celebrated head coach only 10 games into the season. Taking over for the fired Carpenter was his top assistant coach, Tom Watt. Watt had once been a legendary coach for the University of Toronto Varsity Blues before Mike Keenan stepped into the role. He won the Jack Adams Trophy in 1982 with the Jets, then briefly held the head coach job with the Canucks and most notably was an assistant on the Flames' championship coaching staff in 1989.

On top of the personnel changes, panic began to bubble when it became obvious that the Leafs were in a dead heat with Quebec for last in the NHL—without owning their first-round pick, one that could possibly end up being taken on the "Next One" himself, Eric Lindros—a local kid who would have turned backflips to be able to don the fabled blue and white (which he would do as a free agent for just one season in 2005–06, well past his prime despite being only 33 years old).

Should the Leafs have finished last in this pre-NHL lottery season, that future mega-star of hockey would be wearing a Devils uniform instead—perhaps a righting of the cosmos for when the Devils missed out on Mario Lemieux seven years prior? With Jersey being so close to NYC, Lindros was a lot less likely to refuse to report there than he would have if a team like, ohhh, let's say Quebec was the lucky recipient.

Ironically, the Leafs and Nordiques had actually swung a trade earlier in the season that helped strengthen one team while weakening the other. On November 17, 1990, Toronto dealt a prospect plus 1988's slow-developing first-rounder Scott Pearson for some veteran help in Aaron Broten, Michel Petit and Lucien Deblois. That the trio had all seen better days didn't seem to matter, given it took three more proven NHL-level players away from an already floundering Quebec squad. Meanwhile, the previously prized acquisition Kurvers was unceremoniously dealt out of town on January 11 in a straight up one-for-one deal that saw depth centre Brian Bradley go to the Leafs from the Canucks. All told, Kurvers—the intended top defensive solution—had ended up being a Leaf for barely over a full season.

With Kurvers gone, it was possible that all Toronto was going to have to show for what might become the Big E pick was a few warmed-over veterans who would be gone within a couple of years anyhow. No wonder local CFTO sports anchor Joe Tilley called GM Smith "under-qualified and hopelessly incompetent" while declaring he had "turned (the Leafs) back into the laughingstock of the NHL and it's time he was shown the door." Not so shockingly given the seemingly cursed and success-adverse nature of the Leafs in those days, Kurvers would bounce back to his old form once free of his blue-and-white shackles by posting 27 points in 32 games for a Vancouver team that was barely better than Toronto in 1990–91, (albeit a playoff team in the Smythe Division).

After 1990–91, the Leafs under their new ownership went to great lengths to differentiate themselves from the parochial and chaotic Ballard. They made a splash by spiriting GM Cliff Fletcher away from Calgary to reinstate the Leafs as a perennial contender. Hiring him as their new GM after the tumultuous season only slightly took the sting out of having missed out on Niedermayer, a figure who could have made a huge difference in any Cup aspirations as a number one defenceman in the 1991 draft.

While the Leafs had passed on future legends in drafts before and had even blown a shot at taking Mike Modano first overall in 1988 by qualifying for the playoffs on the final day of 1987–88, this time they had added the significant gut punch of wasting a high pick in a short-sighted, impatient zeal to regain respectability.

As a hire tied to Ballard's mismanaging ways, Smith was part of the purge in 1991—despite having only being in charge for a pair of seasons. Once the new ownership, headed by Toronto grocery tycoon Steve Stavro, evaluated the organization from top to bottom, his dismissal was assured. In the summer of 1991, the Leafs bumped him back to a scouting role after enticing the highly respected Fletcher. Niedermayer proved to be the one who got away, though.

Today, many believe the extra glare, scrutiny and drama that Toronto presents compared to New Jersey wouldn't have affected the Hall of Fame path for Nieds, including Eric Duhatschek:

> I absolutely believe that he would have succeeded in Toronto or anywhere. I got to know him a little bit during his playing career, and I think it had a lot to do with the calmness in his personality. There are some players, depending on their nature, who probably shouldn't be in a major market because of how it would affect them. We've all seen examples of that. But I don't think it would be the case with Niedermayer. He was a truly grounded guy. I don't think that the fact the Leafs weren't as stable an organization as the Devils would have negatively affected him, either. I honestly think he would have had a spectacular Hall of Fame career no matter where he played. It just has more to do with the intrinsic qualities he had.

Outside of the Lindros melodrama and the Niedermayer selection, the 1991 draft showed just how essential European talent had become within a few years to building a successful NHL club. The excellent class of Forsberg,

Alex Kovalev, Markus Naslund, Zigmund Palffy, Michael Nylander, Sandis Ozolinsh and Alexei Zhitnik all stood up as useful NHLers, especially when matched against some of the highly ranked North American–developed busts such as Pat Falloon, Alek Stojanov, Patrick Poulin, Tyler Wright, Pat Peake, Brent Bilodeau and Trevor Halverson. Looking back, Ritch Winter muses:

> Around this time, European players may have been getting selected more often, but they weren't getting taken as high quite yet. All you have to do is go back and look at the North Americans that teams were missing on. What would be very interesting to see is the level of misses based on the pick, North American versus European. I've never done that, assigning some kind of weight to the bigger the pick and the bigger the miss. But I think a lot of it had to do with scouting simply not adapting to the reality of where the game was going to be over the next 5 to 10 years.

Falloon in particular was a costly disappointment from the North American crop. It would hamper the brand-new Sharks from hitting their stride in their first six seasons. Despite memorable first-round upsets of the Red Wings in 1994 and the Flames in 1995, they posted losing records, three times finishing last, tied for last or second-last. While number two overall picks just as often end up equal or superior to the top pick, there are choice examples of a clear drop-off, and Lindros to Falloon is certainly one of them. The consensus number two that year, Falloon had blazed through the WHL with the Spokane Chiefs and authored a 61-game showing of 138 points (62 of them goals) in leading his team to the WHL Championship and a berth in the Memorial Cup.

After leading the dismal inaugural Sharks edition of 1991–92 in goals (25), assists (34) and points (59) as a 19-year-old, Falloon began an up-again/down-again habit of seasons. His offence peaked in the NHL as a rookie; a combination of injury and off-ice distractions affected the rest of his career. He would bounce around to Philadelphia, Ottawa, Edmonton and Pittsburgh after the Sharks gave up on him in a 1995 trade. Dogged by rumours of drinking issues, the native of Foxwarren, Manitoba, had gone from great expectations to being derided as "Fat Balloon" by dismayed Sharks fans.

Done after nine mostly underwhelming seasons between 1991–92 and 1999–2000, Falloon was also unable to carve out another role to prolong his NHL employment. Big names at the draft, like the Predators' first-ever choice, David Legwand, have been known to reinvent themselves. Legwand simply wasn't a player you'd build around and never reached elite status despite being a number two overall pick in 1998. Even so, he ended up having a long, respectable career by turning into a responsible two-way playmaker. Falloon, however, couldn't change. Demonstrating both the draft's inherent bias against smaller players and the crapshoot of it all, San Jose found far more fortune in drafting Falloon's linemate Ray Whitney, who had outscored Falloon in junior with 185 points in 1990–91. The 5-foot-10 Whitney fell to the second round at number 23 overall. More of a flashy, offence-first type, he lacked the physical abilities people had projected on Falloon.

Showing how a player's progress is neither linear nor instant in, Whitney didn't blossom as a dependable scoring stud until his mid- to late 20s, when he landed on the Panthers (via waivers from the Oilers, who had signed him as a free agent once the Sharks soured on him in 1997). Florida was the first of four different teams, out of eight he suited up for, where the Edmonton-raised Whitney would notch a 60-plus-point season. Giving up on Whitney proved one of the more glaring personnel errors in Sharks history: he became one of his era's most useful journeyman scorers, playing 20 seasons and over 1,300 games and scoring nearly 400 goals while surpassing the cherished 1,000-point mark, not to mention contributing to the Hurricanes' 2006 Stanley Cup victory.

Nonetheless, it was Lindros who dominated headlines during and after the events of that eventful 1991 day in Buffalo. He was already castigated by hockey types, but his spurning of Quebec had even more impact than imagined. He shunned years of tradition whereby young men hoping to pursue pro-hockey dreams were expected to shut their mouth, keep their head down and be grateful for whatever was given to them. He became a poster child for those growing tired of the modern-day "spoiled rich kid" athlete. But catering to the demands and whims of others was something Lindros and his fiercely protective family would never subscribe to.

RE-DRAFT OF 1991 FIRST ROUND (TOP 11)

#	PLAYER	TEAM	ORIGINAL	ACTUAL
1	ERIC LINDROS	NORDIQUES	#1 (QUE)	SAME
2	PETER FORSBERG	SHARKS	#6 (PHI)	PAT FALLOON
3	SCOTT NIEDERMAYER	DEVILS	#3 (NJD)	SAME
4	MARKUS NASLUND	ISLANDERS	#16 (PIT)	SCOTT LACHANCE
5	ZIGGY PALFFY	JETS	#26 (NYI)	AARON WARD
6	ALEX KOVALEV	FLYERS	#15 (NYR)	PETER FORSBERG
7	CHRIS OSGOOD	CANUCKS	#54 (DET)	ALEK STOJANOV
8	RAY WHITNEY	STARS	#23 (SJS)	RICHARD MATVICHUK
9	GLEN MURRAY	WHALERS	#18 (BOS)	PATRICK POULIN
10	BRIAN ROLSTON	RED WINGS	#11 (NJD)	MARTIN LAPOINTE
11	SANDIS OZOLINSH	DEVILS	#30 (SJS)	BRIAN ROLSTON

CHAPTER 6

SIDNEY'S OPERA (2005)

1. Sidney Crosby, Pittsburgh
2. Bobby Ryan, Anaheim
3. Jack Johnson, Carolina
4. Benoit Pouliot, Minnesota
5. Carey Price, Montreal
6. Gilbert Brulé, Columbus
7. Jack Skille, Chicago
8. Devin Setoguchi, San Jose
9. Brian Lee, Ottawa
10. Luc Bourdon, Vancouver

HOCKEY LOVES THE CONCEPT OF "passing the torch" from one generation's superstar to the next. Greatness recognizing greatness. So it was in the summer of 2002, when a 14-year-old Sidney Crosby arrived in Los Angeles for a training session arranged by his agents at IMG. While skating with fellow clients Henrik and Daniel Sedin, Crosby was studied by a figure on the other side of the glass. A famous L.A. resident had come to see what the fuss was all about with this teenaged prospect from Nova Scotia. That onlooker was none other than Wayne Gretzky, who had barely put on a pair of skates since retiring in 1999. He studied Crosby with the eye of a master examining a pupil. After a time, Gretzky scrambled to lace up a pair of skates and grab a stick just so he could experience Crosby up close on the ice. As he skated with him, Gretzky recognized elements of himself at the same age: the vision, the anticipation, the love of the game. Leaving the workout, he would tell bystanders, "He's the best talent to come around since Mario."

Hockey's greatest legends have typically come from humble origins and acted as such. Author Roy MacGregor called this the "humility gene." That was definitely true in the pre-1990s days, when it was not the major urban centres but smaller communities that produced the elite hockey heroes. Gordie Howe (Floral, Saskatchewan), Jean Béliveau (Trois-Rivières, Quebec), Phil Esposito (Sault Ste. Marie, Ontario), Bobby Orr (Parry Sound, Ontario), Guy Lafleur (Thurso, Quebec) and Gretzky (Brantford, Ontario) were examples. Players from big cities, like Mario Lemieux, usually grew up in the working-class sections. More often than not, these future hockey heroes didn't have means or well-off parents to bankroll their aspirations with private training and the latest cutting-edge technology. But this was before rising enrollment, expensive equipment and training costs priced blue-collar families out of the sport.

Such requirements are now the norm for kids who want the best development. These factors have led to many contemporary star players growing up in or around cities instead of in small towns. That's where all the best training, competition and teaching seems to be found. Despite this demographic swing, 2005 saw a small town on Canada's East Coast defy the odds on the newest teenaged prize in hockey. When Sidney Crosby began dominating his age groups out of Cole Harbour, Nova Scotia—scoring 193 points (95 goals, 98 assists) in 74 games with the bantam Dartmouth Subways—local chatter turned to national hype until, by age 14, he was starting to attract the attention of scouts and hockey writers all over the world. (Amazingly enough, another local boy, Nathan MacKinnon, would also land the top draft selection eight years down the road.)

For the first time, Atlantic Canada had produced one of the game's true greats. Despite never being a physically imposing tyke (much like Gretzky years before him), he torched every minor hockey level. But Crosby could not resist the inevitable tug of the star-making machine forever, eventually leaving home to venture to the United States and Central Canada. Crosby would transfer to the Minnesota prep school Shattuck-St. Mary's to take on a higher quality of opponent—while also earning a high standard of education for the model student athlete that he was. While at St. Mary's he made friends with Jack Johnson, who'd be selected two spots after Sid in the 2005 draft and would later be his teammate in Pittsburgh from 2018 to 2020.

Even though he left home early, he's still considered the pride and joy of Cole Harbour. To be sure, there have been other stars from Canada's Atlantic provinces, including Nova Scotia's Al MacInnis and Bobby Smith, PEI's Gerard Gallant and Brad Richards, New Brunswick's Danny Grant and Gordie Drillon, Newfoundland and Labrador's Michael Ryder and Ryane Clowe. But there have always been fewer opportunities for players born in the remote parts of Canada. Limited by economic factors, resources and competition, many youngsters over the years were forced to move to Quebec or Ontario to advance their hockey careers. While some persevered through the change to a bigger talent pool, a lot of the significant names from Atlantic Canada sank in the more competitive Central Canadian junior ranks.

Finally, the QMJHL expanded east to capitalize on the growing desire for competitive organized hockey. This gave local products the chance to thrive closer to home. With expansion and relocations, new Q teams hit Moncton (the Wildcats), Halifax (Mooseheads), Charlottetown (Rockets/ Islanders), Cape Breton (Screaming Eagles), Saint John (Sea Dogs) and Acadie-Bathurst (Titan). It proved a major aid for Atlantic hockey to excel at the highest junior levels.

By scoring 162 points (72 goals, 90 assists) in only 57 games at Shattuck-St. Mary's during 2002–03, Crosby made it known that he could handle an even greater challenge. Jumping from bantam to the QMJHL in only two years sounds daunting, but Crosby would make it look like child's play. Taken first overall by the Rimouski Océanic in the Quebec league's bantam draft, Crosby amassed one of the best seasons from a 16-year-old in many years. Accumulating 135 points (54 goals, 91 assists) in just 54 games—interrupted by a stint with Canada at the World Juniors— Crosby proved himself head and shoulders above his rivals. Even though his August birthday made him one of the league's youngest rookie skaters, Sid led an Océanic squad that had finished 11–58–3 in 2002–03 to five games above the .500 mark in 2003–04.

After Eric Lindros's ascent to number one overall draft pick in 1991, the hockey media had been on the lookout for the next "Next One." The number one picks from 1992 to 2005 produced some excellent candidates for the Hockey Hall of Fame, but no Next One. Nearly everyone thought there might be a *"grande vedette"* in the entertaining, lightning-quick and prolific-scoring QMJHL phenom Alexandre Daigle, who became the consensus top prospect in 1993. The charismatic Victoriaville Tigres centre may not have been quite as universally praised as Lindros (he had discernible downsides to his game) in the wisdom of scouts. Even with flaws—overlooked, as it turned out—in his drive, character and passion for the game, Daigle was deemed a workable project because of his God-given gifts. He was a veritable can't-miss prospect, especially where teams with a French fan base were concerned.

As Daigle was wrapping up his junior career, the 1992–93 expansion Ottawa Senators finished last place in the NHL. Thanks to a controversial "tanking" race to the bottom with the San Jose Sharks that proved a competitive embarrassment, the NHL followed the NBA's lead and instituted its first-ever draft lottery in time for 1995, which might be Daigle's only lasting impact on the NHL. Ottawa claimed the top pick by virtue of a wins tiebreaker with just 10 compared to San Jose's 11. It was set in stone back in mid-April. Daigle was going to be taken first come draft day two months later.

Instead of a Lindros or Mario Lemieux, Daigle was the successor to Brian Lawton and Doug Wickenheiser as a colossal No. 1 overall bust. While the Big E was the most outspoken and honest top prospect hockey had ever seen, he never bragged about how great he really was. Gifted with skills himself, Daigle possessed a healthy ego as well—one that gave him the bravado of a basketball or football prospect. His swagger would prove to be one of his downfalls; shortly after the draft, he quipped, "I'm glad I got drafted first, because no one remembers number two"—words that would ring hollow and look self-indulgent instead of determined when he couldn't come close to backing them up at the rink. Number two in 1993, by the way, happened to be future Norris Trophy winner, Hart Trophy winner and 2015 Hall of Fame inductee Chris Pronger. (Pronger later joked, "Nobody remembers number two, boys? Nobody remembers number two. Classic all-time quote. Guess who ate the shit sandwich on that one?")

Still, he was bilingual—an added benefit for a player in Canada's capital city and a boon in attracting fans from Quebec's Hull/Gatineau urban area just across the river. Even if the loquacious Daigle couldn't chalk up MVPs or scoring titles, it was believed he could still generate revenue and draw casual fans to Senators games. For that reason alone, Ottawa had zero intention of giving away the Daigle pick in the run-up to the 1993 draft, ignoring lucrative trade offers from the Nordiques and Canadiens—the two franchises that stood to gain the most from bringing in a Quebec-born phenom. (What do they say about the best trades being the ones you never make?) Both the Habs and Nords dodged disaster, as Daigle would likely have crashed and burned even sooner under the microscope of Quebec's capital city or the hotbed of hockey royalty that is Montreal.

Hampered by a lousy supporting cast with the Sens, Daigle never grew beyond his peak in 1993. Any expectation that he would him capture the NHL by storm right away was dashed when he averaged well under a point per game in each of his first two seasons (1993–95). It wasn't until 1995–96, when he dropped to a paltry 17 points in 50 games, that the realization finally hit that he would likely never fit the bill of superstar. His off-ice attributes of handsome looks and a magnetic personality also had led to distractions, as when he briefly dated the pre–Tommy Lee *Baywatch* star Pamela Anderson and showed an interest in getting into acting—all while being far from a superstar in the sport.

Upon his first retirement several years later, Daigle would admit that, while he was very good at the game, he didn't really enjoy it a lot. Hockey was more like a job than a life calling. As the expression goes, "Some guys love to play hockey. Other guys like to play at being hockey players."

With many other young stars improving and leading the franchise to its first of 10 consecutive playoff appearances in 1996–97, the Senators organization found itself ready to bid good riddance to its draft bust. Alexei Yashin had turned into the Sens' franchise centrepiece, and Wade Redden, Marian Hossa and Radek Bonk had leapt ahead of Daigle, the Chosen One. Ottawa dealt the 22-year-old to the Flyers partway through 1997–98. Stops with the Lightning and Rangers didn't go much better for Daigle, and he quit hockey at just 25. A comeback just a couple of years later stalled, and Daigle was out of the NHL once more by 2006—all before turning 32.

Which left the hockey world still searching for a successor to Lindros. Following Daigle, top overall selections such as Ed Jovanovski (1994), Bryan

Berard (1995) and Chris Phillips (1997) were considered ho-hum compared to Lemieux or Lindros. But then, a two-year period from 1997–98 brought a pair of mega-stars in Joe Thornton and Vincent Lecavalier. Both, especially Thornton, would go on to enjoy outstanding careers in the NHL, but the hoopla definitely looked foolish early on as they adapted to big-league play with even more difficulty than Daigle had.

The easygoing Thornton was kept around for 1997–98 by the Bruins, even though he was used on a sparing basis by rookie-averse coach Pat Burns, who frequently kept his ice time low and his press-box trips numerous. A future playmaking dynamo, "Jumbo Joe" scored a measly three goals and seven points in 55 games as a rookie and elicit some cries of "bust."

A year later, Lecavalier went first overall to the sad-sack Lightning. Compared to Jean Béliveau on account of his Quebec heritage, his playing number (4), his graceful style and his tall, lanky frame, the six-foot-four L'Île Bizard native was hailed (or was it jinxed?) by team owner Art Williams upon his selection: "He's going to be a Hall of Famer. He's going to lead us to Stanley Cups. There's no doubt that in three or four years, he's going to be the world's greatest hockey player. He's going to be the Michael Jordan of hockey." Yet again, a top prospect couldn't come close to the expectations heaped upon him at the outset. Lecavalier struggled to play at an All-Star level over his first four seasons before eventually becoming a regular 25-plus-goal, 65-plus-point player over the seven seasons that followed. And he did prove Williams right on the Stanley Cup prediction—even if Williams wasn't around as owner.

During the five years after Vinny Lecavalier was chosen in the top spot, the NHL did see first-overall picks who would enjoy stellar careers (Ilya Kovalchuk in 2001, Rick Nash in 2002, Marc-André Fleury in 2003) and those who didn't come even close to that (Patrik Stefan in 1999, Rick DiPietro in 2000). So enamoured were the Islanders with DiPietro that they dumped their previous goaltending prospect, Roberto Luongo, to clear the decks for him. "Rolling the dice here a little bit," said GM Mike Milbury. "Roberto Luongo is going to be an excellent goaltender. He is a class act and a kid that we would have been happy to ride with. But as the draft progressed, it was clear that the value of Luongo was greater than the value of the first overall pick; but in our minds, if we could get to DiPietro, he possesses an element that Roberto perhaps doesn't possess." Oopsie daisy. DiPietro: 319 games played, 130–136–36 record and 16 shutouts. Luongo: 1,044 games played, 489–392–124 record and 77 shutouts. At least DiPietro earned a 15-year contract whereas Luongo's longest was only 13.

Soon after 2000, the NHL saw a sea change: top overall picks would become more of a sure thing than they had ever been before. Whether you chalk it up to improvements in scouting and development or to Canada's late-1990s grassroots summit to explore why talent was starting to dry up, things began to improve. It began in 2004, when the Capitals selected Russian phenom Alex Ovechkin, maybe the greatest pure goal scorer the NHL has seen. A number one pick who has lived up to the billing of "generational player," Ovechkin maybe would have been even more widely hailed as that "Next One" had he developed under the intense hockey media spotlight of Canada, or North America in general.

Never before had an international player earned the kind of accolades Ovechkin received leading up to his draft year. After all, he was only the second Russian ever to go that high on draft day. But the fact he wasn't a Canadian kid may have tempered the headlines around "Ovie" and made some fans skeptical about his supposed wizardry. He wasn't helped by how easily a stacked Team Canada had handled him and his Russians in the World Juniors of 2004 and 2005. In retrospect, "The Great 8" was actually undersold as a generational legend. But all of this made his majestic rookie season as a 20-year-old in 2005–06 more of a revelation than it would have been otherwise.

While the 2004 draft lottery would transform a sagging Capitals franchise that had just had come off its worst season in 35 years—and had not won a playoff series since its first run to a Cup Final in 1998—the luck of the draw aided the Penguins almost as significantly. Many thought that 2004's draft lottery did not break in their favour because they lost out to the Capitals on the chance at Ovechkin. (Few shed many tears, as they had owned the first overall pick a year earlier in goalie in Marc-André Fleury.) But then the Penguins wound up with perhaps the greatest "consolation prize" ever in NHL draft history, selecting Ovechkin's Russian comrade Evgeni Malkin second overall. In NHL draft history, rarely had falling to the number two pick been so beneficial. With "Geno" in tow next to Sid starting in 2006, the Pens had a legendary one-two punch that would bring them Stanley Cup triumphs and Finals appearances in the years to come.

While the future would prove glorious, the Pens in 2004 were a wasteland of hockey hopelessness run on a shoestring budget. The trouble dated back a decade. On their way to winning the second of two straight Stanley Cups in Mario's heyday of 1992–93, the Penguins saw a change at the ownership level when the DeBartolos, owners of the NFL San Francisco 49ers, sold the club to Howard Baldwin—who was largely financed by Morris Belzberg and Thomas Ruta—in November 1991. Baldwin had first made his bones owning the WHA's New England/ Hartford Whalers back when he was a 28-year-old whiz kid, the youngest owner in a league full of similar hotshots young and old. At the time of purchasing the Penguins, Baldwin had recently sold his stake in the Minnesota North Stars to partner Norm Green, and obviously found even greener pastures to have gotten out so soon after buying the franchise from the Gund brothers.

Baldwin inherited a superb product, and team management was soon given free rein to spend at or near the most of any organization in the NHL. With this lofty budget to keep their core together, the Penguins' talent level was an embarrassment of riches over the next handful of seasons. Of all the NHL clubs in the 1990s, only the Red Wings could rival the dizzying array of skill most Pens teams could brag of. However, it could have been even more glorious if the personnel had been handled a little bit better. After a battered, frustrated and exhausted Lemieux stepped away as a player for the first time following the 1996–97 season—still shy of turning 32 years old—the skies began to darken in Steeltown.

While the burgeoning one-man show of Jaromir Jagr held the team afloat as a playoff-quality squad on the ice, the off-ice health of the Penguins was a different matter. Baldwin and Belzberg were revealed to owe over $90 million to creditors, forcing the Penguins to file for bankruptcy in November 1998. A pall was cast over a once-thriving organization, now likely to be sold and possibly moved to a new city. Yes, the Pens were back at square one, facing relocation like it was 1984 all over again. As he'd done when he joined them as a player, Lemieux stepped in to save the day. Through a series of moves—including turning his own cash plus deferred salary into $25 million and controlling interest—Lemieux was able to keep the team in Pittsburgh.

Even Lemieux returning to a playing career couldn't stem the bleeding, however, and an on-ice decline began soon after. A 2001 Eastern Final appearance against the Devils proved to be the last Stanley Cup playoff action the city would witness for six years.

Pittsburgh in the years before Crosby resembled a glorified AHL team, barely better than their actual minor-league affiliate in Wilkes-Barre/Scranton. Replete with reclamation projects (Rico Fata, Ric Jackman, Dick Tarnstrom), drafting disappointments (Aleksey Morozov, Milan Kraft, Konstantin Koltsov) used in prominent roles and several retreads (Brian Holzinger, Drake Berehowsky, Mike Eastwood, Kelly Buchberger, Marc Bergevin), the 2003–04 Pens were a dire product indeed. Fans stayed away in droves, turning Mellon Arena into a library most of that season—exemplified by a stretch of 18 consecutive defeats that only missed being the official NHL record losing streak thanks to an OT loss in the middle. The many shortcomings would eventually lead to Craig Patrick losing his job in 2006 and Ray Shero being ushered in as his replacement.

From the 2003–04 edition, which won just 23 games, only an 18-year-old Fleury plus young defencemen Rob Scuderi and Brooks Orpik would still be around to taste championship glory down the road. Which is why "Sid the Kid" was made to order. In his last few years, GM Craig Patrick would contribute elements in later-round finds such as Tyler Kennedy, Alex Goligoski and Kris Letang. But in order to become champions, the Penguins would need the generational players soon to be taken in 2004 and 2005. But first, a year-long labour stoppage would descend upon the NHL. Although it represented a grim turn of events for hockey supporters in general, the 2004–05 lockout would benefit the Penguins franchise in ways no one could have possibly dreamt at the time.

Fought over the owners' desire to implement a hard salary cap to curb escalating salaries, the bitter 2004–05 lockout made the NHL one of the few pro sports leagues at that time to outright cancel its championship. Fan apathy and disgust was at an all-time high as the Cup-less spring turned to summer without the usual free agency period arriving on schedule come July 1. But July 13 brought a breakthrough, as the sides ratified a new collective bargaining agreement—one that weighed heavily in the owners' favour, as it turns out. They received most of the concessions the players, under NHLPA executive director Bob Goodenow, had promised to never make. (Goodenow, long demonized by the owners, was subsequently replaced by NHLPA executive Ted Saskin.)

The Penguins turned out to be one of the biggest beneficiaries of this unfortunate lockout. This would first manifest itself in the new CBA's chief result—a hard salary cap for the first time in any North American major pro sports league. Where it became a blessing for the Pittsburgh franchise in particular was with the agreement that a lottery would decide the draft order. The lottery odds would be based on how teams had done over the prior three seasons—not a single season, as in the past. In other words, a mathematical chance to draft Sidney Crosby was presented to each of the NHL's 30 franchises.

The singularity of the 2005 format was one thing, but the fact it was for the most highly touted prospect since Eric Lindros made it all the more compelling. Though televised as usual, the 2005 draft (held on July 30—just eight days after the order was determined by lottery and 17 days after the end of the lockout) was staged at the Westin Hotel in Ottawa instead of the Senators' home rink, the Corel Centre. It was the first draft day not open to the public since 1980.

Once Crosby showed what he could do with the Océanic of the QMJHL, Canadian hockey knew it finally had another player to match the lofty billing of Lafleur, Gretzky or Lemieux. One telltale sign was how he made others around him better. During his time in Rimouski, he gave a glimpse at his ability to turn ordinary wingers into stars by converting Dany Roussin, Marc-Antoine Pouliot and Danny Stewart into scoring sensations. (This would later be a salary-cap advantage, as parsimonious Pittsburgh would frequently saddle Crosby with linemates who were somewhat less than star quality.) Unlike Lindros, Crosby even made a significant attempt to learn French while in Rimouski. It all confirmed the projection that he would become the slam-dunk top prospect heading into the 2005 draft.

Becoming the big catch for this draft was an even more whirlwind process for Crosby than it had been for Lindros 14 years earlier. The reason?

The explosion of sports media. Back when TV first started broadcasting sports to millions of households in the 1950s, newspapers began to expand their sports sections in response to the challenge, as their words no longer were the only way to paint a picture for fans who couldn't attend games and could only listen on the radio. In the long run, this only intensified the attention on sports. The absence of pro hockey throughout 2004–05 meant Crosby had the Canadian sports media stage all to himself as he lit up the Q (and why not, considering the main competitors were *Movie Night in Canada* and the AHL?).

While the constant coverage had led to the formation of ESPN in the U.S. starting in 1979, there was still no 24/7 sports radio in Canada and no all-sports network until 1984, when TSN took to the airwaves (its Quebec equivalent, RDS, was launched five years later). Even then, TSN wouldn't see a head-to-head competitor in Canada—with CBC's coverage only being a part-time aspect of its network—until 1998, when CTV Sportsnet was created. When Lindros rose through the ranks to prospect supremacy in 1991, the print media was still predominant. While the 24/7 sports channels on both radio and TV had made the volume of sports reporting even greater for that 1991 draft, that was nothing compared to 2005.

Once the 2005 draft order and date were revealed, the Crosby selection went under the microscope. The internet only added to the coverage and greatly changed the landscape. Suddenly, it was not only hockey journalists giving their assessments on the sport but also a new generation of online fans who gabbed on message boards and chat applications and wrote blogs. Insists Peter Loubardias, "I think part of the allure of Sidney was he fell into that interesting window when things were changing in the media landscape. Maybe we didn't have smartphone capabilities in 2005 the way we do now, but we did have cellphones. The whole landscape had changed so much in that period of time, whether it was junior hockey that you could now all of a sudden get on TV or just the sheer amount of people writing about different opinions."

CAA agent J.P. Barry concurs that Crosby may have been the trendsetter and the impetus for the current sports-media fascination with that next big thing:

Because of the circumstances of him being the top young prospect in the world and there not being any NHL that year, I recall that he garnered unheard-of attention in 2004–05. His junior games were being broadcast constantly on TV, whereas only a few would be seen for a player of his calibre in the past. There were lots of clips of Sid's games, clips of his goals on a regular basis on sports highlight programs—not to mention the internet. It was really some of the only hockey that people were able to watch for a few months until things were settled with the CBA too. The fact he was so intriguing, plus that his lead-up was during a lockout, really led to an increased attention toward prospects. We've had a lot of young people in the World Juniors, like he was, who did really well but didn't necessarily translate so over-whelmingly well into the NHL like he did. So, yes, Crosby had way more eyes on him. And he justified that because he kept performing over and over to prove his worth.

Blogging became a primary component of average fans getting their opinions circulated in the new millennium, and it proved a vital outlet for the burgeoning hockey analytics community, which used baseball's "saber-metrics," pioneered in the 1980s by Bill James, as its inspiration. With all of these tools, it was much easier to know about Crosby's overall game, be aware of his attributes and see the highlights of his exploits on video without needing to view or tape/PVR the broadcast. While his Rimouski team didn't win the 2004–05 Memorial Cup, Crosby's entire season—not to mention his commanding 2005 World Juniors performance, centring a dream line with Patrice Bergeron (age 19 but already with an NHL season under his belt in 2003–04) and Jeff Carter.

Even Wayne Gretzky's gracious comments that Crosby would break all his records didn't initially deter the doubters. There was still trepidation after Daigle, Thornton and Lecavalier had not immediately lived up to their tremendous hype even as other picks in the intervening years, such as Alexei Yashin, Paul Kariya, Dany Heatley, Jason Spezza and Rick Nash had become impact stars from the get-go. (Still, only one of those names—Kariya—is in the Hockey Hall of Fame, and the others are unlikely to join him anytime soon, if ever.)

The real allure of the unconventional 2005 draft lottery format—who would land the coveted pick—had been decided days before the draft itself. Under the NHL's weighting of the draft, certain franchises had more of an advantage than others when the balls started popping. Teams that had won a lottery in the prior three seasons lost one ball out of a maximum of three put into the mix. A playoff berth subtracted another ball too, but teams could still hold a minimum of one. This set-up ultimately favoured poor performers such as the Penguins, but also the Blue Jackets, Panthers, Sabres and Rangers—all teams that had not made the playoffs even once over the previous three seasons and had not owned the first pick in that time either (the Pens' first overall selection of Fleury in 2003 had arisen from trading up with Florida, who selected Jay Bouwmeester third while the Hurricanes took Eric Staal in the number two slot).

These teams each had three Ping-Pong balls in the lottery mixer, and two other teams were docked a ball for winning a recent draft lottery (Atlanta in 2002, Florida in 2003). The fact that the full draft selection format in 2005 would also be seven rounds and of the snake variety—meaning the top-pick holder wouldn't select again until number 60—was definitely secondary considering the top prize at stake.

With Crosby on the line, the selection lottery held more interest than draft day itself. Some teams had no luck in the process; the Flames had their two Ping-Pong balls gone by the 28th overall pick while the Coyotes two balls were gone by the 17th. Hit worst of all were the Sabres, who saw all three of their balls used up by 13th overall pick. Meanwhile the Rangers' three balls were gone by 12th while Atlanta's were done by 8th. Amazingly, two of the teams holding just one chance made it inside of the top 10: Ottawa lasting until 9th (a climb that ultimately got squandered on bust defenceman Brian Lee) and the Canadiens' gone by 5th (to be used on superstar franchise-lynchpin goalie Carey Price).

With Montreal out of the equation at the number five selection, the intrigue of Crosby going to his professed favourite team was squashed too (Crosby became a childhood devotee of Les Habitants because his father, Troy, was a goalie drafted by the Habs in their 1984 haul, discussed earlier in this book). The rights to the top pick ultimately boiled down to the Anaheim (still Mighty) Ducks and the Penguins. At the time, Anaheim was just two years removed from one of the more unexpected runs to a Cup Final ever seen. Clearly, the Disney-owned Ducks weren't the more desperate of the two organizations—either on or off the ice. The Pens, meanwhile, needed a little Crosby love.

On that mid-July day in 2005, the Ducks' newly hired president and GM, Brian Burke, stood on stage next to Penguins president Ken Sawyer, waiting to see who would receive manna from hockey heaven. And it went to Sawyer's club instead. After a dramatic pause, the winning card was revealed as belonging to the Penguins. For a second time in two decades, they had secured the rights to take a franchise-altering god of the puck trade. The unique scenario, in which all 30 teams had a chance at number one, has never been tried again—not too shocking considering the NHL has always stood by its small markets and struggling teams.

Would it be fairer if perhaps one day the NHL made its top pick a tournament-determined carrot to dangle? Or mandated the lottery as a 32-team affair that gave everyone a certain percentage of a chance at number one overall? "Well, I don't think that they will try it in the NHL as long as Gary Bettman as commissioner," answers Eric Duhatschek:

> It's too innovative for their liking. I do like the idea. The whole mantra at the NHL level right now is parity, though. The gap between the top and the bottom not existing— it's probably the perfect scenario for the National Hockey League front office. I don't think most fans want that, but I do think that the way the system is right now penalizes teams that had been consistently excellent for a long period of time. I like the idea of having every team have some small chance of moving up, even if they're an elite-level team. Because guess what? You should *reward* teams sometimes for competency, not for incompetency.
>
> And that's what ends up happening when you have the draft lottery. Incompetence is incentivized. In the same way you don't want a team dominating for 30 consecutive years,

it doesn't do the league any good if the same team finishes last 10 years a row either. So, you have to give them a little bit of a leg up. The current system does create that possibility where the bad teams don't automatically pick first. I'd just like to see more of that than we have currently.

As it was in 2005, though, the Penguins winning the lottery meant the Ducks would be in the unenviable number two spot, with fewer stars left to choose from. Who knows how different NHL history could have been if they had ended up with the generational talent Crosby instead of Bobby Ryan, who ultimately was a respectable but far from brilliant player? It's likely that Pittsburgh would not be even close to the three Cups it won with Crosby, while Anaheim might have had that many, if not more, had they won the Sidney sweepstakes.

A year later, the Mighty Ducks, rechristened simply the Ducks, switched to gold and black uniforms after being purchased from Disney by the Samueli family. A year after that they achieved Cup glory—two years sooner than the Penguins. Even if Pittsburgh hadn't landed the Crosby pick, Eric Duhatschek contends it might not be that cut and dry as to whether the franchise would have been doomed:

> Even today, it's still hard to know if they would've been in trouble (with) relocation or not getting their new arena. Malkin came the year before Crosby, and he's proven that whenever Crosby's not there, he's a dominant, marquee franchise player in this league. Would the Pens have taken Ryan too, or have gone for a Jack Johnson? I remember Burke saying one time, "We're happy with our guy." Then he paused and said something like, "But we might have found a sweater for the other guy." In that Brian Burke way of his, he said, "Yeah, he would have helped us, but we will be okay." And they were. I mean, they went out and they made the moves to get Niedermayer and then Pronger. Getzlaf and Perry were sort of coming into their own a little bit after that. They were young players and real good supplementary

pieces on a team that already had guys like Teemu Selanne and Andy McDonald.

Other decisions would have had to have been made based on what you eventually had to pay Crosby coming out of his entry-level deal. It's impossible to forecast what that would have done. But, I mean, when you think about basketball rivalries, like Clippers versus Lakers, if you go out and get a Kawhi Leonard type of player in Crosby to go up against the established Kings? Suddenly you're way more interesting locally. It's hard to compete against a LeBron in that market unless you have something similar in terms of star power. Certainly, the Ducks would've had their profile raised with Crosby in their ranks. Still, Selanne was *the* guy in that market of Anaheim. He was, and is, so beloved by Orange County sports fans. So as great as he has been, I don't think Crosby would have ever replaced Selanne in the eyes of the fans there.

J.P. Barry back then worked closely at IMG with Pat Brisson (together they'd co-head the hockey division for the CAA). He feels Crosby could have taken Anaheim to an even loftier level than what they've ever known:

If you look at the history of it, I think it would have changed Anaheim for sure. It would have turned them into a powerhouse, especially if you look at some of the other players they had and would have been able to surround him with. They were more ready to compete right off the bat than Pittsburgh—and even the Pens were in the finals in year three under Sid. He would have been that one more piece for the Ducks, who as we know were already pretty good. I know that Pittsburgh over the years has found a way to put players together, but that lottery 50/50 situation has definitely changed the course of both of the franchises.

Maybe the Penguins needed it more than Anaheim did, but it's already a huge hockey city, and they had Malkin on the way too. So while it's true that Anaheim won a Cup without Sid, maybe they would have won several Cups with him. There's a big difference there.

In a sign of how their fortunes had changed, the Pens had gone from hockey purgatory in 2004 to owning both Sidney Crosby and Evgeni Malkin in just over the span of a year. Pittsburgh's second pick overall (in 2004) became one of the greatest Russian players ever, while the Ducks' own second-overall choice (2005) ended up a sometimes-30-goal winger. Ryan was no project as the majority of scouting rankings had the American-born winger the consensus player to be picked after Crosby. Much like Pat Falloon, Ryan would see his game decline (mainly after being dealt to Ottawa) and become sidetracked by injuries before personal demons halted him later on.

Nonetheless, Ryan is a smashing success compared to a lot of other number two overall picks. Unlike Falloon, he was a consistent star at one point who didn't find himself out of the NHL or washed up before age 27. He even has rebounded to remain a viable NHL forward after undergoing treatment for his personal problems.

Amidst all that hype and approval from scouts, it would have been understandable if Crosby had been unable to handle the pressure at the outset. But he was that rare talent that also had the mental fortitude to withstand the circus. Duhatschek sums up what separated and still does separate Crosby from players of similar skill levels:

> He had this quiet confidence. There's nothing cocky about him, but he always struck me as somebody that had this inner fire, the thing that motivates you to get better. You've seen it throughout his career. I mean, what has marked Sidney Crosby's progress throughout his National Hockey League career? Year after year, he would identify some small part of his game that he felt had to be improved, and then he would work on it and try to make it better. After his success was immediate, he could have just said, "I'm fine." But no. In year three or four or whatever it was, he spent the summer

trying to become a better face-off man, and he became a better face-off man. Nobody talked about him as a candidate for the Selke Trophy at the start of his career, but last year there was a lot of people that were upset that he didn't get more votes for it.

I used to do some reporting for *Sports Illustrated*, and a lot of times what they would do for the season preview is that they would ask you to anonymously interview NHL players on your home team and around the league. One of the questions in 2006 was "Can Sidney Crosby be one of the all-time greats?" This was after he had been in the league only one year. And I thought that there wasn't enough of a body of work after one year to be able to even ask that.

I felt a little bit embarrassed asking the question, to be honest, and yet I was surprised at the number of players that responded, "Yes, we believe he can be one of the all-time greats." I thought to myself that it was interesting, because they had the view from ice level, right? So that's not me in the press box analyzing it. We're not people who are involved in the actually playing of the game of hockey. These are responses from players that were playing against him this rookie year, and collectively they saw something in Crosby that made them believe he could be an all-time great:

Amidst all that hoopla, Crosby never broke stride or tripped up. He never was flummoxed by accusations of him being a "golden boy" or a "whiner" (witness clashes where opposing players and coaches looked down on a rookie Crosby for mouthing off or complaining to the officials when he had a mouthful of blood or had taken a vicious slash). He was continually able to somehow tune out all that noise. Being able to do so "had to do with both his confidence and his drive," according to J.P. Barry:

Sidney knew from a really young age that he wanted to be the best player, he knew that he could be the best player, and he was willing to work hard enough to be the best player. I do think his preparation coming into the league at a young age was more than any other player had previously demonstrated. It might have been some people who thought he was all too much hype, but I think we understood the fuss over him going into the draft and the lottery. I think the majority of people really did know that this was a can't-miss sort of potential generational prospect. There might have been some who were unaware or chose not to see that, but I really do feel the majority knew, based on what he had accomplished, that he was going to be a very special player. Maybe I didn't see any backlash because I might have blocked out a lot of the doubters.

Even those on the broadcast side, such as Peter Loubardias, noticed there was a uniqueness to Crosby compared to all the other highly heralded prospects who had preceded him:

> I'll never forget interviewing Sidney in 2005 and walking out of that room saying to the camera guy and a couple other people that were with me that this is an incredibly special young person who is kind, respectful and aware. Unlike some others that have come along since Wayne, I think Sidney truly understood what it was going to mean, and he embraced, understood it and didn't take it for granted. I think it's why Sidney Crosby has the incredible track record that he's left so far. And that is, as great a player as he's become, I think he's equally someone who we should herald as a person. This guy's never been in trouble, and all he's done is win.

Obviously, Crosby would never be compared to any of his draft-year peers in 2005. Following his dynamic rookie campaign as an 18-year-old, it was obvious in 2006 that Crosby > everyone else from the 2005 draft. In the second of his two fine books written about Sidney Crosby, 2019's *Most Valuable*, author Gare Joyce set up the scenario for the anointed one entering the big time on the heels of a lengthy and bitter lockout: "Into this unpromising situation was thrust Crosby, skating in his first NHL game just weeks after his 18th birthday. In many ways he was set up to fail, and some seemed to delight in the prospect of watching him crash and be exposed as pure hype—not a phenomenon, but an illusion, perhaps even a fraud."

Joyce also reflected on how scouts saw a guarantee of success that may have been hard to understand for fans and journalists who hadn't watched, studied and/or analyzed the play of the Kid to such an extent. On a flight to the August 2003 Under-18 World Cup in the Czech Republic, Joyce talked to Tim Burke, the Sharks head scout at the time, who declared, "I'd pay to see this kid play . . . Yeah, we're supposed to be skeptical about the players we evaluate, but . . . It's not just that this kid can be good in the NHL. He will be—that's something that you can only say about a handful of players over the years. Thing is, he can be good *for* the NHL . . . What's really great is the fact the kid looks after himself on the ice. He fights his own battles. He doesn't just take it. He dishes it out. He's fearless out there."

Joyce admitted that, to him, the lavish praise seemed to be "a stretch at the time—to talk about a kid being an asset to one of the big four professional sports leagues before he'd even entered the feeder system. In retrospect, maybe it wasn't so far out of the box."

Crosby also attracted comparisons and contrasts to the number one pick of a year prior, Alex Ovechkin. The NHL, usually slow to seize upon promoting individual rivalries, began propping up the Crosby/Ovechkin tête-à-tête as must-watch TV from the beginning, especially in the U.S. Any time the Capitals and Penguins clashed, it was featured as a national game (first on OLN/Versus, then NBC after it signed a TV deal with the NHL).

Where Crosby was the honourable good soldier, Ovechkin had a bad-boy image as a pitiless opponent whose goal celebrations were a bit over the top and who threw truly punishing bodychecks (which likely accounts for Crosby having the public adoration that is only grudgingly and occasionally bestowed on Ovechkin). Luckily for the interests of the sport, the two superstars rarely failed to excite fans while achieving their personal success—not to mention whenever pitted against each other. Gord Miller asserts:

The big question for Crosby wasn't if he was going to be better than his draft peers, it was "Who's going to be better, he or Ovechkin?" And you know what? Fifteen years later, it's still a legit question. Most debates get settled quite fast, but this is one that has remained compelling to this day, which is rare. And you know, I think it will never be settled. You can legitimately argue for either guy. If you want to make the case for Alexander Ovechkin being the greatest player of his generation, you can legitimately make that argument. If you want make it for Crosby, you can legitimately make that argument. It's truly amazing that those two guys have come in and been like that.

Joyce has also, somewhat curiously enough, pointed to Crosby not only as the defining star of his generation but also as the most important skater ever to come around. "You could argue that Bobby (Orr) was better, or Wayne, or Gordie. But it would be hard to argue that any of them changed the game as much as Sid . . . In Crosby's case, the entire league was remade in his image," he wrote in *Most Valuable*. "The irony is that Crosby created a league that made it harder for him to thrive. And the tragedy may be that it could bring his career to an end in one fell swoop."

Even setting aside Crosby, 2005 was a superb draft that generated a handful of future All-Stars (and some potential Hall of Famers), not to mention some unlikely stories of making it to the big time. While other players have certainly enjoyed more team success, few from 2005 have enjoyed the individual honours and respect from their peers and opponents that Carey Price has. Though his lofty selection by the Canadiens raised eyebrows at the time—notably current NBC analyst Pierre McGuire, who infamously called the surprise pick "right off the reservation." Said McGuire in his state of shock, "José Theodore, Cristobal Huet, they traded Mathieu Garon, they have Yann Danis, who they signed as an unrestricted free agent coming out of Brown University. This is not a fit for Montreal."

Canadiens fans and NHL followers in general were critical of the choice upon its announcement, given the team's needs at that time. A minority of fans to this day feel the Habs would have been better off taking a strong two-way centre in Anze Kopitar. After all, goalies don't have to be generational to lead a team to a Cup, whereas legendary centres don't just fall off trees—something Montreal fans should be well aware of since the retirement of Jacques Lemaire in 1979. They have not been able to boast a top-five centre since then, the closest versions being Bobby Smith, Vincent Damphousse, Pierre Turgeon, Saku Koivu and Tomas Plekanec—non–Hall of Fame names that generated not a single MVP finalist or major individual accomplishment between them.

Meanwhile highly-regarded centre-ice prospects such as Doug Wickenheiser, Alfie Turcotte, Eric Chouinard and Alex Galchenyuk failed to live up to their ambitious projections. Current names such as Jesperi Kotkaniemi and Nick Suzuki have shown potential but still need more of a resumé to prove their worth. Yet the Price selection was indeed right for GM Bob Gainey and his director of scouting, Trevor Timmins. As McGuire pointed out at the time, Montreal's netminding inventory was already well stocked even without the pick, as they owned former Vezina and Hart Trophy winner Jose Theodore plus future number one netminders Cristobal Huet (acquired that draft weekend from the Kings in return for backup and once heir-apparent Mathieu Garon) and Jaroslav Halak. But Montreal still lacked a goalie with the pedigree of a true franchise backstop, something Theodore had provided in glimpses between 1997 and 2004 but usually followed up with disappointing seasons.

As it was, "Theo" hit the skids again after the Price selection, struggling badly enough to be traded away to the Avalanche for David Aebischer with just a month to go in the 2005–06 regular season. All of a sudden, Price went up a tick in the Habs' goalie system. In the next year and change, he would claim a World Junior gold medal, a Calder Cup and the American Hockey League playoff MVP award (Jack Butterfield Trophy). This was all accomplished less than two years after his selection, we might add. As teenage goalies go, it was a rise not seen since the days of Patrick Roy.

"That was such a good draft and such a deep one too," Mitch Melnick points out:

> The Canadiens needed help everywhere. At that time, they
> needed help up the middle and they needed help on the

blue line. Again, I'm such a great admirer of Bob Gainey's and what he did here as a player, and winning a Cup with Dallas as a GM. I had confidence that Gainey knew what he was doing. Based on the manner in which he spoke about Price, and then to see what he did at the World Junior Championship a year later? Well, I figured there was something to this pick after all. I never really questioned it much, anyway. I know a lot of people did, debating whether it was the right avenue to go down or should they have taken Kopitar instead. I think the error . . . was not building around him sufficiently.

Price had come from a goaltending pedigree, though that's not the unconventional part. The son of minor-league goalie—and 1978 eighth-round Flyers pick—Jerry Price, Carey also was related to Coyotes' mainstay Shane Doan: Doan's father, Bernie, was Jerry Price's cousin. While Carey Price owned good hockey lineage on one side of his family, thanks to his mother's side he became one of the highest-profile players with Métis or First Nations ancestry. Even more interesting, his mother, Lynda, happens to be a Chief of British Columbia's Ulkatcho First Nation.

Price grew up in the small, remote mountain village of Anahim Lake, 320 kilometres to the west of Williams Lake. He attended practices or games three times a week, making the 640 kilometre round-trip by plane, as his father put his pilot's licence to use and flew young Carey to and from games whenever it could be done in the daytime and the weather was fair. While the airborne taxi was a modest operation ("more a lawn-mower with wings," the senior Price told the *Globe and Mail*), it did the job and made for a hockey-parent story that the sports media ate up later, when Carey was on his path to the bigs. So did his Métis heritage. In a sport where Indigenous skaters such as Fred Sasakamoose, Henry Boucha, Reggie Leach, George Armstrong, Jim Neilson, Jonathan Cheechoo and Dale McCourt have made their name, Price is the rare goaltending hero with that background.

A few months after his AHL glory—and just a month after he turned 20—Price made the big club and then was crowned the starter leading up the 2008 playoffs. He has yet to lose control of the number one job since, all the while setting franchise records for the NHL team with perhaps the richest goaltending history of them all. While he gets flak for their Cup-less years of frustration, one can point to the inequalities of the rest of the roster and poor goal support come playoff time as the more obvious culprits (for example, Price posted a 1.78 GAA in the 2020 playoffs, yet only sported a record of 5–5 because his team could barely generate more than two goals per game and were shut out twice along the way). Mitch Melnick laments:

> It's just like it was with Saku Koivu. Same thing, different positions. It was a shame how many lousy teams Koivu played for and how few great wingers he got. This guy turned Chris Higgins into a 28-goal scorer, for crying out loud. If he ever had a proper All-Star winger for 70 games, how much more productive could he have been? At least Price still has some years left in the tank. Unfortunately, his biggest problem is that he wasn't able to do what Dryden and Patrick did, and that's win the Cup and Conn Smythe in his rookie year. He had a good rookie year, and then did fine against the Bruins before it fell apart against the Flyers. But he was only 20! The norm is not to do what Dryden and Roy did. Even then, the 2007–08 Canadiens were good but not as stacked with big names as '86 or even '93, and far from the legendary team of '71. As good as those goalies were, look at all the Hall of Famers they played behind. Truly, Carey Price has never been part of a Canadiens team that was capable of competing for the Cup.
>
> Thanks to his individual merit, the onus has all been on Price, and that should never happen. It's too bad, because the crap that he's taken is completely out of whack. Twenty years from now, people are going to look back and go, "What the . . . ? Why did we do that to Price?" They'll likely be criticizing the goalie they do have and say, "Why can't he win a Cup?" or "Carey Price would've done better than this guy,"

or something nostalgic like that. I mean, just have a look at the centres for Dryden's runs. Even in 1971, you had Béliveau, Richard, Lemaire, Mahovlich down the middle. Hall of Fame central. In '93, on what was far from a legendary team, Roy still had several stars like Kirk Muller, Brian Bellows and Vincent Damphousse not to mention some future Hall of Fame guys like Denis Savard and Guy Carbonneau, who shut down Gretzky after Game 1 of that finals series. Then flash forward to 2017, which was the last time Montreal finished top eight in their conference. Look at the centremen Price had: Tomas Plekanec, Phillip Danault, Steve Ott and Brian Flynn. Yikes, right? He put up a 1.88 GAA and .937 save percentage in that round, but they still lost the series in six games.

People were questioning *him* more than they were asking why the Habs had maybe the poorest centre depth of any playoff team that year. His team in 2020 that got into the play-in and the first round saw his numbers get even better too, but they went 5–5 anyway. They couldn't finish worth a damn. In 2014, they likely win that East Final versus the Rangers if Price never gets hurt, but they got there because they were getting some scoring for once. Over three goals per game, if I'm not mistaken. It's maybe the only playoff run with Price where they were able to provide him some offence on a regular basis. I don't think even Price could have done anything about the Kings winning it all that year if Lundqvist couldn't, but maybe the Price narrative is slightly different if he doesn't hurt his knee and manages to get to that year's finals.

Price came at the tail end of an era when highly touted goalies were still taken as top 10 selections. The strategy of goalies being taken so high in a draft or paid the salary of an elite forward has come under fire in recent years—no doubt strengthened by the Canadiens' recent decline in fortunes despite Price's presence. And yet, they often do help teams strike it when going that high too (see Tom Barrasso, Grant Fuhr, Marc-André Fleury).

Even with his success, the goalie fascination has dropped off measurably in the first rounds. As J.P. Barry explains:

> Some of it has to do with not actually having any consensus on the league's elite top-10 goaltenders. They really don't come around that often. It's rare for a goalie to have developed at that level at age 18. Goalies are generally late developers. You don't really see the dominance of a goaltender until the 22-to-25 range. Even Price's best years didn't start until after turning 23.
>
> The gap has been shrinking between a good goalie and a great one too. It's very difficult to predict a generational goaltender, which really is what it takes to select a goalie that high in the draft. It's an extreme risk-reward scenario. It's a high risk, but it could be a really high reward, and yet it can also be a disaster to your development system if you're wrong. I think there has to be a significant margin over replacement cost for a team to be willing. But Montreal that year was an example of a group that did their scouting, believed in the scouting, stuck by the scouting and took the pick no matter what controversy they thought it could bring about, so I do think that's a good example of stepping out of the box and sticking to your convictions.

To Barry's point, Price's closest competitors from that draft have done pretty well themselves without getting chosen at number five overall selection. While our re-draft of 2005 has Price going after Jonathan Quick, it's a close race considering Quick has less individual hardware and has dropped off in recent years. But Quick's two Stanley Cups—especially his 2012 Conn Smythe Trophy showing—give him the edge as the most accomplished goalie from this particular year. Even if, arguably, his overall talent and technique are not superior to Price's, his peak proved more productive, more significant and more legendary. Plus, he had to fight to reach his esteemed position in the league after being an unheralded third-round pick seven years prior to his 2012 triumph. Let's say he won the battle if not the PR war with Price.

Price, on the other hand, will have to rack up several appearances and wins for another few years before his Hall of Fame case becomes ironclad. That said, no one in their right hockey mind should argue that a goalie from that same draft, such as Tuukka Rask or Ben Bishop, would have been a better investment for Montreal. While those two have a combined three finals appearances to Price's zero, their individual awards case isn't quite as stocked either.

While Price's airlift upbringing is a long-shot story, few could have foreseen a talent arising out of a far-flung non-hockey nation such as Slovenia. Not long after Price was selected in 2005, Anze Kopitar would become that story. While concerns that he may have just been a great talent out of a small talent pool made some back away from putting him high on their projection lists, Kopitar would go on to make the Kings' number 11 "gamble" on him look positively genius. It was one of a handful of draft smash hits that would elevate GM Dean Lombardi's team from doormats to near-dynasty just seven years down the road.

In addition to Kopitar, Lombardi tabbed Quick in round three. At the time, most believed 2006 Kings' first-rounder Jonathan Bernier was the Kings' future in net. Alas, Bernier would never blossom into a go-to goalie, while Quick outplayed him for the top spot in La-La Land. Bernier would be relegated to backup status behind Quick before being dealt to the Leafs in 2013.

Securing two of the best choices in the 2005 draft went a long way to cementing the Kings' contender status for a decade during which they enjoyed two Stanley Cup titles with a Conference Final appearance sandwiched between. While other teams' superb picks that year never got them too deep, the Penguins (who also snapped up future top-pairing defenceman Kris Letang at the start of the third round) and Kings—teams that had both missed the playoffs in each of the three seasons leading up to the lockout—benefited greatly from what they did that year, combining for five Cups between 2009 and '20.

Even the Penguins, after lucking into the Crosby position, didn't entirely cement their Cup years until they still acquired a few more weapons. Meanwhile, taking Price didn't do much for the Canadiens in the way of titles, as they only made a single conference finals appearance with him in net. It only goes to show that a championship team goes far beyond just one home-run selection. A healthy mixture of savvy, patience and—most of all—luck can do the trick.

RE-DRAFT OF 2005 FIRST ROUND (TOP 15)

#	PLAYER	TEAM	ORIGINAL	ACTUAL
1	SIDNEY CROSBY	PENGUINS	#1 (PIT)	SAME
2	ANZE KOPITAR	DUCKS	#11 (LAK)	BOBBY RYAN
3	JONATHAN QUICK	HURRICANES	#72 (LAK)	JACK JOHNSON
4	CAREY PRICE	WILD	#5 (MTL)	BENOIT POULIOT
5	TUUKKA RASK	CANADIENS	#21 (TOR)	CAREY PRICE
6	KRIS LETANG	BLUE JACKETS	#62 (PIT)	GILBERT BRULÉ
7	BEN BISHOP	BLACKHAWKS	#85 (STL)	JACK SKILLE
8	PAUL STASTNY	SHARKS	#44 (COL)	DEVIN SETOGUCHI
9	MARC-ÉDOUARD VLASIC	SENATORS	#35 (SJS)	BRIAN LEE
10	JAMES NEAL	CANUCKS	#33 (DAL)	LUC BOURDON
11	KEITH YANDLE	KINGS	#105 (PHX)	ANZE KOPITAR
12	T.J. OSHIE	RANGERS	#24 (STL)	MARC STAAL
13	BOBBY RYAN	SABRES	#2 (ANA)	MAREK ZAGRAPAN
14	MARC STAAL	CAPITALS	#12 (NYR)	SASHA POKULOK
15	PATRIC HORNQVIST	ISLANDERS	#230 (NSH)	RYAN O'MARRA

EPILOGUE

THE SHAPE OF DRAFTS TO COME

2020 FIRST ROUND

1. Alexis Lafrenière, NY Rangers
2. Quinton Byfield, L.A.
3. Tim Stützle, Ottawa (from San Jose)
4. Lucas Raymond, Detroit
5. Jake Sanderson, Ottawa
6. Jamie Drysdale, Anaheim
7. Alexander Holtz, New Jersey
8. Jack Quinn, Buffalo
9. Marco Rossi, Minnesota
10. Cole Perfetti, Winnipeg
11. Yaroslav Askarov, Nashville
12. Anton Lundell, Florida
13. Seth Jarvis, Carolina
14. Dylan Holloway, Edmonton
15. Rodion Amirov, Toronto (from Pittsburgh)

IN THE FOREWORD FOR SHANE MALLOY'S 2011 book *The Art of Scouting*, Brian Burke, tongue firmly in cheek, wrote "Here's an ad for a scouting position: 'Wanted: NHL Amateur Scout. Need a keen eye for projecting how players who are seventeen will play when they are twenty-five years old in the best league in the world. Pay only fair, hours long, travel brutal. Bushels of criticism and scorn from the media when you're wrong. Faint praise when you're right. Multiple relocations likely over your career.'" Surely it is a thankless task putting values on unfinished young men, as we've seen throughout this book. But that is what scouts, general managers and coaches are paid to do. Sometimes you get a Crosby. Sometimes you get a Dave Chyzowski. Who, you might ask? Chyzowski was a highly rated forward out of Kamloops, taken number two overall by the New York Islanders in 1989, behind Mats Sundin. He was one of those prospects who physically matured at a much earlier age than everyone else, so he used that advantage to overpower the players matched up against him.

However, when he got to NHL, where nearly everybody was physically mature, he didn't have that edge anymore. Chyzowksi played just 126 NHL games between 1989 and 1995. It was a miscalculation on the scouting world's part that he would project well to the NHL game because, as it turns out, he was just using pure size and physicality with only an average skill set to become such an effective junior. It was just an unfortunate projection—one that hurt the Isles for years to come, however. But that sometimes happens—although that is one of the more egregious mistakes.

Chyzowksi is a classic case of overrating a prospect, and while that hasn't been an issue in recent drafts (especially during the size-obsessed late 1980s to early 2000s period of scouting), it still rears its ugly head. Go back a few years to see the reaction to the Canucks selecting 5-foot-10, 170-pound college defenceman Quinn Hughes at seventh overall. J.P. Barry recalls:

> If you'll remember from watching that draft, what did Brian Burke say on the broadcast? "There's not much body. That is one really small frame. That's a small body." That shows you what sorts of biases pop into a scout's head right away.
>
> Now, Burke said that kind of spur-of-the-moment. He's actually friends with the Hughes family. He once hired the dad, Joe, to work for him as his development guy. So he's not neutral, but he isn't biased against Hughes or his family either. Still, it just shows you the initial feelings were along the lines of "Oh, my gosh, you're taking a defenceman this high and he's 5-foot-10 and his weight is that soaking wet!?'" It's like his natural instincts took over to say, "How is that possible?" even though he wasn't a GM or president of a team anymore. Like many others, he was betting he was right about this being a big problem, and he was wrong,

because look at what Hughes has done since then in spite of his frame. That said, I think scouting has more of an understanding of where the game is at now. They know the types of players that are succeeding in the modern game.

So I don't think there's any confusion of size and bulk over skill, especially at the high end of the draft. There's also increased exposure, more events and more watching these kids even at a younger age. I see it as a much more professional world now with an increased size of the staff and members who are more and more made up of a lot of recent players and pros, rather than what was the case 20 years ago. They've got players who recently played the game who are now evaluating where it is. Backing that up with analytics and video. It's really changed a lot in the last decade. Scouting has become so important to the GM that they're not going to just hire based on friends, contacts or old teammates anymore. It's to their own survival that they have to have a good scouting staff, because it's just so hard to make a significant trade in the league now, and it's very difficult to land a prime-time free agent also.

So what are the lessons from these remarkable drafts we've touched on? Who has utilized the draft to their benefit and who has not? Current contenders for bragging rights include teams such as the Lightning, Blues, Capitals, Flyers and Bruins. These squads have not only struck it big on lottery picks, but also found gems in the later rounds—the true key to building a winner. As evidence, witness the struggles of perennial lottery participants such as the Oilers, Sabres, Panthers and Coyotes—clubs who haven't been able to string together great seasons despite a glut of top-five picks over the years. By exploiting the later rounds, the top-performing NHL organizations have managed to surround their elite talents with the necessary complementary picks, more crucial than ever in the current landscape. And to build up a stable of young players that you can use in trades when the push for a championship requires a veteran star. Many try to analyze this landscape in order to determine what it takes to build a modern contender in the salary cap era. But most end up still with more questions than answers on how to concoct that secret formula.

For example, how has the introduction of the salary cap changed the annual talent distribution? And why would teams often rather lose games than miss out on the next great thing coming down the prospect pipeline? Summing up the challenge of being a scout to Malloy in *The Art of Scouting*, then-Panthers director of scouting Scott Luce remarked, "It's easy to go out to a game and pick out the best players. Every fan knows the guy who got the hat trick that night probably is one of the better players in the game. But it's not easy to go to the game and see the guy on the fourth line who had five shifts, did everything right, played his position, had good read-and-react, and is a big skinny guy who, once he gets his strength, is going to be an above average skater and contribute down the road. It takes time and patience and a lot of practice to fine-tune that art."

Summing up the hit-and-(mostly) miss nature of the position, scout Mike Futa tells author Shane Malloy in *The Art of Scouting* that "it's the only job where you can be right 15 percent of the time and be ruled a Hall of Famer or a success. You are going to be wrong 85 to 80 percent of the time, and if you hit on 2.5 home runs every Draft, you are on par with some of the best scouts ever."

"I think there's no doubt that the scouting world didn't evolve and catch up as quickly as the actual development world, meaning the way the game was changing," asserts Barry:

> We've seen that multiple times where you get scouts that maybe are dug into their ways about what a hockey player should be, and you've got coaches the same way. Then you see changes at the younger level in the way the game is played. The second wave probably has been the last decade with the rule changes. You're seeing the speed of the game just increase at an enormous level.
>
> But when the rule changes came, and the players were coming out of a different system where they were playing the speed game, that changed everything. I think in both instances, the scouting hadn't adapted quickly enough, so you

saw teams that had adjusted and teams that hadn't adjusted . . . it's come an extremely long way as far as identifying the right talent, as far as reviewing it, exposing different eyes to it, coming to a conclusion. I do think they still struggle . . . around minor injuries that become overblown. I went through that recently when both Mathew Barzal and David Pastrnak dropped in the draft order due to relatively minor injuries. Boston did eventually take Pastrnak in 2014, but then a year later they passed on Barzal three times in a row right before the Islanders took him. Look at those (Islanders) picks. None of them are even close to his level right now, not even the best of the three in Jake DeBrusk. If you were to do it over again, a team might not take three players over Barzal overall. He probably becomes anywhere from a third to a sixth overall pick in the 2015 draft.

Former Canucks GM and president Mike Gillis claims that "in some circumstances, drafting and scouting has become much more accurate than it used to be. But you know, there is still built-in prejudice and confirmation bias that occurs in that field." Gillis himself was a touted power-forward prototype of his era when coming out of a junior career starring for the OHA's Kingston Canadians (where he had many future big-league teammates who surpassed him—Paul Coffey, Tim Kerr, Ken Linseman, Tony McKegney, Behn Wilson, Jay Wells, Greg Hotham, Richie Dunn, Mike Crombeen). Taken fifth overall by the inept Rockies in 1978, Gillis was handicapped from the get-go. With a combination of injuries, playing for an unstable organization and an inability to translate his game to the top level, he spent a six-year pro career hopping between the AHL and NHL.

Despite a journey that never quite materialized into stardom as a player, Gillis believes that "it was actually really good for me to be such a high draft pick. Because you quickly come to realize that your future is in the hands of others, oftentimes poorly intentioned and incompetent. You learn that you need to take control and not leave it all up to others." After his fruitless experience with Colorado, Gillis would experience a different method of challenge after being traded to the deeper, established contender in the Bruins—a team where finding a regular spot on a scoring line was highly improbable.

In the AHL, where he was used as a prime scoring winger, Gillis put up tremendous numbers, but he could only manage third- or fourth-line duty and some rare power-play minutes on a team loaded with skilled forwards such as Rick Middleton, Barry Pederson, Keith Crowder, Peter McNab, Tom Fergus, and Mike Krushelnyski. All this hard-earned experience served him well in a successful career as a major player agent, then as an executive in Vancouver, where some of his harshly critiqued moves turned out to help the franchise down the road (for example, acquiring Jacob Markstrom from the Panthers when dealing away Roberto Luongo, and acquiring a ninth overall pick that became eventual team captain Bo Horvat when dealing Cory Schneider to the Devils).

To this day, Gillis believes it's hard to evaluate moves right at the start, and that media and fans (sometimes influenced by one another) will attempt to find a verdict too early. "One of my most memorable draft day experiences, in fact, was trading Cory Schneider for the future captain of the Canucks but getting vilified for it at the time," he recalls. "Memorable because of not only how controversial it was, but for the fact it turned out to be a positive move in the long run for the organization when you look at how valuable Bo Horvat has become there."

Projecting is what Flames assistant GM John Weisbrod was doing with unknown forward Mark Jankowski at the 2012 draft. "He's a long way away, he's raw, he's young, he's still got to cross the crocodile-infested waters and develop properly —like, it's a long way from draft day to play in the NHL —but the physical attributes this guy has. The athleticism. The skating. The hands. The fact that he'll likely be playing at six-four, 215. I've said it to our scouts all week long —he's Joe Nieuwendyk," Weisbrod gushed at the time. Sure, Jankowski has succeeded enough to become an NHL player, but he hasn't justified first-round status whatsoever, and he hasn't at all been like the second coming of Nieuwendyk. But that's the way projection goes sometimes.

Drafting becomes even more of a complicated matter when it involves bringing in players from outside of North America where the training, culture and various approaches to the game can greatly differ. After all, the difficulties presented to heavily scouted players are numerous even for youngsters that grow up closer to the NHL circuit and are more accustomed to its parameters. But how about those faced by players from outside that Western bubble? Speaking from the standpoint of someone who's represented many clients from Eastern Europe, particularly the Czech Republic, over his numerous years of service, Edmonton-based agent Ritch Winter has seen how the difficulties are especially great for those from foreign countries:

> I distinctly remember Richard Smehlik when he arrived to his first Sabres training camp. He was saying to me after one of the scrimmages that he was surprised. Surprised because he thought he was as good as, if not better than, some of the guys that he went up against. What's really important about this type of experience for a player is that now you *know* that you are capable of the challenge, instead of just thinking or hoping you are. He got his answer when he got to his first camp, basically. Because of that, he went into an NHL career with a much more confident mindset, knowing he was able to play at a level that was consistent with some pretty good players.
>
> But the language barrier was a very difficult roadblock for sure. You've often got a coach speaking at a mile a minute, sketching something on a board. Look at Dominik Hasek, for instance. He struggled with the language at first too, so it took him a while to adapt. Chicago even sent him to the minors (the IHL's Indianapolis Ice) at least a couple of times. Can you imagine? Not only does that happen, but he was made available in the expansion draft and put on waivers twice! It's mostly because he struggled understanding what was required of him, and this lack of understanding plus lack of good communication led to him losing his confidence a bit. It's a testimony to how important the mental aspect of the game is, because even maybe the greatest goalie in the history of the game can have that happen to him.

There really was just a lot going on in the lives of these Czech players that made it so hard. When they would go on the road and leave a young wife with a child behind, she'd usually be there without a driving license and unable to speak the language at all. Imagine it, when you have to abandon them to go off on the road and make nightly calls from the hotels to see how they were doing. Talk about pressure. Nowadays, it's changed when it comes to drafting in that the younger players have gotten representation at least four years before that. Which, to me, is a bit ridiculous. I don't think they need them so early. I think it creates all the wrong impressions when teenage players should just be out having fun. The big difference now over when I started, is that we have to recruit younger players because by 13 or 14 most of them already have an agent.

These challenges lead teams to still overlook European names even deep into the past decade. Barry points out how that policy has backfired and recalls just how pervasive such biases were:

If you look at the truly amazing seventh-, eighth- and ninth-round picks of the past, the percentage of Europeans on that list would be very high, right? Especially compared to Canadians. One of the few great picks like that from this country that comes to mind right away is Luc Robitaille. But the majority of those steals have come from overseas.

Even as recently as the 2005 draft, the guy who was picked dead last (Patric Hornqvist) has done better than most of those names that went in the top 10! If you re-draft that year, Hornqvist would certainly be picked ahead of guys like Benoit Pouliot, Gilbert Brulé, Jack Skille, Devin Setoguchi, Brian Lee. And here's another question: Who was the first European to go in that draft? It wasn't until Kopitar at 11. So why were all those Canadian kids taken in the top 10 and most didn't pan out? There was a bias going on there, obviously. If I'm an owner in that situation, I'm going to be asking my management team why Pouliot, Brulé, Skille and Setoguchi ended up ahead of Kopitar on their list. I'd want to understand the rationale of that. You can say Kopitar maybe has done better than anyone other than Crosby from 2005, but I won't argue with picks like Bobby Ryan, Carey Price and Marc Staal. The teams who took them at least got quality NHLers.

Even with Russian players, we've seen a hesitance in the past. A few teams have said to me, "Sorry, we just don't draft Russians. End of story." I know of several teams that did make that an internal memo. Some even said, "We can't take a Euro in the first three rounds!" I don't think there's any team that could say any of that anymore, though. Way back when, however, there were these unwritten internal policies that were just silly. There was definitely a period there where teams didn't want to touch Russians because they didn't feel that they could get them to come over. Sometimes they were teams impacted by something negative that happened in the past and let it change their course of action.

Over the years, the draft lottery has been the league's method to prevent teams from tanking. While the reward reaped by bad teams such as the Sabres and Oilers has given them generational talents, the journey from abysmal to champion has not happened overnight. The more random nature of the lottery today has seen the Devils win it twice in three years without ever finishing bottom two in any of those seasons, while the Rangers picked second overall then first overall a year later without finishing even bottom five in either season. (Hmmm, what metropolitan area do those teams have in common?)

Meanwhile, some bottom-dweller seasons from the Avalanche, Sabres and Canucks saw them draw the short end of the stick and not even pick top three. Even the topsy-turvy, COVID-19-forced draft lottery's first phase in 2020 didn't pay off for the Red Wings and Senators after both wallowed near the bottom throughout 2019–20. While each crew suffered through a rather dismal season, Detroit took it to another level with one of the three lousiest campaigns in their history. And yet they could not snag the rights to the number one overall pick—Quebec phenom Alexis Lafrenière. They didn't even grab a top three selection, as the Rangers (an eliminated team from the one-time qualifying round format) were the lucky recipients only a year after jumping up a few spots to get Kaapo Kakko at number two.

Meanwhile in this "phase one," the Kings leapt up to pick second—perhaps a fitting outcome considering they had run their franchise so well and had fallen on hard times mostly due to the capricious punishment that the hard salary cap system enforces on well-run organizations.

As has often been brought up throughout this book, could an all-32-teams NHL lottery be a novel idea to discourage failure and reward success even more? In an era where the best teams can't even dream of a dynasty because of salary cap casualties, the teams near the bottom get to stockpile talented prospects and pounce on free agents or potentially high-priced players freed up from those superior clubs. Mike Gillis believes it should be a direction the NHL goes in someday. "I really do think that the league should try that idea out. It would be a welcome sight. To me, being perennially bad should not result in continuous reward. It doesn't often work to advance badly run teams either, as we've seen with so many struggling franchises that can barely even make a playoff spot if at all." In books such as 2019's *Cap In Hand*, the argument has been made to adopt a model like European soccer, with relegation and promotion for bottom-dwellers—while doing away with the draft entirely.

Surely having some of those picks pan out as projected is essential to an eventual Cup team, no? After all, even the 2019–20 champion Lightning needed lottery fortune from years earlier en route to their championship, owning 2008 top pick Steven Stamkos and 2009's number two overall pick (and 2020 Conn Smythe Trophy winner) Victor Hedman. On top of that, one of their top four defencemen and a possible heir apparent to Hedman, Mikhail Sergachev, was acquired from the Canadiens for 2013 number three overall selection Jonathan Drouin, a highly skilled but injury-prone and inconsistent winger with some defensive issues.

But Tampa's triumph wasn't built strictly on the backs of lottery picks, nor have the poor results that the Oilers, Sabres and Islanders endured over the last several years been prevented by top picks (especially the former two teams, which have combined for a piddling four playoff appearances between 2007–08 and 2019–20). Despite high picks—Taylor Hall, Ryan Nugent-Hopkins, Nail Yakupov, Leon Draisaitl, Sam Reinhart, Jack Eichel, Connor McDavid, Jesse Puljujarvi, Rasmus Dahlin—success has been highly elusive in Edmonton and Buffalo.

Contrary to the beliefs of their doubters (a much smaller crowd since they ended years of frustration by lifting the Stanley Cup in 2020), the Lightning built their second championship team largely without needing to tank for several years. Their back-to-back poor seasons from 2007 to 2009 did net them superstars for sure, and aside from a surprise run to within a win of the finals in 2011, they struggled to get back to respectability for a while (partly due to bouncing between owners: from William Davidson to the disaster duo of Len Barrie and Oren Koules to stable current owner Jeff Vinnik).

Many teams have proven unable to take players with high projections to that enviable level of superstardom. Tampa isn't one of those. The Lightning were able to surround them with talent far more off the radar, cultivated in a model AHL development system with the Norfolk Admirals/ Syracuse Crunch (first with their future head coach Jon Cooper then afterward with Rob Zettler and Benoit Groulx).

A master stroke came with hiring Steve Yzerman as GM in 2010, after he had already apprenticed in the Detroit organization the previous four seasons following his legendary 23-season playing career. That was the turning point in Tampa's rise from the post-2004 Cup malaise to a regular contender from 2014 to the present. While "Stevie Y" inherited a team that already had holdover stars from its glory days in Martin St. Louis and Vincent Lecavalier—not to mention future pieces Stamkos, Hedman and Alex Killorn—he still had a lot of work to do. Revamping the franchise's scouting and coaching, Yzerman notably brought in Julien BriseBois as his assistant general manager—a man who would take over as GM and get his name on the Cup after Yzerman's departure to take the Detroit job from former boss Ken Holland in 2019.

From there, the organization began to score draft and development wins even when the main club wasn't tearing through seasons quite yet.

They dug up smart undrafted free agent finds in Tyler Johnson and Yanni Gourde. Tampa Bay's 2020 playoff MVP turned out to be Hedman, but he still received stiff competition for that honour from teammates who weren't heralded as future linchpins on their draft day: 2014 third-rounder Brayden Point and 2011 second-rounder Nikita Kucherov (already the league MVP and scoring champion from 2018–19 and a two-time 100-point scorer to boot).

If the Oilers were on the verge of a title, could anyone envision anyone other than McDavid or Draisaitl being close in a Conn Smythe race? The failure of "tank-happy" teams to find important elements outside of the draft's top 10 is what sets apart teams like the Lightning, Blues and even the Capitals, who were a long-suffering bunch come playoff time before they finally came through in 2018. While the Penguins benefited from lottery picks more than perhaps any team has by finding generational talents in Malkin and Crosby, it wouldn't have mattered if not for shrewd picks outside of the first round.

Even with that, one could argue Pittsburgh has just as often let down their dynamic duo and should've had a dynasty instead of three Cups spread out over a nine-year period. Despite being outside of Conn Smythe consideration in 2020 for the Lightning, the team's fourth-most offensively prolific member, Ondrej Palat (11 goals in 25 games), was not a heralded name when he was picked. He was the Bolts' last selection back in 2011, at 208th overall in the seventh round. Hardly the part of the draft where integral Cup contributors get taken. Even before that epochal 2011 draft, the Lightning pulled off a savvy discovery by signing undrafted free agent Johnson, who would build his reputation off a tremendous 2015 playoff run and several 20-plus-goal and/or 50-plus-point seasons without being a top-line centre. Even though he was no longer that same impact forward, he still was around to contribute to the 2020 championship run.

A year after the tremendous prospect haul of Kucherov, Palat and Johnson, the Lightning made more gains toward their NHL supremacy by taking eventual starting goalie Andrei Vasilevskiy 19th overall and even securing a valuable energy liner in Cedric Paquette in the fourth round, at number 101 overall. In 2014 they repeated the Johnson home-run signing by inking another undrafted free agent in QMJHL scoring star Gourde.

A year later, Tampa would find speedy two-way penalty-killing threat Anthony Cirelli at 72nd overall in round three. Even draftees that wouldn't contribute a ton to Tampa's overall fortunes would be put to good use, as first-rounders Vladislav Namestnikov (number 27 overall in 2011) and Brett Howden (also number 27, in 2016) would secure them Ryan McDonagh at the 2017–18 trade deadline——an important component of their blue line when they ultimately did win it all.

One of the more amazing aspects of that Lightning triumph was how they did it without team captain and oft-labelled franchise linchpin Stamkos, who only suited up for a single Stanley Cup Final game during his team's ultimate title run (and, for good measure, scored the opening goal in it after reinjuring himself on the same play). Even with his recurring injuries keeping him sidelined, the Lightning barely missed a step in their 2020 "COVID/Bubble Cup" playoff drive. How many championship teams could say they did it with their long-time superstar staple (and one who had been taken first overall years earlier) mostly sidelined along the way? Not many, if any. Even the 1992 Penguins had Mario Lemieux most of the way, though they had to muster up some big-time courage to survive in the six games he missed to injury that spring.

Tampa Bay is a case study for the importance of draft brilliance, but they aren't the only one in recent years. Even less reliant on the top end of the draft to get to the promised land, the 2019 Blues triumphed with just one top-10 pick of their own (2008's Alex Pietrangelo) and one top 10 pick from another team (2009 Kings pick Brayden Schenn). The majority of their roster was constructed through wise non-draft acquisitions in the preceding years (Ryan O'Reilly, Schenn himself, Tyler Bozak, Jay Bouwmeester, Alex Steen), their own first-round successes (Jaden Schwartz, Vladimir Tarasenko, David Perron, Robert Thomas) and some of their deeper draft finds (Vince Dunn, Colton Parayko, Ivan Barbashev, Sammy Blais, Jordan Binnington).

Going back just a year before that, the Capitals ended a long-suffering franchise drought as well as 11 seasons of knocking on the door without so much as a conference final appearance despite the presence of one of the most dominant goal scorers of all time in Alex Ovechkin. Sure, Ovechkin and his playing partner Nicklas Backstrom (fourth overall in 2006) were the rewards for dreadful Caps seasons from 2003 to '06. But aside from that, their core was found outside of those cushy picks. Goalie Braden Holtby was snapped up in the fourth round in 2008, while John Carlson at number 29 in the first round that year turned out to be a steal (and wasn't even Washington's top choice, as they took Anton Gustafsson at number 21). Picked a year later, Dmitry Orlov also played an important role in the eventual Cup team. Even just a couple months after one of their many playoff failures—a stunning conference quarter-final loss to the mighty underdog Canadiens—the Caps made that defeat a footnote by using their number 26 overall pick on Evgeny Kuznetsov.

Subsequent top-round picks kept up the Capitals' drafting excellence (Tom Wilson, André Burakovsky, Jakub Vrana, Ilya Samsonov), even when such players (like Filip Forsberg) didn't go on to be a part of the team's future success. Although supplemented by some nice trade acquisitions (Lars Eller, T.J. Oshie) and free-agent additions (Matt Niskanen, Brett Connolly, Brooks Orpik), the 2018 Capitals were primarily put together from scouting home runs that boosted already having a generational superstar left winger and future Hall of Fame centre to rely on.

Even before these recent teams that finally broke through, the importance of drafting had been apparent in the Penguins, Blackhawks and Kings combining for eight of nine championships won between 2009 and 2017.

While those powerhouse multiple-Cup teams were no doubt aided by core stars gained via tanking— Sidney Crosby, Evgeni Malkin, Jordan Staal, Marc-André Fleury, Patrick Kane, Jonathan Toews, Drew Doughty, Anze Kopitar—they were also just as much led by players acquired in exchange for solid draft picks or players taken outside the "surefire" part of the first round, if at all.

Prior to 2005–06, drafting was still important, of course. But with no financial limitations, not hitting it big on prospects could still be overcome if a team had deep enough pockets to attract prime free-agent talent. Titles won by the Red Wings, Avalanche and Stars in this time of steadily rising salaries showed that aspiring to a Cup team had become a rich man's game, leaving smaller-market clubs in the dust and making them clamour for the "fairness" a salary cap could bring. There were exceptions. The middle-of-the-pack Devils claimed three Cups despite the growing economic gap.

Then there were the finals appearances of the small-budgeted Panthers, Sabres, Hurricanes, Mighty Ducks and Flames during the 1995–2004 period between NHL lockouts. Many good teams had to keep shuffling in new faces and sometimes make tough decisions by letting free agents walk or dealing them for prospects/picks before losing them for nothing.

Dallas, owned at the time by Tom Hicks, would unload big money to land names like Brett Hull and Ed Belfour, while the Red Wings in 2001 also brought in Hull, as well as Luc Robitaille and Dominik Hasek, and the Avs used their depth and wealth to deal for high-priced names such as Claude Lemieux, Theo Fleury, Ray Bourque and Rob Blake. It wasn't all a cushy holiday for the free-spending, of course, as the Rangers routinely led the NHL in payroll by spending upwards of $80 million a year just to disappoint and miss the playoffs for seven straight seasons, from 1997–98 through 2003–04.

The fact that most title teams of the salary cap era have eventually found the right formula may give hope to those in playoff agony despite their mighty potential. While the Maple Leafs, Predators and Jets have been enduring frustration, their chances of one day getting it right are much better thanks to the top draft picks and depth of talent they have already stockpiled. From there, it doesn't always come automatically. It takes some tinkering, experimenting and plugging in holes to eventually strike a "perfect balance"—and luck and timing, often necessary features of success.

The hockey gods are capricious, and many a championship has been lost through pure circumstance. As the Lightning showed, you can make your own luck sometimes. Even though they were required to grab six overtime victories along the way, it was one of the more decisive Cup runs in recent years. The Lightning are one of the few teams since 1998 that didn't need to win a seven-game series en route to hoisting the Cup (along with the 2007 Ducks, 2008 Red Wings and 2010 Blackhawks).

If anything, it was the opponent they defeated (Dallas) that seemed to always have the right answer when a comeback, fortunate bounce, big save or timely goal was necessary. Then again, sometimes it can still go sideways when it seems a Cup is inevitable; recall the Sharks of 2000–19, the Rangers of 2005–15, the Canucks of 2001–13, the Senators of 1998–2007 and the Flyers of . . . well, most seasons since 1976. Even the expansion Golden Knights have seen what roadblocks exist, having had nearly everything roll their way, only to see a 2019 collapse to the Sharks and 2020 let-down in the West Final versus the Stars.

Vegas is a classic example of leveraging assets to acquire picks, as before they even played an NHL contest, they were able to not only take advantage of a more favourable expansion draft system for their league entry but also use the bluff of taking valuable assets to leverage draft picks in trades. In all, the Knights' 2017 inaugural draft saw them land two extra first-rounders and an extra second-rounder, used to take Nick Suzuki (shipped to Montreal to land 30-plus-goal sniper Max Pacioretty) and Erik Brannstrom (sent to Ottawa in a package to land star winger Mark Stone).

All in all, the lifeline for a franchise in the modern NHL has been its ability to find a special talent in the NHL draft and not only incorporate that into their fabric but turn it into a thriving catalyst of victory. The last few Cup-hoisting clubs stand out as a testament to that way of thinking.

No one can be sure how the blight of COVID-19 has altered the 2020 development and drafting process. Certainly, it adds yet another variable to the chemistry of the process. Will Alexis Lafrenière, the number one pick, be added to the list of greats or busts? Will the restrictions of the virus be a bump on his road to stardom or an insurmountable hurdle? No one can say yet. And with minor pro leagues and junior hockey also hammered by the pandemic, how will the names following Lafrenière make out? The OHL talked about eliminating bodychecking as a security measure. How will that affect the more physical prospects? And so on.

This year's heirs to a tradition stretching back to Gilbert Perreault in 1970, the first year of the open draft, will face unique challenges. It will be fascinating to see how they measure against their predecessors. That's what makes the draft an inexact science.

ACKNOWLEDGEMENTS

EVAN

I would like to thank a number of people for making this publication a reality. For many years I've wanted to delve into the fascinating history of hockey for a book project, and I have many people to credit for helping it happen. ECW Press and all the fine people working there have been a huge help every step of the way, especially Michael Holmes. A big thank you to him for his guidance, enthusiasm and faith in this book. Also to Shannon Parr for her helpful editing.

I'd like to thank my parents (Bruce and Meredith) for their great support and nurturing me to be who I am today. Added thanks to my father, of course, for his help in writing this book and offering his unique wisdom, expertise and experience as an accomplished author. I'd like to thank the folks I've worked closely with at TSN's Sportscentre, too. I've been very thankful to find my niche there, and especially grateful for the opportunities provided by Scott Hart and Jason Palter. Thanks too, to the co-workers who have encouraged me along the way and made the job even more fun than it already was. Chief among these friends are fine gentlemen such as Jeremy Visser, Adam Dunfee, Desmond D'Souza, Jason Davidson and Brian Hastings.

I'm also very appreciative of my lovely wife Hannah throughout this process. She has been a big supporter of my work and has allowed me to pursue it despite the time it consumes (and the annoyance of having to hear passages read aloud to her non-hockey-fan ears). It's been a much easier endeavour thanks to her patience. I'm grateful and so lucky to have had such a support system from her, as well as from her parents, Patty and Gerry Vandergrift (not to mention the devoted love of our pet dog Pekoe and cat Toby) through the past couple years. The days spent writing at their cottage on Lake Huron made the process go smoother. Without the efforts of my family and the team at ECW Press, this book would never have come together as well as it has. I'm grateful for them all.

BRUCE

It's always been a goal of mine to work with my kids on a project, and with *Inexact Science* I've realized that with Evan. From research to writing, it's been his project. I just got a close-up view. Meredith and I—and his brother Rhys and sister Clare—are very proud of his diligence and hard work. Hope everyone enjoys his work as much as we have done. And once again, thanks to Michael Holmes for another successful project at ECW.

EVAN DOWBIGGIN is the sports statistical researcher and writer who runs TSN's StatsCentre Twitter. He has been on SportsCentre's behind-the-scenes team for over a decade—at first, covering news and game events, then over the last six years helping to dig up unique stats, build graphics and conduct research for the show's production side. Born and raised in Toronto (but having spent time in Calgary and Lethbridge in between), his passions include following sports, history (especially sports history), collecting music, playing music and writing. He lives in Toronto with his wife and their dog and cat.

BRUCE DOWBIGGIN's career is unmatched in Canada for its diversity and breadth of experience. He is currently the editor and publisher of *Not The Public Broadcaster* and is also a contributor to SiriusXM's *Canada Talks*. Bruce's career has included successful stints in television, radio and print. A two-time winner of the Gemini Award as Canada's top television sports broadcaster for his work with CBC, Mr. Dowbiggin is also the bestselling author of *Money Players* (finalist for the 2004 National Business Book Award) and other notable hockey releases such as *Ice Storm: The Rise and Fall of the Greatest Vancouver Canucks Team Ever* and *Grant Fuhr: The Story of a Hockey Legend*. His ground-breaking investigations into the life and times of Alan Eagleson led to his selection as the winner of the Gemini for Canada's top sportscaster in 1993 and again in 1996. This work earned him the reputation of one of Canada's top investigative journalists in any field. He was a featured columnist for *The Calgary Herald* (1998–2009) and *The Globe and Mail* (2009–2013), where his incisive style and wit on sports media and business won him many readers.

This book is also available as a Global Certified Accessible™ (GCA) ebook. ECW Press's ebooks are screen reader friendly and are built to meet the needs of those who are unable to read standard print due to blindness, low vision, dyslexia, or a physical disability.

Purchase the print edition and receive the eBook free!
Just send an email to ebook@ecwpress.com and include:

- the book title
- the name of the store where you purchased it
- your receipt number
- your preference of file type: PDF or ePub

A real person will respond to your email with your eBook attached. And thanks for supporting an independently owned Canadian publisher with your purchase!

MARQUIS

Québec, Canada

Printed on Rolland Enviro.
This paper contains 100% post-consumer fiber,
is manufactured using renewable energy - Biogas
and processed chlorine free.

100%

PERMANENT